HIGH

For Your Amazing Birthday!

Pamala DB.

Enjoy the

HIGH

life

An X-Rated Marijuana Memoir

Leonard Lee Buschel

Logan House PUBLICATIONS

HIGH

Logan House Publications
PO Box 1745
Studio City, CA 91614
First edition, 2023
Print ISBN: 978-1-66789-985-5
eBook ISBN: 978-1-66789-986-2

Dedicated to Robert Downey Sr. (A prince)

HOW NOT TO DIE
Around people
if I feel I'm gonna die
I excuse myself
telling them "I gotta go!"
"Go where?" they wanna know
I don't answer
I just get outa there
away from them
because somehow
they sense something wrong
and never know what to do
it scares them such suddenness
How awful
to just sit there
and they asking:
"Are you okay?"
"Can we get you something?"
"Want to lie down?"
Ye gods! people!
who wants to die among people?!
Especially when they can't do shit
To the movies—to the movies
that's where I hurry to
when I feel I'm going to die
So far it's worked

— Gregory Corso, Herald of the Autochthonic Spirit

Contents

Keep your face always toward the sunshine - and shadows will fall behind you.
— Walt Whitman

Acknowledgments

I have many people to include on the acknowledgment page. Most are living, some are deceased, and a few are fictional.

My son Ben comes to mind first because when he was 14, I told him about one of my smuggling trips to Israel, and a week later he asked me to tell it to him again. Like a bedtime story.

So, I wrote it down.

Cut to: Years later at Los Angeles Community College in the substance abuse counseling class, we had to write an essay about the bad choices we had made in the past, and did we really have a choice. A couple years ago I found those old assignments and decided to fill in the blanks. I hope you like the book.

Thank you, brother Bruce for always being my big brother, and bringing writing into my life. My mother, Rose Lily Buschel, for always seeing the glass half full, and allowing me to get lost, and found. Thank you, Cheech and Chong, for making me think there was nothing wrong with smoking ridiculous amounts of pot every day for 26 years. Thank you, Bill Wilson, Dr. Bob Smith and Mrs. Betty Ford, for showing me the light at the end of the joint. All of my AA sponsors: Philip A., Tony D., Robert T. Also Bettina Buschel for continuing support and family values. Burl Barer, a legend in his own minds, for encouraging me to keep writing. Prof. Karl Abrams for answering all my science questions for 40 years (without Google). Ron Tannebaum and Ken Pomerance for publishing excerpts on Intherooms.com

William Saroyan for making writing look easy. Martin Amis for making writing look impossible. Tom Robbins for making writing look fun.

My very own leprechaun, Gerry 'Wildurbangarden' Thompson, for never taking himself or me too seriously. Jewelle Sturm for reminding me drugs can kill. I miss you every day.

Ahbra Schiff for typing up my horrible handwriting and creating the cover design.

Papillon for making life look like a death-defying adventure. Nicholai Hel for his Zen-ness. Seymour Glass, Buddy Glass, Franny and Zooey Glass, and Les, Bessie and Walt . . . for giving me the family I will always have. Billy Phelan for almost bowling a perfect game. Matthew Scudder for taking me to AA meetings in New York. Captain Nemo for hoisting the sails of my imagination.

Unconditional LOVE to the canine Gods and Goddesses: Spook, Lala, Goliath, and Lolita

And special thanks to my editor who never judged or abandoned me, Karen Chernyaev.

And it would be heartless and thoughtless not to thank Dr. Wen Chung, my heart surgeon, and Dr. Ray Chu, my brain surgeon.

Preface

If this were a movie, it wouldn't be a Woody Allen film; there are no nerds or molesters. Not a Sam Peckinpah film; not enough violence except for a few choking scenes. Not a Scorsese film; not enough sleaze bags, but a lot of drug dealers, gamblers, and loose women. And criminal behavior on every page, because whenever you spend untaxed income, it's an illicit purchase.

François Truffaut. That's who I feel should have been directing my life—lots of lovemaking and characters as cool as iced espresso and hot and smoldering like a Gauloises.

However, none of them French. Actually one, but she was French Canadian, and that affair went nowhere. I don't think Parisian street walkers count. On second thought, let's face it, it'd be more Barry Levinson. There's way more *Diner* in me than *Shoot the Piano Player*.

I think of things in terms of movies a lot. They seem to be markers for events in my life. Films are my newest drug of choice. That's why in 2008, I started the REEL Recovery Film Festival & Symposium with Robert Downey Sr.

At the REEL Recovery Film Festival & Symposium, we showcase filmmakers who make honest films about addiction, alcoholism, behavioral disorders, treatment, and recovery. We started in Los Angeles and expanded to seven other cities over time, including Ft. Lauderdale, New York, and Denver. We are still adding other locations. During the COVID-19 pandemic of 2020, we went online with our own REEL Recovery Film Channel, available nationwide to anyone in any state.

I like a good movie, and I worship a good foreign film, like the 2019 masterpiece *Portrait of a Lady on Fire*. I was transported back to the 1700s in this somber French tale.

My friend Steve Seid was a curator at the Berkeley Art Museum's Pacific Film Archive for 25 years. He revered film as an art as much as I do. In 2021, in response to the San Francisco Museum of Modern Art closing its Film Program, he wrote the following on Facebook:

> "I propose that Cinema, the seventh art, be promoted—promoted to the first art because it contains aspects of each of the "lesser" arts. Cinema encapsulates aspects of its lesser brethren and though Cinema was formulated after the assumed perfection of Painting, Architecture, Sculpture, Literature, Music, and the Performing Arts (theater, dance, symphony, opera), the medium in its many forms arrives at a cumulative impression that is greater. Cinema can mesmerize as it transits upon a whited screen or delight and absorb as it engulfs its environs with dazzling abstraction. Cinema can be encountered as a language-based experience or absorbed as non-verbal recitation. Cinema can dance upon the architectural space or illuminate a multitude of dancers. Cinema can tell vast stories or reduce experience to a pigmented utterance. Cinema can depict the world with photographic insistence or astound with graphical departures. Cinema can occupy complex interior spaces or reflect back your colorful claustrophobia. Cinema can dazzle the impatient ear with mellifluous sonorities or flow frantically forward with an airy musicality. Cinema can be painterly, sculptural, literary, theatrical, architectural, musical, simultaneously."

Movies are about telling stories, and they've done so beautifully for well over a century.

Showcasing films about addiction and recovery is deeply personal to me because, as of the writing of this book, I have lived the last 27 years sober . . . without a drink or a drug (except for some Dilaudid after open-heart surgery and Percodan after brain surgery).

For 25 years, I dealt drugs, got high every day, and lived under the daily specter of arrest, incarceration, and violence. I travelled the world, met brilliant charismatic men and women, ate in fine restaurants and had orchestra seats for plays by Tom Stoppard, Sam Shepard and every Sondheim musical on Broadway. I avoided the cops when it counted, welcomed poets and musicians into my life regularly.

Since December 12, 1950, I have been floating down the stream of life in a rowboat that could have sprung a bad leak at any moment. Too often, I was gasping for breath (fucking asthma). Breaking the law. Worshipping nature, art, literature, and females. Getting high as a kite. Being funny, because if you can't play an instrument, you better make people laugh. And always looking for love, sex or the Benjamins. I spent my whole life climbing to the top of the mountain, and when I got there, I realized, *oh fuck!* Wrong mountain.

Welcome to the world of a five-foot, eleven-inch Jewish Sagittarian dilettante's drug-addicted life. No one would ever guess this edge-of-the-cliff dance ends with a most miraculous miracle and recovery from drug and alcohol addiction. I don't know if my story can help anyone. I hope so. Maybe there is someone reading this who only smokes pot every day because it seemed like a good idea 40 years ago. No, it's because you're addicted. The highest you can be is when there is nothing between you and reality. Reality, the ultimate natural high, is more exciting than any drug-induced roller-coaster ride.

Marijuana is often called the lazy man's way to enlightenment. It can also be called a lazy man's way to creativity. And it is, until it's not. If you think there can be heaven on earth with a joint in your mouth, then it must be very good weed. No, that's bullshit. Drugs wear off. Reality never does. My son often reminds me of what Timothy Leary said: "The goal is not to get high, but to be high."

v

The idea of writing a memoir never occurred to me until I was taking classes at Los Angeles Community College to get my certification as a substance abuse counselor. The classes were pretty much made up of recovering drug addicts, rappers, and ex-cons. I felt right at home.

The teacher wore sweaters every day probably bought on sale from Banana Republic. The class worked from a paperback textbook called *Did I Really Have a Choice?* Every week I had to write an essay about my formative years and the "choices" I made along the way.

Discussing "free will" with a 10-year-old is a moot point. I was programmed to be me by my environment, mother, brother, and the cataclysmic death of my father. The actual dying was not cataclysmic (quiet heart attack in his sleep while being driven home from the night shift at the post office) but the effect on my breast feeder and my sibling were life changing, shattering, and a fucking bummer.

When I was young, around 17, after just having been introduced to the works of Henry Miller, I read several volumes of *The Diary of Anaïs Nin* (Miller and Nin were *very close*) and was blown away thinking I'll never lead such an interesting life, such an introspective life, or be able to write like her. Yet here I am . . .

My brother has always been the writer in the family. Brother Bruce wrote lots of great magazine articles for *GQ, Forbes, Medium*, a column for the *New York Times*, his own memoir for Simon and Schuster in 2007, *Walking Broad: Looking for the Heart of Brotherly Love*, and in 1973, he co-wrote the pre -*All the President's Men* exposé on the Nixon Watergate break-in, *The Watergate File: A Concise, Illustrated Guide to the People and Events.*

I think there a few well-known Jewish writers hanging around on our family tree—the editor for the *Forward*, a legendary newspaper founded in 1897, and the author of *Famous Jews in Sports* (a very slim tome). *Famous Jewish Chess Players* was more substantial. If any readers are about to throw this book into the fireplace because I seem to be bragging about the innate and superior intelligence of Hebraic peoples, *stop*. Achtung, halt, STOP. I promise you there are some pretty idiotic tales to come.

"A book lying idle on a shelf is wasted ammunition. Like money, books must be kept in constant circulation... A book is not only a friend, it makes friends for you. When you have possessed a book with mind and spirit, you are enriched. But when you pass it on you are enriched threefold."

— Henry Miller

Part I

What It Was Like

"REALITY is what you can get away with."

1. Rehearse successful outcomes in your mind's eye.

2. Expand your ability to feel gratitude and appreciation.

3. Don't demand all or nothing answers: accept partial solutions.

4. Interrupt you negative chains of thought by forcing yourself to visualize the crazy sweet adventures you plan to enjoy someday.

— Robert Anton Wilson 1932 – 2007

Chapter 1

Grief Like a Torn Dress Should Be Left at Home

I am not what happened to me, I am what I choose to become.
—Carl Jung

OPENING MONTAGE: Camera descends through the delicious mists above a pot of simmering chicken soup at 4639 N. 10th Street—the house where I grew up. There I am, having just been born into an idyllic Jewish family unit smack-dab in the middle of the twentieth century, with a working father, a beautiful, house-wifey mother, and a strong handsome three-year-old brother. I started life in the North Philadelphia neighborhood called Logan, in a row house with mortgage payments my parents considered affordable.

When Mom and Dad brought home their bouncing baby boy from St. Joseph's hospital, my mother pressed her tender ear to my tiny chest and heard a heartbeat that was anything but regular.

The next day my mom called the delivery doctor and told him she'd heard something strange when she put her ear to my chest. The doctor had already detected a loud murmur associated with a bicuspid aortic valve disorder. The doctor didn't want to tell my parents right away about my defective heart and ruin the family's first night home with their new beautiful baby boy.

There was an operation available to repair said defect, but in the 1950s, 1 out of every 10 kids who went under the knife to repair the errant valve never made it back home to watch *Howdy Doody*.

In those days, there was no heart-lung machine. The surgeon would have had only three-and-a-half minutes to replace the little piece of shit valve in my heart. Mom was not about to play *Beat the Clock* with a life-threatening experimental surgery. But she was willing to bet that operating room technology would advance faster than my valve's health would retreat. Mom was certainly right on that estimation.

Three weeks after I took center stage, my daddy dropped dead of a heart attack on his way home from working the night shift at the post office. He was 34 years old. Suddenly there was a gaping hole in our lives. No husband, no father, no breadwinner.

January 5, 1951 Bad News

Mom was a grief-stricken and frightened widow. Shock prevented her from breastfeeding, so at three weeks old, my first bartender eighty-sixed me. Mom had no job and the mortgage became unaffordable. She was now confronted with a new reality: How was she to have the time to raise my brother and me into men when

2

she needed to get a nine-to-five job? How would a 100 percent woman manage to raise two sons without a father around? Could her instinct and intuition carry her through? *The Common Sense Book of Baby and Child Care by Dr. Spock* was not in her library.

I was a particularly large drain on family emotions. Before I could even walk, I was faced not only with a life-threatening heart condi-tion but with a gnarly breath-taking case of severe asthma, which ultimately led to numer-ous emergency room visits.

My lucky brother's life started with daddy's gen-tle masculine push. Over the years, I've seen 8 mm home movies of my brother Bruce, being pushed by my father on a swing and another home movie shows him being held

What Me Worry?

above the cresting waves in the Atlantic Ocean off Atlantic City by the proud, strong hands of our daddy. Others called him Morris. I called him deceased.

For my brother, our father's death was much more of a loss than it was for me.

I'm sure on an unconscious level, I must have been devastated. Though at the time I probably didn't notice, being so focused on Mom's fountains for youth. Who was going to hunt for food, gather wood, and keep our row home supplied with heating oil to stay warm at night? At three weeks old, I had to metaphorically stand on my own two feet while actually only able to lie on my back or stomach, as newborns do. I was already starting a new chapter in my life, as I did again 44 years later when I got sober. It's not like I was on one uninterrupted trajectory from infancy to the Betty

Ford Center. I did stop at nursery school, public schools, weddings, fatherhood and racetracks. But at three weeks old, without realizing it, I was pretty much faced with having to fend for myself.

Being brought up by a single mom is like being an electrical plug with only one prong. The energy is not a balanced flow. A missing father is a missing prong. A missing father short-circuits a child's learned response to stimuli. As a man, he may overreact to everyday problems as if he were from Venus and not from Mars.

How would I learn the aplomb a father uses to smoothly carve a holiday turkey? Or repaint the bedroom or change a flat tire? I would never know how to safely experience the fear and unsteadiness that come when Daddy takes off the training wheels to unleash the careen of the bike on the asphalt. Or feel his love, assistance, acceptance and protection at the same time. When I had my own son, I told him the first thing to learn when riding a bike is how to fall over (on a grass field), and the second thing is how to get up and keep pedaling. Somehow, I managed to master this life lesson without a daddy of my own.

When I started to attend elementary school, I heard kids in the playground talk about their fathers and the jobs they did. I would slink away embarrassed that I didn't even have a father. Heretofore, I never really knew what I did not have. I did have some older guys in the neighborhood who took me under their wings from time to time but never like a father would.

One of the best realities of my life was that my family lived in the same house for 20 years. I felt secure in the Brigadoon-like neighborhood of Logan in North Philadelphia. I say Brigadoon because to me Logan was like the mythical village in Scotland that rose out of the Scottish mist once every 100 years, for only one day of joy and splendor.

Logan, built on top of a buried creek, existed as a middle-class Jewish ghetto for about 50 years, before three square blocks (including my house) sank into the mud, disappearing off the face of the earth forever. There is no old block to go back to visit. Except through memories, and in family photos, 10th Street will remain forever a shimmering universe of childhood adventures and fantasies. And where my creation story started off with a death and a wheeze.

My mother, Rose, only drove a car twice in her life; once for a lesson and then to get her driver's license. She really didn't need one because she usually only travelled with her boyfriends or took public transport. We never owned a car. As a kid, the only modes of transportation I ever knew were buses and subways, walking, riding my bike, and hitchhiking. I hitchhiked to Olney High School every day for three years. When I was late, the teachers understood that I didn't get a ride fast enough to be on time.

I grew up self-reliant, with two bus stops a block from my house and with only a 20-minute walk to the Broad Street subway. Our station was the Wyoming Avenue stop. From here, for a five-cent token, I could travel up and down the spine of this city of neighborhoods or to where the Declaration of Independence was birthed and to the home of comedian W. C. Fields. One story has it that Fields had the following words engraved on his tombstone at Forest Lawn Memorial Park in Glendale, California: "All things being equal, I'd rather be here than in Philadelphia."

School was a challenge to my developing ego. I attended a big school that had three floors and two elevators. My heart problem, a bicuspid aortic valve that should have been tricuspid, got me a special elevator pass (like a seat on the "special" bus).

I was never allowed to participate in the regular gym class, so I took remedial gym where the only equipment was a Ping-Pong table. And there wasn't always someone to play against. I became bored with boredom.

My special pass to use the elevator was necessary all winter, when my ridiculously bad asthma caused me to wheeze like an out-of-pitch accordion. That wheeze embarrassed me greatly. I didn't want the other kids to know I had any physical defects, so I would wait for everyone to go into their classrooms before I slipped into the elevator. Self-stigmatization. If a guy saw me and asked what I was doing taking the cripple's elevator (kids are cruel)—because they all saw me playing basketball and other ball games at lunch and recess—I would make up a story (lie).

I got along with pretty much everyone in the neighborhood, a skill that would eventually help get me through some of life's biggest challenges. Luckily I was born in the Chinese year of the chameleon.

I grew up playing sports on neighborhood streets every day and was able to do more than my doctor advised. The rules for street games weren't set like in Little League. The guys would have to renegotiate the rules and boundaries every day. One day, first base was the black Chevy, second base was the old Fairlane, and third base was the blue Caddy. We debated every little disagreement but not for long. We wanted to get on with the game.

Whatever game we were playing became the most important thing in our otherwise dull lives. Physical exertion and competition made us feel more alive than any homework assignment or family chore. We knew our dream game would be cut short when someone's mother called them in for dinner, or the darkening sky would call the game.

The first time I needed emergency medical attention was at age 10 in Rockaway Beach, a neighborhood in Queens, New York. Almost dying in Rockaway Beach prior to puberty is a depressing and enervating concept, especially for someone whose entire life consisted of just one decade.

The cast of characters leading up to my potential last gasp consisted of Mom, Brother Bruce and the relatives we were visiting on December 25 to celebrate the birth of that famous Jewish stuntman who is probably rolling over in his grave because he didn't get credit for teaching Houdini everything he knew. Uncle Larry, Jewish, married Mary, Catholic and very Italian. Aunt Molly, the spinster, was there too. So were Larry and Mary's two sons, both real rednecks.

Much like the Three Wise Men arriving at the manger, we three managed to make it to Rockaway Beach, with Mom and Brother Bruce carrying the gifts. I arrived with a deadly cat allergy—a "gift" I would have gladly returned with no refund. Italian Aunt Mary and Uncle Larry had two cats. I don't remember their names, but I will always think of them as Sacco and Vanzetti. Except these little fuckers were guilty.

I'm sure my aunt and uncle didn't acquire them with nephew-murder in mind, but as we sat down to an authentic Italian feast, my breathing became somewhat labored, short and difficult.

Wheezing is what it's called. Mine was louder than a cat's purring.

Not one to draw attention to myself, I refrained from mentioning my lack of oxygen for as long as possible, until I was compelled to rasp out, "Mom, I'm having an asthma attack."

"Relax," she whispered to me, "just try to get through dinner."

It's Howdy Doody Time

By now, my wheeze was quite audible, and they all probably heard me, even if their gazes never lifted from the authentic homemade lasagna on their plates. "Relax," Mom said. Relax my ass. I wasn't having a fucking anxiety attack. I was having a cat-dander-provoked major asthma attack.

Not a hard time breathing. *Not breathing.*

Mom didn't want to be embarrassed by her little Lee, not after being so embarrassed losing her husband 10 years before. After all, hadn't we taken the train from Philly to New York, the subway all the way from Penn Station to Far Rockaway, and hadn't our relatives bestowed upon us a duffle bag full of Christmas gifts?

Ironically, the gift I most needed was a new pair of lungs, but I wasn't holding my breath.

I told her again, which wasn't necessary because my wheezing was now louder than the Mario Lanza album on the Victrola. Eventually, I was given the only ingestible remedy at that time: a noxious slime of liquid. Aminophylline in a vulgar- tasting pink colloidal cocktail. The taste always made me gag and occasionally, throw up. An even more unpleasant intervention was my mother giving me Aminophylline suppositories. To this day, that's why I'm only comfortable with fingers in my ass and never cocks or dildos.

I kept the vile medicine down and was taken to my Aunt Molly's apartment nearby to wait for the wheezing to diminish. All through the night, I had to sit up and fight for every breath. In retrospect, I think that if someone, such as a loving family member, had gently rubbed my back and put their warm soothing hands on my shoulders, the breathing would have calmed down.

Such was not the case. Swedish massage or the laying on of hands were not among my family's established healing practices. Many Jewish families don't touch. For the Hassidic, they are afraid a woman might be on the menstruation cloth, and a man might have Hep C. This is perhaps a cultural trait. Indians put their hands together and say *namaste*. The Japanese don't shake hands. They bow to your aura. The Jews don't bow to your aura. They just ignore it altogether.

Mom and Aunt Molly waited till sunrise to make an emergency call to Molly's general practitioner because no one should bother a doctor in the middle of the night. Arriving in his obligatory Buick, black bag in hand, the good doctor whipped out his somewhat sterilized reusable syringe, filled it with adrenaline, and poked it into my arm.

I'm sure it hurt, but I was too busy struggling for my next shallow breath to notice the pain. Within minutes, I was out of danger and suddenly aware of the three facts leading to one unasked question. The three facts: (1) the black-and-white television was on; (2) I was very hungry; and (3) I could breathe again. The unspoken question: "Why the hell didn't any of you take me to the emergency room?" I think I knew the answer. It was bad enough to bother a doctor in the evening and even worse to inconvenience an entire hospital.

Asthma was my constant companion. I was 10 when Brother Bruce had his Bar Mitzvah. Mom wanted to make sure Brother Bruce and I knew how to dance for the occasion, so she hired a very attractive, tall, buxom instructress to teach her little men to cha-cha. I think the big hit at that time was *Moon River* by Henry Mancini.

Brother Bruce and his face stood exactly chest high to the big-breasted dance teacher. It was in that well-cushioned environment that he experienced the reality of erections. Weeks later, when he finally intoned, "Today I am a man," it was true with intention, if not in consummation. I made it through the Bar Mitzvah and the cha-cha sessions without becoming breathless—a glorious accomplishment in those days.

Not breathing is also exceptionally inconvenient and potentially life threatening. Oxygen deprivation is known to cause irreparable brain damage and can lead to erratic and bizarre behavior. I am still capable of both with a perfectly healthy brain.

A few years later, while playing touch football in the street, I had to quit the game because I was having an asthma attack. My brother got pissed off because the game had to stop until a new player showed up. What Brother Bruce didn't know was that wheezing might be hellish and scary, but I really didn't want to take that truly vile pink shit, the Aminophylline, with its ammoniacal odor and a bitter taste.

Shortly thereafter, a miracle of modern medicine occurred. Our family physician, Dr. Doodies, made a house call to see about the heavy wheezing. Sitting next to me on the sofa, he reached into his black bag like a magician with his hat. Instead of pulling out a live rabbit, he pulled out one of the first albuterol asthma rescue inhalers in America.

My life changed forever when my doctor gave me that inhaler.

"Hold it in your hand and press here and breath in, then do it once more," he said with the confidence of a confidence man.

I pressed it in and breathed in as deeply as I could and then did it again. Thirty seconds later, I wanted to get back into the game— the game of football and the game of life. The attack stopped on a dime. It was a miracle. It saved my life, many times, and gave me a mobility I would have never had if I needed to be rushed to a hospital for every difficult bout of wheezing. However, as I was perpetually abusing myself with pot and coke, the Ventolin inhaler didn't always work. As it is, I have been 911'ed and ambulance driven to ERs about a dozen times in my life. After all, take away someone's breath and what do you have? A corpse.

I can easily sum up my youth. Defects of the heart, problems of the lungs. That sentence fragment, although grammatically incorrect, is absolutely true in characterizing my life. It wasn't until a little later that compulsive gambling became my favorite problem.

#

Growing up my home routine was just that—very routine. Every day, Mom went to work, and I went to school. After school, I was alone for a few hours, and if I couldn't find a ball game to join, I would set fires, steal things, shoot sparrows in the backyard with my dead father's .22 single shot Remington rifle, hang out at Cooper's (the corner candy store) or watch TV. The shrinks call that acting out. I called it solving loneliness, boredom and existential angst.

When I was 12, I was addicted to Classics Illustrated comic books, such as *Moby Dick*, *Treasure Island*, and *Dr. Jekyll and Mr. Hyde*, and they were my constant companions. While Mom thought I was sleeping in the next room, I was actually counting Robinson Crusoe's footprints in the sand or wondering whether Captain Nemo was still 20,000 leagues under the sea.

My favorite day was Tuesday, not for the television shows that were airing but because that's when the *TV Guide* came in the mail. It was like receiving a new lease on life every week. Other people's lives to watch every day. My life was focused on TV, what was on, and what was on *next*. I would underline (no highlighters back then) all the shows I didn't want to miss, like an executive whose entire life is chiseled in their day planner. The *TV Guide* listed all the TV shows I wanted to watch and couldn't live without.

On cold winter afternoons, *The Three Stooges*, *Boris and Natasha*, and *Sally Starr* were my only companions. One day, many years later, I turned on the TV and had a neurobiological revelation. Just as the TV was starting up, making its usual crackling sounds, I could feel my brain turning off, see my brain cells diming, shutting down thoughts and feelings, suddenly stuck in time, like in suspended animation.

My First Love

Looking back, I realize that every time I came home to an empty house after school and turned on the television, it helped assuage my burgeoning youthful existential angst. I didn't feel so alone. Of course, all these shows were interrupted every 10 minutes by commercials. Childhood brainwashing. In 2013, children saw an average of 40,000 commercials a year, and many more if you include the Internet and social media. If you see enough advertisements, you eventually stop existing as an original human being. You are now no longer you. Now, I try not to have the TV on. My fear was that, when I die, it won't be my life passing before my eyes but Jerry Seinfield's.

In 1965, when I was 14, my mother took me to the Locust Street Theatre (on Locust Street) for a matinee performance of *The Roar of the Greasepaint—The Smell of the Crowd*, by Anthony Newley and Leslie Bricusse. Much of the cast was my age, except for the leads.

This singular stage show helped me to understand love, politics, hope, oppression, war and nonviolence all in one afternoon. At 14, I was just waking up to politics. John Kennedy was offed just the year before. I agreed with Dallas D.A. Jim Garrison and didn't think the assassination was just the efforts of a lone lunatic with the best aim ever. The show's dramatically powerful portrayal in music was one of those magical experiences I have not forgotten to this day. Resembling a music hall production more than a sit-com style musical, the plot examines the maintenance of the status quo between the upper and lower classes of British society in the 1960s. My 10-second summary boils down to this: The play is about the tension and class disparity between two characters—a rich man and a pauper, Sir and Cocky, the oppressor and the oppressed. It was an allegorical plot with characters named for who and what they are; Sally Smith played the Kid, the Girl was played by Joyce Jillson, the Negro was Gilbert Price, where he introduced the world to the classic of classic songs, *Feeling Good*, recorded by dozens of artists but made most famous by Nina Simone.

When I realized that Anthony Newley wrote the show, composed the music, and lyrics (with Leslie Bricusse), directed the production, sang, danced and acted in it, my admiration for him was set forever. Years later, my friend Jesse Jones worked for Mr. Newley as his personal concierge. Jesse told me that after Newley's divorce from Joan Collins (yes, the Joan Collins of film, TV and theater fame), his entire tour entourage consisted of only one person—his mother. This, I could relate to. Jesse also assured me that Mr. Newley was the sweet and classy gentleman I imagined him to be. This brilliant artist and perfect gentleman died on April 14, 1999.

All of the shows that I had seen before had many set changes. When I realized the set of *The Roar of the Greasepaint, The Smell of the Crowd* was not going to change, I was focused on every aspect of the production. Anthony Newley, Cyril Richard, and Gilbert Price gave performances that blew my 14-year-old mind. The memory remains so fresh that listening to the original cast recording still moves me to tears.

I had the pleasure of introducing my son Ben to the score by playing "A Wonderful Day Like Today" on many mornings before school. Once I came home to find Ben listening to the CD on his own. I was proud and happy that I could pass something on to him that meant so much to me. And I don't even think he was getting high yet. And he wasn't going gay. If I had caught him listening to "Cabaret" or "Funny Girl," I may have thought otherwise.

In sixth grade, my homeroom teacher, Mrs. Forman, brought in a record player one day and put on "In the Hall of the Mountain King," from the *Peer Gynt Suite*. I was moved in a way that Sinatra (the most listened-to artist at home) never did move me. I could feel dormant parts of my little brain start to come alive. I also felt my heart skip a beat, in a good way. My teacher told us about a place called Norway. Never heard that word as Mom didn't sit around the dinner table discussing Scandinavia. I ended up loving Björk.

Mrs. Forman put on "Morning Mood" from the same suite. I needed to hide my face because I didn't want my girlfriend, Jeanette Jekel, to see me cry. Hearing the two superb musical masterpieces exposed me to the alpha and omega of emotions that classical music inspires. (Facebook, being what it is, I sent this chapter to an old friend from the same elementary school I attended to see if she had similar memories of Mrs. Forman's class. She sent back this note. I will let it speak for itself: "I hope you include in your memoir that Arlene Marinoff sat behind you in sixth grade and scratched your back with a ruler in exchange for pictures of Ben Casey and Dr. Kildare that your mom got from Perfect Photo. I would have done it for free as I had a crush on you. You were adorable.")

A similar experience happened 10 years later, in 1969. I was with Brother Bruce, in his Opel Kadett, a fairly nondescript vehicle. It takes some living to know what kind of car you should be wearing. For years I drove a Volvo. The automobile most favored by pot dealers. Big trunk, low profile. No cop ever stopped a professor in his Volvo mistaking him for a pimp or drug dealer.

Brother Bruce and I decided to use the East River Drive to get home. We were cruising along the Schuylkill River when Brother Bruce turned on Temple University's full-time jazz station, WRTI. What was about to happen in that Opel Kadett was anything but nondescript. The song that came on was like a psalm, a chant, a prayer, a beseeching voice, like a shot of caffeine that percolated into a frightening cacophony. We drove home in silence and sobs for exactly 37 minutes, until we parked in front of our row house on 10th Street. The music? It was "The Creator Has a Master Plan" by Pharoah Sanders and vocals by Leon Thomas. You probably think I was high? No shit. I was high every single day of my life from the age of 18 to 44. But the piece sounds as good today sober as it did 50 years ago. I'm listening to it right now, not high, not stoned, just in tears. It's about the horrors of slavery . . . freedom and enlightenment.

Years later I would often see Mr. Sanders hanging out in various jazz clubs around San Francisco. It was like having royalty in the room. His countenance was truly regal. It was as if on that afternoon in 1969, God came down and gave unto me the world of jazz, a world that makes life worth living. Although really good jazz makes you feel as if you might be dying.

Before music CDs, we collected vinyl discs. There were 45 rpm (revolutions per minute) singles, and 33 1/3 rpm long-playing albums—LP for short. I ordered my first 33 1/3 rpm record player when Columbia House advertised a very special offer in a magazine: a real stereo, long-playing record machine with detachable, extendible speakers, plus six "free albums," for only $14.99.

Being a bit flippant, I ordered it without asking Mother whether it was okay, because she was after all going to get the bill when the stereo arrived. Which reminds me of a story told by Marie-Louise von Franz sometime in the '80s, a story that has guided me all through my life ever since. She tells about a friend on the subway platform in Prague, looking down and seeing a lot of cigarette butts. Feeling like lighting up herself, the woman asks the nearby station master if it's okay to smoke there. The station master responds very emphatically, "No, it is VERBOTEN."

"What about all these butts?" "They didn't ask."

So I got an Andy Williams LP, some Frank Sinatra (we share a birthday, 12/12), and the Dave Brubeck Quartet's *Time Out*, which included the jazz standard "Take Five." Also, the life-changing *Judy at Carnegie Hall*. Maybe I was gay after all. (Not that there's anything wrong with that! Thank you, Jerry Seinfeld.)

Soon after I received the LPs, I traded *The Andy Williams Christmas Album* for an LP by someone named Bob Dylan. Brother Bruce got very angry because he had never heard of Bob Dylan, and he loved *The Andy Williams Show*. Then Brother Bruce smokes his first joint while listening to the Dylan LP. Moved to such intense emotions never felt before, Brother Bruce went into the basement and masturbated.

If Mr. Dylan (a.k.a. Robert Zimmerman) reads this, I hope he takes Brother Bruce's response as a compliment. Lord only knows how Brother Bruce handled himself after accepting Dylan as the troubadour of our generation.

#

I don't ever remember doing any homework on my own volition. I did as little homework as possible, just enough to get C's. That's because A's didn't matter much to my mother. She was more concerned with me being street smart than school smart, like she was.

At the end of a long day at work, Mom would come home and prepare dinner. She had a very special way of lifting the foil off the Swanson TV dinners. We ended the evening watching TV and eating Breyers vanilla fudge ice cream. In fact, I had a horrible sugar habit. (It's only a moderate problem now.) I would buy cases of Coca-Cola with my own money and drink up to six small bottles a day. They were only a little more than a dime each. Sugar. The cheapest antidepressant on the planet.

I was one of the only kids in the neighborhood with a charge account to go into the corner grocery store and get whatever I needed—or wanted. I could also do that at Jack Parrish, a classy men's apparel store. I never abused the privilege. I knew we only had the money my mother earned at Perfect Photo, a photo-finishing plant, where I got my first job in the eighth grade. Looking back, I'm sure my strong independent decision-making powers came from those shopping experiences without Mom.

When Mom sent my brother (age seven) to boarding school, I felt like an only child. Really, I was a lonely child. Brother Bruce would come home for the weekend every Saturday morning. I would be waiting for his bus at the corner, unless he called to tell us he was in trouble at school and not allowed his weekend pass. Sadly, that happened a lot.

When the Number 75 bus rolled down the street, my anticipation would be gleeful or painful. Because when the door swung open, Brother Bruce wasn't always on the bus. So, I would wait, almost in a trance, another 20 minutes for the next one. When he finally arrived, the weekend began, like the beginning of a great buddy movie. That's how I learned to love waiting. The anticipation was so delicious I was in heaven, not thinking about anything mundane, knowing my Jesus had arrived again.

We would play sports, fight with each other, pal around, and go to the movies. On Sundays, the bus that delivered him would take him away.

When Brother Bruce wasn't visiting or on the 75 bus, he was at a boarding school/orphanage called Girard College. Founded in 1833 and opened on January 1, 1848, Girard College was created by provisions in the will of Stephen Girard, the fourth richest man in America at that time. He saved the U.S. government from financial collapse (loan shark?) during the war of 1812. He also envisioned a school for "fatherless and poor white boys." Yep, that was the Buschel boys.

Girard wanted to educate boys who might otherwise be lost, whose mothers would be forced into prostitution or waitressing, to prepare them for useful, productive lives. I was exempt from this heartfelt act of ego-driven and racist social generosity because I had a loud heart murmur only spoken of in quiet whispers. Exempt isn't the right word. Rejected is more accurate.

They didn't want me there, and my brother didn't want me to go there. At the time, I did not know why. He later said he wanted to spare me the unpleasant (horrible) experience, which he revealed in his memoir, *Walking Broad*, 2007.

Brother Bruce advised our mother not to send me (for my own good).

It's highly likely that the officials at Girard feared that I wouldn't withstand the nightly buggering that so traumatized my elder brother. He later spent a small fortune on Freudian therapy—good money on bad memories.

Girard's painful initiations into the world of unwanted intrusions allegedly softened considerably and withdrew completely when this educational facility went coed in 1984. The anticipation of midnight rides having nothing to do with Paul Revere are, as far as we know, no longer a concern.

But I was desperate to be near my brother. And family members made Girard College sound like an excellent opportunity to get a fine education at a private school, at no cost! I did not go to that hideous place but instead hit the Oedipus jackpot. I got to stay home with Mom, watch TV, eat Breyers ice cream, and hang out at Cooper's candy store.

Still, on weekends when the fatherless boys' orphanage kept Brother Bruce grounded for some infraction, and kept him from coming home for the weekend, my boredom would set in. At around 10:00 a.m. I'd start looking for something to do or for trouble to get into. One noncompetitive game I played was called step ball. Sort of the equivalent to solitaire. It wasn't a very complicated game. The player (me) would throw a rubber ball against a flight of steps and then the other player (me) would catch it in the air. Over and over and over. It was like having a catch with yourself.

One of my favorite escapes was to go to the cinema. I lived within walking distance of three movie theaters, and I was at one of them at least once a week. When I heard about Saturday matinee double features (and I could cross the street by myself), I walked there to be immersed in three hours of total stimulation and escapism.

Sometimes, a friend and I would go for the Saturday matinee and then afterward hide in the balcony playing gin rummy and parsing out Raisinets to sustain us until the evening features. We saved money by not paying another admission fee and enjoyed watching the more sophisticated films at night meant for grown-ups. Those were some of the happiest days of my life.

The correlation between happiness and cinema is forever linked in my consciousness. The first movie theaters were referred to as "dream palaces" not only for their ornate architecture but for the altered state achieved by patrons for five cents. I learned to love the movies, except the time my mom took me to see *Psycho* (child abuse), and it scared the crap out of me.

A mama's boy, one competition for my mother's affection had died and the other was packed off to boarding school. Father dead . . . brother excommunicated . . . and she was all mine. For years it made me a very possessive and jealous lover. For years? Bullshit! Forever.

Bruce, Rose, Lee

Chapter 2

The Starting Gate

I educated myself. To me, school was boring.
—Van Morrison

CUT TO: Beth Judah Hebrew School. Mr. Silver is sending me to the principal's office . . . again. I was caught taking bets on that Sunday's Eagles game.

The Philadelphia Eagles were a 14-point underdog against the New York Giants. My young classmates, who didn't know what a point spread was, were all betting the Eagles would win outright. (No way that could happen against the New York Giants— not in 1962.) By the tender age of 12, I was well-versed in both the concept of the point spread and its profitable application.

I had learned these lessons at Cooper's—not your ordinary corner confectionery. Cooper's was the kind of candy store you'd see in an old Bowery Boys film or a Paul Mazursky movie or read about in *The Plot Against America* by Philip Roth. It's easy to picture handsome Jacob Garfinkel buying a pack of Chesterfields and telling the guys, "If this horse I have in the fifth at Garden State wins, I'm buying a one-way Greyhound ticket to Hollywood and changing my name to John Garfield."

For a Jew, Cooper's was the equivalent of an Irish pub, where neighbors often meet to have a few Guinnesses. But rather than a few pints, the magnet for me and some of these other brazen gamblers was placing bets with Moxie, the resident bookmaker; eating ice cream; drinking fountain sodas; and shooting the shit with the guys. I never felt alone or out of place there, even though I was the youngest patron. A real regular.

The younger of the guys (average age 30) and I played half-ball or handball out in front on the street every day, weather permitting. Meanwhile, to conduct their business, gamblers and bookmakers used the old-fashioned candlestick telephone. And I mean old-fashioned. The earpiece was separately tethered by a wire to a big black box with a protruding part, like an inverted megaphone to place your mouth against and speak. Very film noir if you ask me.

We played pinochle, rummy, or five-card stud and sometimes chess in the three booths at the back of the store. Always for money. Even chess. This was the kind of place where if two raindrops hit the front window at the same time, someone would bet you which drop rolled to the bottom first. However, it was the pinball machine that seemed to call my name, especially when I had someone to play against.

The Pinball Wizard at Coopers

If a game is fun to play, it's always more fun and way more intense if you have a bet on the outcome. A game of pinball only cost a nickel, but our bets could be up to 15 or 20 cents. To get those nickels, I would steal bottles off back porches and return them to the store for the deposit money. On a five-ball machine, I could play for 10 to 15 minutes on one game. That meant that for 10 to 15 minutes, I wasn't thinking about anything else, like homework or chores or where I was going to get my next nickel to play another game.

Pinball took all the powers of observation and finger dexterity I had. At 12 years old, playing pinball was my first compulsive habit. When I was old enough to go to Las Vegas, and before Atlantic City drained every last dollar from New Jersey's senior citizens and pie- in-the-sky lottery addicts, I would gamble on anything, but mostly on sports, poker, and other casino games.

Stooped over with age and experience, Benny Cooper was the owner of the candy store. For how long? Nobody knew, but definitely pre-Civil War. He was old. His smile was as bright as the gray hair on his shiny Jewish kup, a smile that would not quit. On Sunday mornings, the store became an eye-burning experience from the cigars and cigarettes smoked by all the regulars. Cooper minded his own business and never said a cross word to anyone. He also ignored any illegal transactions going on right in front of his Coke-bottle thick eyeglasses. Thankfully, I could owe him for anything I wanted whenever I ran out of money. Later, when I had a son of my own, I named him Benjamin. We called him Benny.

Cooper's was home to a cast of characters who were as colorful as anything from the pens of Damon Runyon or Saul Bellow. With no daddy, I leaned on these paternal role models—the gamblers, bookmakers, convivial conmen, scholars, poets and hucksters from the streets of Philly. I gathered with my surrogate tutors, embroiled in discussions about politics, literature and the arts. Fights were rare. Firearms were unheard of. Although before I left the house, my mother warned me not to get hit by any stray insults. It was, after all, a Jewish neighborhood.

Moxie, who always wore a suit and a tie on his medium build, had an engaging smile that never really looked full—more like a stifled grin that was deciding which way to go next. He was the top bookmaker in the neighborhood.

Fixie must have been Sephardic. He had a dark, almost Latino complexion. Fixie was slender and flexible but not a big gambler. He had impressive eyebrows— cathedral round, not too bushy. But his eyes were expressive enough to make you think that he knew what he was talking about. He did odd jobs and small scams whenever he could. He was also the best half-ball player in the neighborhood.

Fox was bulky but not overweight. He was a solid, all-American guy who always needed a shave. His smile was pearly white. He was plain spoken and direct. And very good looking. He always had a girl stashed somewhere.

Bruce the Flying Goose was annoying yet very charismatic. He was five foot eight and had wavy dark hair, which he never combed. His Adam's apple was noticeably large (he would not have made a convincing tranny). He was always trying to make some deal or another. Goose's brother was called The Geese. He was odd-looking, almost Picasso-like. Together, the two of them could've starred in a buddy movie directed by Robert Downey Sr.—a movie that would be funny, nonsensical, absurd, and good-natured.

The know-it-alls who hung out at Cooper's were always ready to share their advice. Two days after I had sex for the first time, I walked up to the corner, and future lawyer Big Ed hands me a book by Henry Miller. "I heard you had sex. Read this," he said. "Now you can have an opinion."

For me, the streetwise guys of North Philly offered needed fatherly advice. They had near-rabbinical insight regarding romance and finance. Sure, I could ask my mother for answers to life's nagging questions, but she was too exhausted from working every day to give me anything but a woman's perfunctory answer. From the guys on the corner, I would get answers from a man's point of view, something my mother could never give me. Answers that sometimes were more like questions. The ways Jews so often do:

"Do you think it's going to be a hot summer?"

"Do I think it's going to be a hot summer? What am I, a weatherman?"

"If I dream about having sex with my mother, does that mean I'm going to become a Freudian therapist?"

"Does it mean you're going to become a psychoanalyst? No, it means you better get laid soon."

These men revered Isaac Bashevis Singer, Bobby Fischer, Arnold Rothstein, Sandy Koufax, Lenny Bruce, and our new young president, John F. Kennedy. In some ways, years later, I intellectually (and emotionally) adopted these men, along with Robert Bly, Tom Robbins, Hunter Thompson, Alan Watts, Martin Amis, J. D. Salinger and most influential of all, Henry Miller, the author dubbed the "Buddha with a penis," to be my surrogate fathers. The poets who most moved me were Allen Ginsberg, Walt Whitman, Carl Sandberg, Gregory Corso, Rainer Maria Rilke, Rumi, Lawrence Ferlinghetti, Gary Snyder and Lew Welch.

As for the arts, the one taken most seriously was cinema. Jumping into a car with a couple of guys to go downtown to see a first run film was heavenly. First for the camaraderie, second for the film but only if it was a good one. And if someone (like me) didn't have enough money to get in, somebody would always offer to treat. If someone offered to cover your ticket, you had passed the initiation. You knew you belonged. Who knows, maybe the guys were all actually just hoping to get under my mother's skirt. But those were some of the happiest days of my life. Going to the movies with friends, then and now, always puts a skip in my step. (Come to think of it, Mom did wear a lot of skirts.)

The complimentary social matrix of my maturation was Logan's black-market society, where commercial transactions took place devoid of check-out counters and cash registers. Sales were undocumented, untaxed and most likely illegal. This was, of course, perfectly normal.

When Jackie Pants, with Cheshire cat grin, excitedly pulls up to the corner candy store, opens his car trunk filled with new Brooks Brothers suits, and offers them at 80 percent below retail, you know this is a deal made in the shade. The best deals are always too good to be true and too shady to withstand the bright light of ethical inquiry.

I don't think the suit I wore to my Bar Mitzvah was "hot," although it is an appealing picture stuffing a stolen suit with honest money, after phonetically mouthing a religious incantation without a spiritual experience anywhere in the room until my mother's boyfriend gets the bill for the whole shindig and cries, "Jesus Christ, who ordered the two extra cases of Smirnoff?"

In truth, if my mother had happened to be coming out of the candy store with our biweekly supply of two half-gallons of Breyers vanilla fudge ice cream, and if the trunk of a late-model Chevrolet Impala were openly revealing teen-sized suits for sale at seriously marked-down prices, she would have bought one. Why not keep the money in the neighborhood and save a trip downtown to Wanamaker's or Gimbels?

I followed their example, and what it got me at the Beth Judah Hebrew School was a lot of dough and a little trouble for taking bets. What did I know? I was only 12.

So there I was in Principal Rothenberg's office. I was angry because I wasn't done collecting bets, although the assorted lunch monies I had stuffed into my pants pockets were substantial enough to create a comfortable bulge. Being in the principal's office was very awkward, for him not me. Rothenberg, a married man, was having an affair with my mother. I knew it. He knew that I knew it. When two enemies share the same secret, silence is their mutual friend. I protect his indiscretion, and he overlooks mine. Mr. Rothenberg's affair was my first lesson in the practical application of "it's not what you know, it's who you know . . . and what you know about them."

"Lee" (my name before sobriety), advised Rothenberg, "just sit here for 10 minutes, then go tell your class I gave you a stern talking to."

Deal!

Had I been the adult, I would have given him the stern talking to. I may have been only 12, but I already felt like a man. Who needs a Bar Mitzvah? Although, one year later, we made it official, at least according to Jewish custom. I became a man raised by a woman.

Mom was very discreet regarding her affair, although her teen years were fairly risqué. Every year on her birthday, a large carton of 24 assorted gift boxes of Cherrydale Farms chocolates were delivered to our house. It was only after her death, when Brother Bruce and I read her diary, that we learned she, at the age of 16, was knocked up by Mr. Cherry (oh, the irony). He paid for the abortion and soothed his conscience by gifting Mom a lifetime supply of chocolate-covered cherries every Christmas. Although a gift for having an abortion should rightly be delivered on Good Friday.

Looking back at Mr. Principle (intentionally spelled like the synonym for morals), I'll bet that my first lawyer, the very well (mob)-connected Rob Simone, would have told me to blackmail the bastard. I could have had gifts for all eight days of Hanukkah or a scholarship to the yeshiva. Yeah, as if that's where I was headed.

Gambling can be as intoxicating as alcohol—and sunflower kernels. For the entirety of my youth, I had enjoyed eating sunflower seeds, cracking off the shell, and eating one kernel at a time. In 1965, on my way to the movies to see *The Sound of Music* in Atlantic City, all alone, I stopped by Planter's Peanuts to buy a snack. The store had bags of unshelled sunflower seeds. I had never seen that before. So I bought a 16-ounce bag. Halfway through the movie, I realized I'd eaten the whole bag and was now physically ill. I sat through the film feeling uncomfortable but not knowing which way the seeds were going to exit my body. But still loving the movie as much as one could love any Nazi-inspired Broadway musical brought to the screen by born- Jewish geniuses. That is my first memory of addictive behavior. I would create many more.

Although alcohol has never been my drug of choice, alcohol can taste and feel like the nectar of the Gods. In Greek mythology, the Olympians were said to drink ambrosia, which bestowed upon them immortality. When reality sets in, mortality can be sobering and frightening. An ancient Hebrew legend tells the difference between moderate and irresponsible drinking. When Noah planted grape vines, Satan revealed to him the possible effects of alcohol. He slaughtered a lamb, a lion, an ape and a pig. He explained: "The first cup of wine will make you mild like a lamb; the second will make you feel brave like a lion; the third will make you act like an ape; and the fourth will make you wallow in the mud like a pig." It's when the wallowing episodes outnumber the bravery escapades that you have to STOP.

Famed comic Dick Van Dyke, after some time sober, remembered calling the AA office while drunk in the middle of the night during one of his drinking and crying binges. "I slipped off the wagon," said Van Dyke. "I bought a bottle, had four drinks, and got sick to my stomach. I thought I might become so hooked again I was terrified, and I poured the rest down the sink. I haven't had another drink since."

Later in my life, in a dream that felt very real, the poet, novelist, and short story writer Charles Bukowski tried to kidnap me. I told him to go fuck himself with a beer bottle. He grabbed a Heineken and did so gladly.

In real life, I used to see Bukowski every time I went to the racetrack, usually Hollywood Park or Santa Anita. I later heard that his doctor told him if he didn't stop drinking, he would die a mundane, miserable alcoholic death. Since Bukowski never wanted to be considered mundane in any way, he put down the bottle and replaced drinking with nonstop horse betting. In fact, he bet on every horse in every race. He never lost a race. He only lost money.

After a period of time, Bukowski's doctor told him that his health had improved, and he could try drinking in moderation. As we know, moderation is not in everyone's vocabulary, but Bukowski did his best. He turned drinking and gambling into two interlocking hobbies and was happy as a clam. Those who warned that booze would be the death of him were dead wrong. He died of leukemia in 1994, still holding onto his love of writing, women, booze and horse race gambling.

In my early twenties, I worked as the trophy photographer at Northfield Park Racetrack on the outskirts of Cleveland. It was harness racing, not thoroughbred racing. I shared an office with the security department. One night, my office mate, a retired FBI agent, made an announcement over the public address system, paging a male patron to come to the security office. When he arrived, racing form in hand, the officer told him they had received a call from the hospital: His wife had just died. Heartbroken, he left the office a little dazed—but not to call family and friends or get in his car and drive home, as you would think. No, he went right to the $100 window and made a bet. No photograph I could take could have captured that profoundly addictive moment. (Who knows, maybe he was celebrating.)

#

As a kid, I loved not only playing and betting on sports but watching and following all the action and intrigue that come with them. At 14, I was a devout Phillies fan. I kept a scrapbook filled with every story about "my team" and firmly believed they were a lock for the 1964 World Series. I cut out each day's box scores from the morning *Philadelphia Inquirer* and glued them into my scrapbook. They were 10 games ahead in the standings in the National League, and I was on cloud nine with puberty behind me and a pennant in front of me. And then . . . it all went to hell in the debacle known as The Phold of '64.

On September 21, 1964, Chico Ruiz of the Cincinnati Reds stole home plate from third base, starting a losing streak for the Phillies, and that same day the St. Louis Cardinals started a winning streak. They went on to finish in first place and win the World Series against the New York Yankees.

I was heartbroken. No, I was beyond heartbroken. Overtaken by fate and massive depression, I put my scrapbook in a cardboard box and never looked at it again. I had invested an enormous amount of adolescent emotional (possibly sexual) energy in identifying myself with the Phillies. Their victories were mine; their ignominious defeat was mine as well. I vowed to no longer pin my self-image to the success of anyone else, nor fall for the hype of self-esteem by proxy.

If there were to be victories for Leonard Lee Buschel, they would be mine, on my terms, my way and not dependent on the fate of others, especially those who I had semi-worshipped but who never knew my name. Being a '64 Phillies fanatic was a dream gone bad.

#

In some areas, people are judged by how rich they are, what kind of family they come from, what country club they belong to, and what kind of Caddy Daddy drives. In my neighborhood, there was no such crap. Instead, the most valuable thing we had was our word. If people couldn't trust you, you were shunned because they couldn't include you in their scams or be privy to their backdoor romances. The deal was: You lie=You get ostracized. I learned there is honor among thieves, so to speak, and in my neighborhood, that was equivalent to equality and acceptance.

Some folks may regard my old neighborhood as "dangerous." Nonsense. It was only dangerous if you were seen doing anything suspicious or, worse yet, arrested. The day before I started Olney High School, Brother Bruce and I were taken into custody for "corner lounging." This was a pivotal moment in my psychological and emotional development. It instilled in me an unwavering oppositional attitude toward authority.

You've never heard of the horrid crime of corner lounging? Well, that may be because the Constitution of the United States assures you of the right of free assembly, a concept unfamiliar to some local law enforcement officers. In truth, corner lounging is a crime in Philadelphia of long-standing reputation. In 1880, the mayor's office reported 198 cases of corner lounging in the annual crime report, yet there were fewer than 10 charges of unlawful assembly, one crime of sodomy, and two folks arrested for bastardy.

Corner lounging is, as one would surmise, the crime of lounging on a corner. Mid-block lounging isn't serious enough to merit incarceration. What happened? Brother Bruce and I went to the movies and took the bus home. Dropped off at the corner bus stop, we walked over to Cooper's to see if anyone was hanging out, someone we could shoot the shit with or talk about the movie we'd just seen. Shortly after we got there, a red and white pulled up, two cops lumbered out of their cop car and grabbed us before we had even the slightest opportunity to start lounging. The cops took us to the slammer at the 35th Precinct. That's where they lock you up before taking you downtown to the Round House to be booked and fingerprinted.

Brother Bruce, being over 16, was released on his own recognizance. Being under 16, I didn't have sufficient recognizance. Mom couldn't come get me because she was unreachable at the Ben Franklin Motor Inn with her married lover. He, however, did experience release, while I languished behind bars on the night before my first day of high school. Maybe that's why I named my son Ben.

On a side note, believe it or not, I prefer the pre-cell phone era, when we were not all accessible anywhere, at any time day or night. Anyway, my brother called my best friend Joe D. His father, Shep, was our local "Committee Man" (politically connected). Joe asked his father to come to the 35th Precinct and get me out. He signed me out of jail at 2:00 a.m. In Philly, a neighborhood Committee Man's personal power outweighs the beat cop and trumps the perversity of a corner lounging arrest.

Once, when best friend Joe borrowed Shep's car to drive us to the yearly Strates Carnival, he opened the glove compartment and showed me a hundred parking tickets Shep had gotten and just ignored. That was the way Philly politics worked. We needed the car to go to the yearly Strates Carnival because it was a couple neighborhoods away and too outside our comfort zone to take the bus.

The rides were dangerous, the food was dangerous and the girls were extremely dangerous. And we were only going for the girls. The girls were dangerous because it seemed like whichever one was anxious to talk to you had two boyfriends who were anxious to beat you up. (Probably whacked around by their fathers and just living up to the adage, "Hurt people, hurt people.")

Before Shep "got me sprung," I was starting to fantasize—or hallucinate—that I could slip through the bars of the jail cell.

Obviously, I could not. Luckily, when 2:00 a.m. rolled around and I was set free, I could go home and sleep for a few hours before my first day at high school.

Orientation Day? I thought I had just had initiation night. The hard floor-to- ceiling iron bars, the single phone call, the gestapo feel of the backseat of a cop car, and *no* idea what I had done wrong.

Sleep deprived, I stepped foot into the high school auditorium with more than 1,500 excited students chattering and yammering for the "welcome new students" assemblage. I was yawning like I had been up half the night planning my escape from jail, because I was! That's alright. It was all bullshit anyway. All I could do was percolate in my mind my brewing, strong distrust for author-ity because the night before, I was arrested for nothing. It must have been a slow night at Logan's 35th Precinct. That distrust for authority followed me through my high school years, at that very big (1,823 boys and girls) and oppressive educational institution.

If I couldn't trust authority, I could trust the guys in the neighborhood.

She told reporters, "Parce-que je ne sais pas, mes chéres. (Because I don't know my dears). Yes–I have visited Sally Tomato. I used to go see him every week. What's wrong with that? He believes in God, and so do I...Then, under the subheading ADMITS OWN DRUG ADDICTION: Miss Golightly smiled when a reporter asked whether or not she herself is a narcotics user, "I've had a little go at marijuana. It's not half so destructive as brandy. Cheaper, too. Unfortunately, I prefer brandy. No, Mr. Tomato never mentioned drugs to me. It makes me furious, the way these wretched people keep persecuting him. He's a sensitive, a religious person. A darling old man."
— Breakfast at Tiffany's by Truman Capote (Vintage Books, 1950)

Chapter 3

Let's Make a Deal

Everybody says sex is obscene. The only true obscenity is war.
—Henry Miller

There is a scene near the end of *The Graduate* when Benjamin, not knowing what direction to take in life, gets advice from his uncle, who sidles up next to him by the pool and whispers, "I have one word for you. *Plastics*." In Logan, that one word was *whiplash*.

When you're old enough to drive, you're old enough to sue. When I turned 16, I was introduced to the wonderful wide world of insurance fraud. I was always happy to be asked to "take a ride" with Elliott Fisher, my former camp counselor who was now my instructor in the art and science of whiplash.

Elliott would drive downtown to City Hall Circle and circle until we were in front of an obviously well-insured driver, preferably in a Lincoln or a Cadillac. Soon enough, Elliott would tell me to brace for the imminent collision. He would hit the brakes with a suddenness that gave the driver behind us no choice but to plow into us. Then, depending on how dramatic we were feeling, we'd throw open our doors and fall or stagger out of the vehicle crying, "Oh my back! I can't walk! My head is bleeding. My knees are broken. Whiplash, Whiplash!"

Whiplash is usually the injury that comes the day after a crash, a delayed reaction revealing the body's actual injuries after shock's hyped-up adrenaline wears off. We would never go to the hospital, where honest doctors might see us. Instead, we went to a crooked lawyer who sent us to a crooked doctor, all of which resulted in documented medical bills in the thousands of dollars. We would all make out pretty good.

After one brilliant crash, hit from behind by an elderly woman driver wearing horned rim glasses, we filed a very sizable claim. Two months later I was visited at home by the insurance company investigator pretending he was Perry Mason. He asked a lot of difficult questions. The guy had significant attitude, and I was nervous as hell. Thank God for all those acting classes Mom paid for and my membership in my high school theatre club, The Footlighters. The driver's insurance company eventually settled, and I collected enough spending money for a year. This was the only time I ever made money from my acting skills.

This was my entree into bilking the system. I knew the insurance company wasn't going to suffer, and for the first time I felt like a real wage earner.

What did I want to be when I grew up? From the time I was a teenager, my dream was to be a successful entrepreneur. At different times, I also fancied being an actor or a lawyer. Mostly, I wanted to make money and work independently.

When I was 15, I would tell friends and family: "I don't want to be a lawyer. I'm *going* to be a lawyer." That's how sure I was about my future—and not just because I loved the TV show *The Defenders*. After experiencing the mind-expanding properties of pot, mescaline, and LSD, I realized that being a defendant could be far more fascinating and profitable than being an attorney. Plus, I preferred fiction to law books. Also, I was aghast at the glaring inequities of the legal system. "He who owns the gold makes the laws."

Greed is a wicked mistress, and at the time, I believed that human happiness was directly related to material wealth. Hence, if I had become a lawyer or stockbroker, I would have pushed the limits. Insider trading, stealing, and selling corporate secrets, along with aiding and abetting all manner of nefarious activities committed by immoral clients, could well have been my eventual, well-earned downfall and disgrace. I would have gone to jail. Because after all, don't attorneys study the laws to know how to break them, consiglieri?

I could have blamed my crass materialism on Warner Bros., producers of the TV show *Maverick*. I recall a scene where someone asks Bret Maverick, "How free are you?" His reply was, "I'm only as free as the size of the roll in my pocket." As an impressionable youth, I took this to heart. I had a hunger for cash growing up, even though my mother never mentioned our precarious financial situation. We always had money for everything we needed. No more, no less. She never once kvetched about our middle-class cash flow or talked about finances, mortgage payments or utility bills. All I knew was if I needed a new pair of corduroy pants for the coming winter, I had them.

No wish to be in corporate America—it's a trap because you become a cog in their wheel. I knew well what I did not want to spend my life doing. The majority of people have to do what they do to make a living, to provide food and shelter for themselves or their loved ones. Or it depends on what their families did, or what they studied in college or maybe what they are good at. I always believed my destiny was entrepreneurial success.

In my twenties and thirties, my entrepreneurial tendencies got me to open a restaurant in Boulder, Colorado, for several reasons. One was to meet an interesting woman as a restaurant owner. The other was to serve Allen Ginsberg lunch. (I did get to serve Allen lunch a couple times.) My fantasy of owning the coolest vegetarian restaurant in Boulder and sleeping with a few hot angel-headed hipsters attending Naropa University never materialized because I brought my own soon-to-be pregnant girlfriend with me. And because my career as a restauranteur never got past the appetizer.

When I bought the restaurant, it was called Corn Mother. But my Genius Cousin Bobb, who I brought in from Los Angeles to run the place, thought the name Corn Mother was too hippie-ish, so we renamed it The Yarrow Stalk. Genius Cousin Bobb promised to give free I-Ching readings to all our patrons. When he threw the coins for himself, the *Book of Changes* told him to change his mind. Not a single reading ever took place. Turned out the restaurant was too close to an elementary school to get a liquor license, and without being able to serve beer or wine, we lost money on every meal served.

Being a risk taker is part of being an entrepreneur. It's not healthy living in fear all the time. Still, some things don't feel risky at the time.

#

As a young man, I wanted to consume life as if it were going out of style. Before drugs became my significant other, my insatiable appetite was completely satisfied with nature's natural high—sex. I'm glad the first time I had sex I wasn't high. I had sex for sex's sake, not unlike Adam in the Garden (with the same intensity as a man wanting to start the human race). Every girl I hooked up with in Philadelphia seemed to be named Kathy. But I thought of them all as Eve.

If you were a boy, growing up in Logan usually meant your first sexual experiences were of the homosexual nature, unless you had a sister. At 15 years old, I didn't really care who was going down on me. It was the thrill, the feelings, pleasurable sensation, and orgasm that mattered. Years later, I participated in a number of sing-a-longs with Allen Ginsberg. He loved to play the harmonium and sing his poems. One song lyric I remember so clearly was, "Everyone's a little homosexual, whether they like it or not." When I told my therapist that I often dreamt of Ginsberg, I asked him if that meant I was gay. He said no, but that somehow, Allen had become my guardian angel.

I knew I really wasn't queer because when I was 23 and living in Amsterdam for the summer, I did a little experiment to see where my sexual chips would fall on their own. Living in the sexiest city in Northern Europe, very far from home, without a friend or family member within 3,000 miles, I was feeling bold. My research results would guide me for the rest of my life.

One afternoon, I went to the Red Light District and made a date with a woman to have sex with me that night at 8:00 p.m. Then I made a date with a man to have sex with me a block away from where I was meeting the lady. At 7:30 p.m., after a few pipefuls of opiated Afghani hashish, a couple shots of Stoli, and a whiff of MDMA (I liked to snort it), I started walking to my pair of paramour providers, emptying my mind of any judgment, shame or guilt and just letting my body decide which way to amble to see which gender I was most attracted to. It wasn't even close. As I approached my chosen hooker, her miniskirt looked like a sequined curtain about to rise on my next act, which would last for the rest of my life. Selling drugs=money=sex equals e=mc2. I did feel a modicum of relief I wasn't 100 percent gay. "Not that there's anything wrong with that." (Thank you, Larry David.)

A collateral benefit of this experiment in the Netherlands was that whenever quick homosexual opportunities did arise, I was able to partake and not be afraid I would go that way forever. Just like being back in Logan.

Funny coincidence. In 1973 the New York Times bestseller was *The Happy Hooker*, by Dutch-born Xaviera Hollander.

#

Back in my teens, my friend Joe D. and I were always looking for girls. On the street. At school. At fairs. At parties. Everywhere. One night, around nine o'clock, we were supposed to meet some girls we knew when they got off the subway at the Broad and Wyoming station. There was nothing special planned other than hanging out together. Drugs had not yet made their way into my scene. I was still a virgin in every way.

Joe and I showed up on time, but the girls failed to ascend from the subway. While waiting, we saw an attractive woman walking down the street in our direction. She was tall, slender, and seemed to be on her way nowhere. Taught to never let a beautiful woman walk by without at least trying, I started walking with her and engaged her in some light conversation, saying things like, "Do you need a light?" I always carried matches because, while I never smoked cigarettes, most sophisticated (loose) women did. Joe stayed back at the subway station waiting for our alleged dates to arrive.

I was well-schooled in the Zen of Picking up Girls: "Never use a pick-up line. Only speak of the here and now. Stay in the moment. Authenticity is a powerful aphrodisiac." Brother Bruce, the horny Zen Master, was correct, and his advice served me well.

I convinced the young woman to come back to my house. Mom was out of town and my brother was home watching television. The girl and I went upstairs to my bedroom, and I was rejoicing that I was going to get to at least make out with this wayward beauty.

Sitting on my bed, I tried to unbutton her blouse. Her hands went up immediately, to block me? so my hands stopped in mid-button. What was this—a sudden rejection? Or the firm setting of boundaries. I had to ask.

Me: "What's going on?"

Her: "You want me to take off my blouse, don't you?"

No argument from me. I answered positively with an enthusiastic little asthmatic pant.

She not only took off her blouse, but she also took off her pants. And MY pants too! We proceeded, for lack of a better phrase, to "make love." This was my first experience with full frontal nudity and my first sexual act involving penetration and not just prostration. It was spectacular.

I was awestruck upon the Mount Sinai of sexual revelation. It was as if God was a ventriloquist speaking divine words of encouragement, praise, and appreciation via her enchanted vagina. I felt at one with Moses. But instead of tablets, Allah sent down unto thee a labia majora. A constellation I would travel through space to visit often.

Afterward, she smoked cigarettes, and we talked up a storm. I am grateful to this day that I wasn't smoking pot yet. This was a completely sober experience. So, years later, after joining Alcoholics Anonymous, I could remind myself that sex is the best natural high in the world.

In the middle of my postcoital revelry, I hear a classic pulp fiction/porno cliché. She asks, "Isn't there someone else downstairs?"

"Yes," I replied suspiciously, "My brother."

"Maybe he wants to come up now," she said smiling.

I put my underwear back on, went to the staircase, walked down a half a flight, and confusingly proclaimed the glad tidings.

"Bruce, you're next!" I announced.

"What do you mean?" he asked.

"She wants someone else now," I answered.

In the blink of an eye, Brother Bruce and I traded positions. I was downstairs watching TV, and he was having sex with that cute woman I'd picked up. About 10 minutes later, while I'm watching Johnny Carson, Joe returns from his stakeout at the subway.

"They never showed up."

"Doesn't matter, Joe. You're next," I said.

"What do you mean?" he asked befuddled.

"That girl I picked up just hit the trifecta."

Let the games begin—and continue. The three of us, one by one—never all together—took turns satisfying the young woman's yearnings till dawn. No drugs. No drinking. Just pure, unadulterated sexual pleasure. At my young age, and due to inexperience, I didn't know the difference between a nymphomaniac and a sex addict. Neither did she. And none of us cared. We were into some antics, not semantics, and all of us were in seventh heaven, on cloud nine.

At six in the morning, surrounded by the heady aroma of all-night sex, we entered a local diner for breakfast, and suddenly the odor of frying bacon vanished, and it Smells Like Teen Spirit. When the final triangle of toast disappeared down the throat with which we were all familiar, she had us drive to her neighborhood, near her house. Before getting out of the car, she gave us her phone number.

"You have reached a number that has been disconnected or is no longer in service. If you feel you have reached this number in error..."

The number was phony, and the name she used (was it Misty, Trixie, or *Kathy*?) probably wasn't the one on her birth certificate. Sadly, she was probably just a living example of the adage, "Sick in the head, crazy in bed."

If there are any therapists or trauma specialists reading this, I apologize for being 17 and a human.

None of us ever saw her again, although I thought of her often. If, by some twist of fate and destiny, she is reading this right now . . .

"Thank you for one of the most wonderful and memorable nights of my life. You were my Annie Sullivan, my personal miracle worker, who opened new vistas of communications beyond sight and sound—full of squeals of delight and sighs of the supranatural. Wanna go have breakfast?"

What made the night spectacular transcended the sexual experience. More than losing my virginity, I was able to do a favor for my brother and a good friend. Our hearts were now bound together stronger than ever.

#

By my senior year, something else was also happening to me. J. D. Salinger explained it in "A Perfect Day for Bananafish." The story describes this fish who's always hungry. One day, he swims into a cave full of bananas. He eats one, then another, and then another. He is consumed with eating all of these bananas because they satiate his hunger, temporarily. When all the bananas are gone, he swims to the mouth of the cave, but he's too fat to get out. Captive in the cave, he dies of malnutrition (and loneliness). Pot and hashish would soon become my bananas.

It may have started with my best friend, who was a bookmaker and five to ten years my senior. Mom said to him: "Why are you hanging out with my son?" She was streetwise to the way of the world of creeps.

He told her, "We just get along. We became fast friends when we met at Cooper's. Your son is a cool kid, and we have a lot in common."

Eventually, the bookmaker would be the first person to lend me money to score drugs to sell (and to take me to a brothel). But I didn't tell Mom that. Or maybe she already had an inkling about it.

Funny thing, looking back I realized that cruising Columbia Avenue for hookers was a little like Forrest Gump's box of chocolates. You never knew what you were going to get. You never really noticed what sex they were until after you had an orgasm.

The first time I got high on marijuana, I knew that I had found a friend for life, a tool for living, the key to the magic kingdom. From my high school senior year on, no matter where I was, I always had pot in my pocket or shoulder bag. Right next to my asthma inhaler. Sounds like a scene of a self-fulfilling prophecy. From my first exhale I was hooked. The weed gave me that indescribable feeling of ease and comfort, inherent human qualities I sorely lacked as a teenager. Shortly afterward, I was turned on to the superiority and compactness of hashish. I can only describe the experience as mystical and earthly. If it was good enough for Victor Hugo, who was I to dispute its wonders?

Reality can slap us in the face or embrace us when we're young. The irony is, I think I only started to create my own reality after I started getting high. But even that can be an illusion. Everybody has a choice, or do they? I thought getting high every day was my choice. Or was it my medicine? People can stop getting high with a little effort. Or not.

Once I started getting high, I needed to make sure I knew how to make and follow plans because if you're high all the time you can become more like a leaf on a branch instead of like a root anchored to a timetable as accurate as Mussolini's train schedule. Occasionally, I do live life by the seat of my pants, preferably without them on.

I clearly remember the exact moment I decided to make smoking marijuana part of my life on a daily basis. When I was 18, I dropped some acid. Not an exorbitant dose, just enough to hallucinate my ass off, astral travel, and see God as energy in everything. Just the usual LSD trip. I was blessed/cursed with the realization that as much as I loved the experience, I could not drop acid every day and be a coherent functioning member of society. But I could smoke pot every day to suggest the essence of the essence of being at one with everything. Like the old man ordering a hot dog from a vendor in Central Park:

Vendor: "What do you want on it?"

Me: "Make me one with everything."

I cut class a lot in the 12th grade, as the mood struck me. Some days the only reason I went to school was to sell pot and football pools. And to check in with my clandestine girlfriend Sandy. We had to keep it a secret because she was engaged and the only woman in our class who already had a daughter. We rendezvoused outside school at least once a week. It went something like this: After doing his popular radio show, Sandy's future husband would drop her off at home, usually well after Sandy's mother had put the baby down to sleep. I was ninja-like, hiding in the tall bushes in front of her house. After the fiancé drove off, I would go through the alley next to the back of the house and she'd let me in. I would climb up the backstairs, stay all night, and split before Baby and Grandma awoke the next morning.

Maybe it was the pot that stole my motivation to go to school. But in all honesty, I had perfected this habit of cutting class over the years, well before I was introduced to marijuana. When I was at Jay Cooke Junior High, older friends of mine would come by during lunch, on their way to the track, asking me if I wanted to join them. I would walk out of the schoolyard like a man who could not refuse such an offer. Social studies or Secretariat in the fifth? Maybe they called roll after lunch, but I was on a roll. Which would later in life be described as "self-will run riot." School was no longer interesting. I just didn't care.

Daytime TV sucked, so if I wasn't gambling, getting high, or having sex, I would ride my bike, trying not to be seen by the truant officers, who usually didn't patrol my neighborhood as much as they did the "bad" neighborhoods. After all, what Jewish kid isn't anxious to go to school, even just to get away from his mother for a few hours? Mine was always at work, so that wasn't an issue.

#

Drugs were quickly ruling out some of my career choices. Until I started smoking pot, I took acting classes and performed in small theater companies. For several years every Saturday morning, I rode the train from Philly to New York's Penn Station. From there I took the subway to Greenwich Village to attend classes at the legendary Circle in the Square Theatre. There I started to wonder about my potential career as an actor. On stage at this iconic theater, I noticed all my classmates could sing beautifully and dance like pros, while I couldn't carry a tune or touch my toes. I felt like a mutt at the Westminster Dog Show. However I did score the starring role at the Rising Sun Theater on Rising Sun Avenue in Philadelphia, playing Aladdin in *Aladdin*. I loved being on stage and spending time with the cast and crew. The time and effort we put into rehearsing and preparing for opening night was time I wasn't spending alone.

I wish theater acting had been my bananafish, a way to satisfy my hunger for more in life, but when I smoked my first joint, I went on stage and suddenly, as if cursed by Shakespeare himself, became so paranoid that nothing came out of my mouth. It was

LOGAN TIMES

April 15, 1965

Thespian

Lee H. Buschel, 14-year old student at Jay Cooke Jr. High School, is appearing at the Abbey Stage Door Theatre in "Aladdin and the Wonderful Lamp." Lee has the leading role in the fantasy.

I Could Have Been a Contender or My First Notice

41

as if Will was saying, "Get off my fucking stage you no-can sing, no- can dance blossoming hippie!" I knew I had to make a choice: acting or smoking marijuana. Naturally, I gave up acting. The satisfactions from performing take hard work and patience and a good voice. Screech. With pot you're high on the spot. No work, no waiting.

I always got high to improve my emotional condition and the ambiance of my surroundings. I see clearly now that my overuse, misuse, and self-destructive indulgence with mind-altering chemicals probably weakened my performance on the stage of life too.

#

One day in my senior year of high school, Sy Schultz, wearing spectacles as thick as 6-ounce 7- Up bottles, told me that if I could score him some weed, he would pay me 10 bucks over cost. I had never scored weed before, but that $10 bonus was an excellent motivator.

"Yes," I said, "I can get that for you."

"By Tuesday night?"

"Yes. Tuesday night, 8:00 p.m."

Being a man of my word, I kept my word. I said yes. The second time I ever scored weed, I bought enough to sell some and get mine for free. Fast cash and entrepreneurialism. I was charting a path.

#

"Ma, I know what I want to do for a living," I proudly announced the night I fulfilled my promise to Sy. "I want to be a drug dealer."

"Why?" Her question was her response. There was no tinge of judgment or condemnation, only curiosity.

"Because you can do it seven days a week, and you can do it at night, and you can do it on weekends. I'll never be bored," I explained. "I don't want to work from 8:00 a.m. to 5:00 p.m., come home, put some steaks in the oven, little red potatoes in boiling water, and after dinner just watch TV and eat vanilla fudge ice cream every night like we do . . . like you do. I want to have interesting things to do, places to go, and people to hang out with. I want to buy things and go out with more interesting women."

I didn't quite realize that what I wanted—expensive clothes, high-stakes gambling, attractive women, or even more attractive women offering vastly entertaining sex by the hour—was not attainable if I didn't continue my new career as a drug dealer.

Sung to the tune of "Maria" from *West Side Story*:

> *DRUG DEALER, say it loud and it's music playing, say it soft, and it's almost like praying,*
>
> *DRUG DEALER, DRUG DEALER,*
>
> *I'll never stop be'n a DRUG DEALER.*

Yet somehow I knew I wanted all these things from the bottom of my heart. I thought there was nothing I wanted more than money and sex. What else is there? With money in your pocket, you can travel, not shudder at prices on menus in nice restaurants, buy artwork, treat friends to shows and concerts, bet frequently on horses or Phillies games, and drive a car that won't break down every other month. And you can engage in sex whenever you want.

I really didn't expect Mom to say anything other than, "Good for you, Son. Could you get me some more ice cream?"

She surprised me by giving me one solid sentence of good advice before requesting the ice cream. "Be careful who you deal with because someone will drop a dime on you. Someone will get busted and turn you in."

She was correct. It was good advice. A Jewish boy's best friend is his mother. But I *never* took a **big** bust or did time. Had a lot of close calls, but by the grace of God or Lady Luck, was always free to do as I pleased but never truly free until I got clean and sober at Betty Ford's in 1994 and did the 12 Steps of AA (except the anonymity step).

Thank God for my mom—she was even keeled, even when expressing her deepest concerns about me. She was even funny when the tension needed breaking. Years later, when I came back from Israel and dumped the red Lebanese hashish I had smuggled onto our dining room table, she looked at me, she looked at the three 200-gram slabs of Lebanese hashish, and said something only a Jewish mother could say at that moment: "Are you hungry?"

Time to Graduate

Where there is excitement and danger, there's no boredom, no middle-class slumber of mind-numbing conformity. There is an alluring danger to a career in which the consequences for failure are more than just a write-up, suspension or docked wages by a moronic manager or a stupid supervisor. Extended imprisonment or death by misadventure were excellent motivators not to fail. I was determined to stay awake—madly awake.

No falling asleep on the job when you're driving through downtown with 10 pounds of pot in the trunk of your low-profile Volvo or when driving across the Florida-Georgia border with 300 pounds of weed wrapped in six burlap sacks just off the boat from Columbia. Nope, no dozing on the job on the 95.

HIGH

In the Halls of Justice the only justice is in the halls.
— Lenny Bruce

Chapter 4

Fortune Will Always Come to a House with Laughter

Mom was right. It didn't happen right away. In 1968, I graduated from high school high and happy. Shortly afterward, I was busted for possession.

The cops kicked in the door to my mother's house—not difficult as it was a warm July evening and only a flimsy wooden screen door separated us from the local gendarmes—brandishing guns at Mom and me. It was a nightmare scene from a low-budget Michael Haneke film. I don't recall them showing us a search warrant, and my mother felt their aggressive behavior was unwarranted.

"You can't go in my bedroom," insisted Mom.

"Oh, yes we can," replied the cop.

"Oh, no you can't," was Mom's motherly retort.

She tried to block their way. Fat chance. Good thing she wasn't black. Then both my parents would be dead.

They didn't listen to her and went in the bedroom, and while they didn't find the hash, they did find two bags of pot prepackaged for sale. They arrested and handcuffed us both, luckily not to each other. They tossed us both into a paddy wagon. Since that night, I have a PTSD-like reaction whenever a woman pulls out handcuffs.

Shaking and shackled, I said, "Someday pot will be legal, Mom, and they won't bust people for it anymore. It's not even as dangerous as alcohol. You wait and see."

As far as I know, that was the first time my mom had seen the inside of a jail cell. She wasn't angry with me. She wasn't finger-printed, but I was. No bail was set, as they released us on our own recognizance.

My mother, street smart and savvy, retained a mob attorney who only charged us three thousand dollars to beat the rap. He knew what he was doing, and clearly explained his Temple University School of Law defense strategy: $750 for the judge, $750 for the prosecutor, $750 for Mayor Rizzo, and $750 for him. Brilliant, succinct, and effective.

"Case dismissed!"

I had heard there was a Crime Menu in Philly—a list of crimes and prices for how much it cost to buy your way out of whatever you were charged with. Italians got a discount, the Irish paid list, and Jews paid double.

You can have these things dismissed from court but not from memory. This was not an event my mom treasured in her memorabilia basket. Just being in her own home now triggered reliving the trauma of Philly's finest waving a gun in her face.

She had another kind of PTSD (Police Traumatized Single Dame) syndrome. Feeling vulnerable in her own home, she sold it two years later—and she did so at a profit. An enterprising real estate agent offered her an extra five thousand dollars to be the first homeowner in the neighborhood to sell to a black family.

Once that historic breach was made in our all-white, primarily Jewish enclave/ghetto, more families followed my mother's example. This would later be termed "white flight," meaning white people escaping a Negro invasion. If you refuse to sell your home to African Americans, you're a racist. If you do sell to black people, you're running away. In my mother's case, it was "white fright."

The neighbors were not thrilled. But they never did like my mother anyway.

She was a leggy, attractive widow, prancing to work down a block dense with married couples and *mieskeit* wives. Every woman on the block lived in fear that their husband would make a pass at Mom and she would catch it in her end zone.

Busting the Buschels was popular in 1968. It happened again— this time to Brother Bruce. Brother Bruce, Joe D., and I did a midnight radio show in Atlantic City on WLDB (AM) six nights a week (yes, a good radio voice is one of my attributes). We had a contact at CBS Records who kept us well-stocked with the latest hit LPs by hot acts such as Chicago and Blood, Sweat & Tears.

The three of us lived together in a boarding house in Atlantic City. One night, I didn't go to the radio show, *The Underground Shoots Up at Midnight*, because I had an arrangement to buy some real Panama Red from Tyrone at the 500 Club. While I was out having a liberal black- and-white malted, cops raided our apartment looking for drugs. All they found was opium incense, a thick substance with absolutely no opium in it. Sort of like opium perfume.

Not being adept at discerning thick black incense from thick black hashish, the cops put out an arrest warrant for Brother Bruce and me, as our names were on the rental agreement. When I got back to the summer rental house, the other residents excitedly warned me.

"You better get out of here," they said. "The cops have an arrest warrant for you and your brother."

"What about our Joe?"

"No," they explained. "His name wasn't on the warrant."

I immediately called Brother Bruce at the station. "You want me to forget the deal and come meet you?"

"Hell no. If it's real Panama Red, we're going to need it now more than ever."

I took the Jitney to the 500 Club and scored some real Panama Red. The 500 Club, popularly known as The Five, was a nightclub and supper club at 6 Missouri Avenue in Atlantic City. It operated from the 1930s until the building burned down in 1973. The Five had become one of the most popular nightspots on the East Coast.

Our radio show was on until 4:00 a.m. on the weekends, but Brother Bruce left at 2:00 a.m. in case the cops were overly ambitious and on their way to the station to arrest him. Joe finished the show by himself. After I scored the weed, I waited at the bar and nursed a Tom Collins for a couple hours. I wasn't 21 but I had a driver's license in my name, printed to perfection by a guy at Cooper's Corner. I had it laminated and could use it to get into any club or bar in Philly or Atlantic City.

Eventually, Brother Bruce picked me up and we headed home on the White Horse Pike. As the sun rose behind us, the radio played Buffalo Springfield's "For What It's Worth." Written by Stephen Stills, the song is based on a spontaneous conversation he had with his friend P. F. Sloan when the two stepped outside of Pandora's Box nightclub into a riot on the famous Sunset Strip in 1968.

For What It's Worth

There's something happening here

What it is ain't exactly clear

There's a man with a gun over there

Telling me I got to beware

I think it's time we stop, children, what's that sound

Everybody look what's going down

There's battle lines being drawn

Nobody's right if everybody's wrong

Young people speaking their minds

Getting so much resistance from behind

It's time we stop, hey, what's that sound

Everybody look what's going down

What a field day for the heat

A thousand people in the street

Singing songs and carrying signs

Mostly say, hooray for our side

It's s time we stop, hey, what's that sound
Everybody look what's going down
Paranoia strikes deep
Into your life it will creep
It starts when you're always afraid
You step out of line, the man come and take you away
We better stop, hey, what's that sound
Everybody look what's going down
Stop, hey, what's that sound
Everybody look what's going down
Stop, now, what's that sound
Everybody look what's going down
Stop, children, what's that sound
Everybody look what's going down

The lines "a field day for the heat" and "paranoia strikes deep" captured the fear and emotion Brother Bruce and I were experiencing. Suddenly our eyes filled with tears. We were crying so hard, we couldn't see the road and had to pull over to gain our composure and roll a joint.

After a few days back in Philly, Brother Bruce decided to go back to AC and do the radio show. That's dedication. On the first night back, Brother Bruce was arrested live on the air, with Joe doing play-by-play commentary (as if it were a ball game), as handcuffs were being slapped on Brother Bruce's wrists and he's hauled out of the station and off to jail.

Brother Bruce made bail, but we needed to get him a lawyer. I had stayed back in Philly, and I saw a newspaper story about cops finding wild marijuana growing in a vacant lot in South Philly. Where there is one vacant lot, there must be more. I was right.

My childhood friend and fellow vandal, Frankie, grabbed his dad's car and we went cruising around South Philly looking for some pot plants. Eureka! We found dozens of plants growing like weeds in a vacant lot (occasionally the police are accurate). We armed ourselves with sickles and saws, chopped 'em down, and stuffed them in the trunk. They were too big to fit in the plastic bags we'd brought. No one knew what pot plants looked like in 1968. However, these were not the resin-rich female plants we had hoped for. These were skinny male plants with barely a single grain of THC-rich pollen anywhere on them. With the branches and green leaves hanging out of the trunk, we got out of the neighborhood. Nobody paid any attention. Just a couple of punks, a Jew and an Italian, trying to earn some money to pay my brother's legal bills.

Our harvest was all leaf, but we sold enough to fund Brother Bruce's successful defense. The cops had no case as incense is not illegal. We now had cash and an un-jailed brother.

Because of the bust, the radio station cancelled our show. With Brother Bruce a free man, we all headed to the Atlantic City Pop Festival where Janis Joplin was performing, along with The Byrds, Joe Cocker, Jefferson Airplane, B. B. King, Little Richard, Santana, Joni Mitchell and so many other *greats*! Even with all these headliners, Janis's set illuminated the firmament with white-hot energy. Too bad two years later some couple stood her up at Barney's Beanery. Disappointed, horny and alone, she drank vodka and shot heroin. The Los Angeles coroner ruled her death accidental.

Speaking of music and accidental death, the following year I almost died of asthmatic embarrassment in the company of several folk music icons. I was invited to spend the weekend at the Woodstock home of famed folksinger Tim Hardin by a mutual friend, Fat Anne. Our transportation was my buddy Joe Brodsky at the wheel of his new Fiat. After a four-hour drive from Philly to upstate New York, and up a windy unpaved road to Hardin's home, Tim meets us outside. Impressed with Joe's new Fiat, Tim asks if he could get behind the wheel for a short spin.

"No," said Joe flatly, "I don't lend out my car."

I jabbed Joe in the ribs and said, "Joe, you mean you aren't going to let Tim Hardin drive your car? *The* Tim Hardin?" Famous for "If I Were a Carpenter," "Misty Roses" and "How Can We Hang on to a Dream," to name a few.

"No," said Joe.

"You're an asshole," I said.

Hardin too was taken aback a bit. Eleven years later, long before the opioid crisis was a trending topic on Yahoo, he died of a heroin overdose. As for Joe, he had what a 1960s astrologer would term "a weird Capricorn self-centeredness characterized by overprotection of personal property, as if sharing diminished dominion." In other words, Joe didn't like lending out his car.

Being in that same room with Fred Neil was like being in the same room as Walt Whitman, if Uncle Walt had been a functioning heroin addict and the composer of "Everybody's Talkin'" (from *Midnight Cowboy*), "Dolphins," "The Other Side of This Life" and so many more.

To add to Tim's Fiat disappointment, several hours later, I was about to make a visit to the coroner's office, except that Hardin, Fat Anne, Joe, Fred Neil, Bob Gibson and Odetta saved my life.

It was after midnight when an unscheduled asthma attack came to call. I attempted taking a blast off my trusty inhaler, but it was empty. An empty inhaler after midnight, high in the hills of Woodstock, New York, was a nightmare. The panic of needing a rescue blast is only exceeded by the panic of realizing your rescue inhaler is empty and that you're about to choke to death in the pristine air in the mountains far from home.

I don't recall which folk music luminary heard my post-midnight screams first, but the entire household arose to my rescue. Someone called the hospital and arranged for an ambulance to meet us down on the highway. I was bundled up into the Fiat, Joe behind the wheel, racing down the road to my life-saving rendezvous. Flashing lights and wailing sirens in the distance augmented my embarrassment at inconveniencing famous folk singers—a faux pas worse than inconveniencing a family's Christmas dinner.

The ambulance met us on the highway and sped me to the hospital tasked with saving my dying life. An injection of this, and an injection of that, some top-shelf O2. I did not sleep at all but stayed awake to make sure I was still able to breathe. I was released the next morning. Joe had found a motel nearby and slept with sweet resolve to not blame me for ruining an all-star weekend.

I Was There... On Acid

My near-death experience at Woodstock did not prevent me from returning to that same neighborhood a few months later for one of the most glorious and significant musical cultural events in the history of America. Going up to Yasgur's Farm anyone? Woodstock here I come. If you haven't seen the film, please do. Words alone could never do justice to the life changing/affirming explosion of love and musical genius that happened in Bethel, NY, August 15–18, 1969. Or measure all the pot I smoked and mushrooms I nibbled.

After a day and a half, my asthma treated me to a foreboding attack of claustrophobia and I was afraid that 500,000 people all exiting on Sunday afternoon would cause a historic traffic jam, and if I needed an ambulance, I was fucked.

It took me five hours to hitchhike home from paradise (usually about a three-hour drive). My ride dropped me off near 10th Street. I had to walk a few blocks to get home. It was Saturday night at 3:00 a.m. Doors locked, no one home, and no keys. The only expression of joy I could muster was to masturbate off my front porch. My neighbors slept not knowing that The Chambers Brothers had proclaimed "Time Has Come Today" and Jimi Hendrix had just liberated the Star-Spangled Banner, forever.

The sixties and seventies produced some of the greatest folk music and rock 'n' roll ever, and where there was music, the drugs and sex were not far behind. My girlfriend, Kathy Mayers (see, I told you about the Kathys), could easily breathe through her nose, a requirement for performing oral sex, which is exactly what she was doing while I drove us back to Philly from a Grateful Dead concert in Scranton, Pennsylvania.

Still seeing trails from the LSD we dropped at the concert, it suddenly felt as if a hot tub had sprung a leak in my lap. I was still hearing the music in the distance, and it turned out to be "One More Saturday Night." My head was in the clouds and hers in my lap, life was a delightful all-paisley pleasure zone. Until she unexpectedly and involuntarily threw up all over my private parts and custom-made bell-bottom pants. (I had an old neighborhood tailor with numbers on his arm. I taught him how to take inexpensive pants and turn them into designer bell bottoms.)

Kathy and I were both embarrassed, me for her and her for her, and we both laughed uproariously at the absurdity of life and the Dead needing two drummers. It was the middle of winter and I thought if we opened the windows the throw up would freeze and we could pick it up off my crotch in one piece and throw it out the window.

Life's absurd, silly, or self-effacing moments comfort us as we age. Somehow, they are proof that we exist. When every day is the same, the stress of predictability drains us of vitality. The universe, including humans, favors novelty. The novelty must be balanced with familiarity. Hence, the proven maxim of Top 40 radio stations: Too much of the familiar is boring; too much of the new is baffling. Moderation in all things, including moderation.

Another memorable concert took place May 16, 1970—Jimi Hendrix headlining with the Grateful Dead (never again would this happen), the Steve Miller Band, and three other acts at the

Temple University stadium in Philadelphia. Tickets were $6.50 for general seating at this small football field.

The concert started at 3:00 p.m. The Steve Miller Band was on when we arrived. By the time Jimi Hendrix took the stage, night had fallen. In a harmless act of solidarity, people started ripping out the benches and throwing them into a huge bonfire in the middle of the field. It wasn't dangerous or hostile. It was tribal and prehistoric. It was beautiful. Just a way for everyone to feel cozy and cast a warm light onto the stage.

Before the concert, I took a hit of LSD and felt like I was teetering on the precipice between a field of daisies and a field of disaster. Back home after the concert, my brother had to keep dropping the needle on "Turn On Your Love Light," on the *Live/ Dead* album, over and over and over again because if that song wasn't playing, I thought I would freak out and have a bad trip. The music kept me in a blissful, unearthly state. Since the album version was only 15 minutes, Brother Bruce had to get up four times an hour. When the Dead play it live, it's usually over a half hour.

When Jerry Garcia died of an overdose, it helped save my life. On August 9, 1995, the sixties finally ended, again. I remember the day like it was yesterday. I was out on the back deck of Café Nuvo, the local coffee shop/hangout in San Anselmo. Five days before that, an AA group had presented me with a One Year medallion celebrating being clean and sober for 365 continuous days. We love to acknowledge people's sober time in meetings. But that made me start to think that maybe this last year, this "sober thing" was just a fad, or a passing fancy for me, and enough was enough and it was time to start getting high again. After all, I had proven I wasn't a drug addict because I just went a whole YEAR without using. And now, 2 miles from where I stood, JERRY GARCIA was really DEAD from a drug overdose. What the hell was I thinking? Of course I had made the right decision and saw Jerry showing me the light, in which I have lived every day since. I knew I did the right thing. Hopefully lots of his fans stopped doing drugs after that day.

#

The radio show, the cops, "the field day for the heat," the Panama Red, the music, the energy of the late sixties and early seventies. Some of us thought a peaceful world was possible. Woodstock proved it; it was certainly *The Time of Your Life*. Yes, I love William Saroyan. But sure enough, Altamont and the Hell's Angels came along to remind us that violence has always been and always will be with us.

Chapter 5

Do Everything You Can and Don't Get Caught

A man is a success if he gets up in the morning and gets to bed at night,
and in between he does what he wants to do.
—Bob Dylan

I can't call it a smuggling "career" since I only did it twice—first in February 1969 when I was 19 years old, full of wanderlust (my love of travel is a Sagittarian trait) and dealing small amounts of hashish in Philly. My second smuggling adventure took place late in 1971, after I started working my chosen profession more regularly.

The mission in '69 was to buy red Lebanese hashish in Israel and bring it back through Kennedy Airport in Queens, NY, down the Jersey Turnpike, and to the streets of Philly. Joe Brodsky, gay and astrologically Capricorn, came with me on the first trip.

Israel was a decent source of hash—fourth behind Lebanon, Pakistan, and king of all hashish producing nations, Afghanistan. Oh, and Nepal, which was famous for its powerful Nepalese Temple Balls.

Going to Israel for hashish made perfect sense. Our families thought we were going to the Holy Land to discover our roots. Our friends and fellow hash-heads assumed we went to make money. Actually we needed to go because neither of us could imagine living another day without taking a hit off a pipe filled with dope. There was *no hash* in Philly or New York. Every dealer we knew was out of stock.

We planned to pay for the trip by selling three-quarters of what we brought back and keeping the rest for ourselves. Joe B. and I really didn't think of it as smuggling—more like just having to go out of the neighborhood to score.

We boarded an airport bus at Kennedy filled to the brim with Hassidic and other assorted Jews. We were driven up to the El Al 747 that would fly us 13 hours nonstop to Ben Gurion Airport in Tel Aviv.

Hashish in the Holy Land

Joe B. and I had met when we were in a few plays at Olney High, as members of The Footlighters theater group. After having sought the spotlight, we now were aching to play the invisible man, or Harvey the rabbit.

To make this trip, we had each taken a semester off from our studies at Philadelphia Community College, where we spent more time focusing on getting high than achieving a higher education.

Our return flight was in three weeks, when we would be cruising though the New York airport named after our most recently assassinated and much-loved president. Both of us returned to the U.S. with 600 grams of hash stuffed in our pants . . . well, not exactly in our pants. The night before our flight back home, we went to a lady's intimate apparel store on the main drag in Tel Aviv and purchased flesh-toned girdles (nothing sexy about these embarrassments). They were not the whalebone rib- crushers with leather laces but the thigh-to-ribcage, super-slim kind so popular with women who wished to appear more svelte.

"I'm buying this for my girlfriend," I explained. "She's built just like me."

"So's mine," said my accomplice in deception. The shop-girls either took our word for it or knew we were neophyte hash smugglers.

The next morning, we helped each other slide the three 200-gram canvas-wrapped bricks into our girdles. Fifty years ago, there was much less airport security, even in Israel. The era of skyjackings didn't start until 1971. We boarded our return flight unmolested and then realized we had both forgotten to buy silver-plated mezuzahs like normal tourists would. A half-day later, we were back in U.S. airspace.

When our plane started to descend to Kennedy Airport, I leaned over Joe's lap to look out the window at the teeming populace of Long Island—7.5 million people. From his crotch, I could smell the distinctly subtle aroma of red Lebanese hashish rising into the stuffy airplane air. Subtle to humans maybe, but like a runaway slave to a Confederate soldier or a customs inspector's German

Shepherd. We had talcum powder with us, and through my teeth I said, "You've got to go to the bathroom and use more talcum powder. But don't let any fall on the outside of your girdle and descend like snow out of your pant leg, onto your Florsheim shoes, and leave a trail all the way to Rikers Island."

Bringing in drugs from outside the country is serious business. It's called "smuggling." I remember waiting in the customs line that I held my breath almost as often as I breathed. It wasn't anything floating in the air outside my nostrils that triggered the response. It was the fear inside my bones. That fear gripped me the entire time.

The Shepherds must have been having a lunch break when we came through. As I cleared customs, I could picture the ump behind home plate at Connie Mack Stadium yelling, "*Safe!*" Joe got through safe and sound also.

Once I was back home, selling the hash was no problem, until I was dealing my last quarter ounce to some guys in a friend's basement in the Kensington and Allegheny neighborhood of Philadelphia. Instead of reaching into their pockets and pulling out money, they each reached into their belts and pulled out a handgun.

One of them put a revolver to my head. The other pressed a .45 automatic to my heart. I remember looking at the revolver pressed at my temple, seeing bullets in all the chambers, and deciding not to give them an argument, or say anything funny. You know the expression, nervous laughter? Well, imagine frightened-to-death, about-to-shit-in-my-pants nervous laughter. Yet I acted calm and nonthreatening. I wanted them to feel happy—happy about their career choice and not trigger happy.

Many thoughts went through my mind. The one I remember most vividly: *If I ever get an acting role that requires me to be scared to death, this experience will come in handy.* Having done plenty of neighborhood theater, this thought was not as far-fetched as you might think.

They took the hash plus the two hundred dollars I had with me and then slowly walked me to my car. I wanted them to know that I wasn't going to panic or do something stupid. I also wanted them to know that I was taking them seriously, and I wasn't making light of being ripped off. Deciding they were unconcerned with either issue, I kept my mouth shut.

As I drove slowly off, tears started streaming down my face, realizing how my life could have come to an end during the loaded drama I had just lived through. At that seminal moment, I came to a firm and unshakable realization and formed an irreversible resolve.

Never again, I said to myself, *I'm never selling drugs in that neighborhood again.*

It never entered my mind to quit selling drugs. Before long, it would become my livelihood, my full-time occupation, my *raison d'être*. Drug dealing was in my blood. A calling if you will. Capitalism in its purest form, just like the cocaine I would soon buy and sell for 13 years.

#

A year later, I made my way back to Israel, sans Joe. I wasn't necessarily planning on doing any smuggling. Rather, I was going to meet Brad Terran and see more of the ancient land I had missed on my first three-week stoned adventure. Brad was a high school friend spending time at a kibbutz. I had made plans to meet up with him at the King David Hotel in Jerusalem on November 15, 1970. I took a flight from New York to London, with a plan to take a student flight from London to Tel Aviv.

When I got to London, I found out that the last student flight of the fall was full. My only other option, considering budget restraints, was to take trains across Europe. I was disappointed but not disheartened. I had taken trains regularly during my whole short life, starting with the Broad Street subway and, later, taking Amtrak up and down the East Coast. I've always loved trains and their mysterious Agatha Christie–type allure. I'll bet more spontaneous romances start on trains than planes. Murders too!

I took a train from London to Dover and the ferry from Dover to . . . well, I didn't know where I was. I noticed a moneychanger was offering francs, so I wrote home, "Hi, I have landed safely in France." I was actually in Belgium, the port city of Oostende.

I did know I was about to traverse West Germany with my personal stash of hash in my underwear. I would change trains in Cologne, Germany, and then head southeast to Athens. I rode through the most colorful explosion of fall leaves. In Albania, the leaves seemed as if they were trying to escape Communist oppression by pretending to be birds floating above the rivers. I watched Austria through the train windows—trees, mountainsides, dying autumn leaves. Trying not to think of the *The Sound of Music* or the Holocaust was exhilarating and painful.

I got to grab a snack (just a chocolate bar) at the magnificent station in Sofia, Bulgaria. The city itself dates back 7,000 years. And I thought Philly, with its 200- year-old Independence Hall and Betsy Ross House, was old.

When the train finally rumbled into the station at Thessaloniki, its first stop across the Greek border, my compartment mate asked me if I was from England. I hadn't spoken a word in two whole days, not wanting to be pegged as an ugly American, though I was no Marlon Brando, and this wasn't Southeast Asia (*The Ugly American*, 1963). Everywhere I went, I tried to blend in. I preferred wearing a cloak of invisibility, never really wanting people to notice me. Not easy to do in a six-seat compartment.

I told him I was from the States. Reaching out the window to the roving food vendors on the platform, he bought me my first skewered stick of shashlik and my first demitasse of Greek coffee. To this day, whenever I have a cup of Greek or Turkish coffee, my taste buds' brain cells transport me back to that train station and to one of my most happy and flavorful memories.

The train ride took about three days, so I was going to miss my scheduled rendezvous with my friend at the King David Hotel. When I got to Athens, I stayed a few extra days at a hotel on Omonoia Square. The area was full of men, hundreds and hundreds, sitting at the outdoor cafes smoking from a thousand hookahs. Just like they do now in Encino, California.

The final weeks of November were cool and sunny, perfect for the wonderment of traipsing around the Acropolis, climbing up to the Parthenon. It's hard to get pictures of this more than 2,500-year-old Greek temple without tourists intruding on the stunning visuals. I waited until the achingly beautiful stoic sun was setting and all the tourists were gone. Alone, I took photographs until the armed guard escorted me out.

Sunny Athens

Earlier in the day, I stood onstage at the Theatre of Dionysus (talk about name dropping), the oldest theater in Greece—and once capable of seating 17,000 patrons. There I stood, arms raised high toward all the ghosts, finding my inner orator and reciting my favorite line from *A Thousand Clowns*, when Jason Robards Jr. tells his ward to "go to your room," and the kid says, "I don't have a room. I live in the alcove." And Robards says, "Then go to your alcove." The line still cracks me up. And years later when I got to have lunch with Jake Robards, Jason's son, I had to tell him that story and how much pleasure his father's performances had given me.

That weekend in Athens, all alone with my pipe, smoke, ashes and endless tiny cups of Greek coffee, remains one of the most glorious weekends of my life, when history came alive for one young college dropout with a sock (or underwear) full of hash.

I was in service to hashish, like a worker bee to his queen. A day without hash was like a day without humor, beauty or a raison d'être. I had a pipe made from a Bic pen. In the stem of the pen, I kept the ink cartridge. Somewhere else in my suitcase, I had a little brass lamp piece that served as a bowl. When I was alone, I would take the cartridge out of the pen and put the bowl with a little rubber hose onto the pen so it became a pipe. I was high as a kite walking around Athens. I enjoyed every moment, and this experience is inscribed forever in my memory. Greece was no longer Greek to me.

Every addict has their drug of choice—or maybe some will use them all. On the East Coast, hashish was king. Until pot came along. As you can surmise, I was quite a fan of hash and its pungency. As more people were getting into pot, the pot connoisseurs would say that weed from Mexico was good; from Colombia, it was better; and from Jamaica, it was the best in the world. Wait, that was before we discovered Hawaiian pot. And Hawaiian pot growers realized the soil on the Big Island was some of the youngest, freshest soil on God's green earth, or God's blue ball, and perfect for producing weed that tasted like the sweetness of honeysuckle with mild hallucinogenic properties.

When it came time to leave Athens, I couldn't afford the airfare to Tel Aviv. My only choice was to take a Zim passenger-freighter to Haifa, Israel's only port. The first night they showed a film in their dining room, on a 16 mm projector, for the ship's 15 passengers. The flick was *Susan Slade*, a trashy Peyton Place–type movie starring Connie Stevens and Troy Donahue. While watching the movie, I noticed two girls clutching cups of herbal tea, paying more attention to Connie on the screen than Troy.

I later found out they were both from Boston. One was very attractive, one not so much. I tried to engage them in conversation but was gently rebuffed. They quickly let me know that they were a couple and I should take my peripatetic penis elsewhere, although those were not their exact words. I respected that, and we didn't speak again during the voyage.

After the ship docked in Haifa, I took a bus down to Tel Aviv. I was five days late for my rendezvous with my friend Brad. I knew he wasn't still going to be waiting at the King David Hotel. This was long before cell phones or pagers, and I didn't know where the hell he was. So I got a cheap room and just kept checking the American Express office for a letter from him because that's how we did it back then—General Delivery, American Express office.

I'm walking through downtown Tel Aviv and I spy the two girls from the ship. They were happy to see a familiar face. So was I. I went over and talked to them and asked what was going on.

They said the ritzy kibbutz where they had intended on staying was full and not accepting any new kibbutzniks. They had no place to go. So, I said, "Well, why don't we go to Jerusalem?"

We took a bus to Jerusalem and got two rooms at an old hotel in the Old City, which is literally like walking into the first century—the stones are the same, the streets and the people are the same, living in alcoves behind ancient walls and dressed the way they were 2,000 years ago. If the walls could talk, they would be speaking in Aramaic.

After checking into the funky little hotel, I show my new friends how I assemble my hash pipe and get ready to light up. Jesus Christ, I ain't got no matches. Nobody has any matches. Neither of them smoked or were in the habit of lighting incense or candles. It's ten o'clock at night and it's not like there's a 7-Eleven on any corner. There's no one on the streets, except maybe the ghost of the Christ and his executioners. But I figure there's got to be a stand or a homeless guy I can ask to sell me a box of matches.

Walking all alone, in the ancient night air, in the birthplace of so many competing religions, I had my first religious experience. (My next one was 24 years later at the Betty Ford Center.) I was only 20, and because of my unstoppable need to get high every day, there I was following in the footsteps of Jesus the Christ. Not dragging a cross, just a drug habit.

A few blocks from the hotel, I'm on this tiny little side street in Old Jerusalem, where in front of me, maybe 50 yards away, I see a dark figure approaching whose silhouette reminds me of my friend, Brad, who I was supposed to meet in Tel Aviv. There are some noticeable differences: this guy has a beard on his face and a beautiful woman on his arm. There's also a redheaded boy with a Jewfro walking beside them.

As I step closer, I realize that it is, indeed, Brad!!! At that same moment, under the hazy dim light of an old streetlamp, he sees it's me. We both scream in joy, as if meeting the Messiah or counting the money you collected at your Bar Mitzvah. We yell and we run, throwing our arms around each other, crying and laughing at this extraordinary, almost biblical coincidence.

"Oh, my God! What are the odds?" Incalculable . . . worse odds than a camel making it through the eye of a needle.

Accidentally meeting in Old Jerusalem at 10:30 at night with no plans to meet there at all was divine intervention. And there was certainly no better place for it.

Brad introduces me to his new girlfriend, Ione from Wales, and his friend Albert from New York. They came to Jerusalem because Albert's an opium addict, and he needed to score. So far, they haven't scored any opium, but they - do - have - matches.

Brad tells me that they are living at Kibbutz Metzer about 30 miles away. He is fairly certain that my new lesbionic friends and I would be welcomed to stay there as long as we worked our asses off. We parted that night grinning from ear to earringless ear. The next day, Gertrude Stein, Alice B. Toklas and I hitchhiked the 30 miles, and the kibbutz took us in with open, unnumbered arms. It was a young, very progressive kibbutz, and they needed workers.

This place wasn't one of the showcase kibbutzim where parents on the Upper East Side or Beverly Hills would pay to have their kids put to work to teach them how to break a sweat on a communal farm before they returned home to get a job on Wall Street or at the Bank of America. Kibbutz Metzer was a real working socialist-style collective where they raised chickens for their eggs and grew avocados and bananas. Lots of avocados and bananas. I really never saw myself as a kibbutznik growing up, but I'd been called worse.

The two women got their own room. I stayed with Brad and Ione in their cabin. We worked wrapping bananas in burlap to keep them frost free, and in the avocado groves, where we used shears mounted on long poles to cut off the avocados that would fall into little canvas baskets positioned directly under the blades. Then we would empty the baskets into a crate hooked behind a small tractor. Eventually, the avocados went by train to Haifa to be shipped to grocery stores all across Europe, well before guacamole was on everyone's lips.

We also walked behind flatbed trucks, throwing rocks and small boulders onto the truck to clear the land for plowing and planting. Removing detritus from your environment helps new things grow and yield nutritious goodies. This lesson wasn't lost on me.

After about five days, holding my BFF (a paperback book) and lying on the floor on my flattened mattress and impromptu sleeping bag, I hear Ione and Brad whispering in bed. Brad peeks out from under the covers, looks at me, and says, "You don't have to sleep down there if you don't want to."

"Yeah? Where should I sleep?"

"Up here," he explained, "Ione wants you in bed with us."

"Really? Do you mean like three parallel bananas? You're in the front and I'm in the back?

"You can have the front," Brad said graciously, "and I'll take the back." It was easier for Brad to diagram the logistics than for me to diagram this sentence.

Ione wasn't saying anything. Masterminds rarely do. It was all her idea, but Brad was making the presentation. As Oskar Schindler said, "Presentation is everything," and a good presentation can work wonders, whether it's to seduce members of the opposite sex or smuggle hashish.

It's got to be warmer in bed with them than here on a mat on the floor. I wasn't really sure if they were asking me to a kosher ménage à trois or just wanted to warm up, a la a three-dog night. After all, it was a cold December in northern Israel.

"Do you mean like the Jefferson Airplane song, "Triad"?" I asked. Ione's mouth turned into the Cheshire cat's smile. Didn't François Truffaut make a film called *Jules et Jim* and Ione?

We three had an amazing relationship for the next few weeks. No jealousies or competition. They were planning on traveling to Afghanistan next. Maybe Israel wasn't old enough for them—or the red hash not strong enough. And I was going home, eventually, so the third wheel (me) would be coming off soon enough.

Brad and I worked our asses off every day and ingratiated ourselves with the Kibbutz administrators while repeatedly penetrating Ione in combinations of sexual positions that would send a Kama Sutra expert screaming for a chiropractor.

Ione worked in the kitchen every day. She was enthusiastic, versatile, and maintained her pre-established boundary—I believe it's called the perineum. There was no sex between Brad and me, although occasionally we did bump heads in the night. Our little Welsh rabbit was very sweet—like an incredible and edible cookie one can share with a pal. She knew what she wanted, and being gentlemen, we graciously complied.

I assure you that neither Brad nor I felt exploited in any way. But since Ione was not even Jewish, Brad and I said our Berakhahs softly, or in a silent way if we were feeling jazzy. We weren't sure which prayer would be most appropriate—the one for breaking bread or sipping wine.

We took a few days off from working on the kibbutz to explore the Sinai Peninsula. We got as far as Dahab, really just a scuba diving and snorkeling outpost waiting to be spoiled by some capitalistic developers. While exploring the outskirts, a Bedouin woman approached us beseechingly, asking us if we would accept as a gift the baby in her arms, flies on his eyes. We knew we could provide the child with a better life in America, but we weren't sure if we could get him through customs. None of us had ever been confronted with such an example of third-world poverty.

It was heartbreaking realizing that this probably went on in one form or another all over the world.

A couple weeks into my stay, Yahweh provided a new miracle. The good-looking lesbian, Ellen, suddenly redefined her sexuality by inviting me to privately engage with her. A gracious invitation indeed, and I eagerly complied with her request. Remember, I had been given an assortment of Henry Miller books by Big Ed at Cooper's Corner the day after he heard I went down on a girl for the first time. Big Ed had said that act gave me the right to have an opinion, and I had to read some Miller to learn about how the world really works. And what men and women are really thinking but are too polite to say out loud. He was right!

Ellen's requests continued, as did my compliance. She also requested that we keep our affair a secret from her girlfriend. Secrecy, sexuality, and betrayal are fraught with potential peril. Perhaps that adds intensity to the sex.

For a young man on an Israeli kibbutz, secretly pleasing a lesbian while having three-ways with my best friend's enthusiastic Welsh girlfriend is as Jewish as I'll ever need to be.

By this time, Brad and I had decided to try smuggling some hashish back to the mom-and-pop basement drug dealers of Philly. We would take a break from banana bagging, clipping down avocados for grocery stores in France, and our nightly sex capades to travel to Tel Aviv to score.

In addition to penetrating Ellen sexually, I had firmly implanted another kind of seed in her mind—that she should become my drug mule.

"You'll fly back to New York," I tell her, "wearing a full-body stocking, and you'll have twelve bricks of hashish taped to your body and you'll be given $1,000 by my brother at the hotel at Kennedy Airport. You can continue home to Boston, and you'll be a thousand dollars richer ($1,000 in 1971 is equivalent to $6,300 today). Perhaps infatuated with my sense of style and confidence, she agrees.

Before her planned departure from Ben-Gurion, we heard a rumor that airport security was starting to search people flying out of Israel. We had some friends who were flying to Istanbul, so we asked them to send us a telegram when they arrived to let us know if it were true, about the searching leaving the country. Sure enough, the next day we got a telegram saying, "WAS SIDETRACKED SLIGHTLY." Oh, *fuck!*

I had already bought five pounds of hash in a very dark empty lot in Tel Aviv, doing math by longhand, using butane lighters as our only

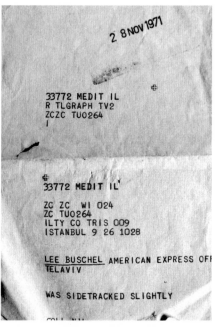

Sidetracked Slightly = Searched

source of illumination. I had to change plans. Ellen and I left the kibbutz and took a bus to Haifa so we could leave the country by ship. Two hours later, the police raided our kibbutz. Our friends assumed the guy we bought the hash from turned us in, thinking he could make money selling us the hash and then buy it back from the police. When the police arrived at the kibbutz, we were already long gone, and our friends at the kibbutz pleaded ignorance as to where we were. For weeks they thought we were in an Israeli jail somewhere.

There was an alternative lifestyle conspiracy theory that Ellen's lesbian girlfriend ratted us out in a fit of jealousy, vindictiveness and her version of betrayal, motivated by my exodus out of the Holy Land with her Last Supper.

That experience certainly confirmed Mom's prediction that people ratting you out is a treacherous occupational hazard. If I've learned anything since then, it's that there's a knack to knowing who to trust and who not to trust. That's the advantage of having a well-developed bullshit meter.

Ellen and I planned to board the ship separately and pretend not to know each other. We were definitely not going to talk or otherwise associate with each other. We were traveling separately. Maybe we'd exchange a casual "hello" that one would kindly give a stranger. We'd meet up in Marseille, after she cleared French customs.

The first morning on the ship, Ellen comes over and sits down at breakfast with me as if we'd been best friends forever. So much for my strategy. The first morning also found us still in Haifa's port. I had thought the sea was very calm the first night of our voyage. That's because the captain had decided to wait in the harbor while foul weather passed over the Mediterranean. For a brief moment, I thought the ship was still in the bay so the authorities could come aboard and take us away. I had reason to be paranoid after all.

By noon the captain decided to shove off and try to get back on schedule. I learned on that voyage that it's not the captain who makes the schedule but the sea. So much for avoiding annoying weather because we soon hit a terrible squall, a violent storm that rocked the boat like a little boy with ADHD on too much Ritalin in a bathtub with his Mermaid Ariel doll who rejected his advances. For about a day, I could not leave my bunk, at all. I couldn't even keep water down. I don't think a pound of Dramamine would have helped. Luckily, I did have my BFF, a well-worn copy of *Raise High the Roof Beam, Carpenters and Seymour: An Introduction*.

The ship made an unscheduled stop for one day in Genoa, Italy. I had claimed this day for myself to be alone, walk around the docks, and explore the side streets downtown. Everyone was so stylishly dressed, like extras in a mid-career Fellini film. I'd never been to Italy. And here I am drinking the best espresso I'd ever had, dipping in a biscotti under the gleaming Mediterranean sun, not knowing whether I would be going home to handshakes or handcuffs. I should have been more nervous, but I still felt the invincibility of a teenager, even though I had just turned 21 two weeks before. And it certainly helped to be high the whole time.

I decided to buy a fancy designer sweater with no label off some guy on the street. I wore it for years as a memento, and to keep warm. Being in Italy also reminded me of one of the few mementos my father left us when he croaked at 34. It was a gray marble ashtray shaped like the island of Sicily. That's where he fought off Mussolini's men as an anti-aircraft gunner.

When we finally get to Marseille, Ellen and a guy from San Francisco we had befriended were walking off the ship when one of the bricks of hash drops out of her pant leg and hits the wooden gangplank with an audible plunk! Walking behind her, I smoothly picked it up and slipped it in my new sheepskin coat pocket. The guy from San Francisco is drop-jawed.

"Are you guys crazy?"

Yes, but undiagnosed. The accusation of crazy was one with which I was becoming more and more familiar. That was 1971, New Year's Eve Day. From Marseille, Ellen and I immediately took the train to Paris, got into a taxicab, and told the driver, "We need a room."

I assume what he said in French was, "Are you fucking crazy? It's New Year's Eve and this is Paris!"

Nevertheless ... "Yes. Please help us find a room. Merci, merci, merci."

He takes us to a snazzy little hotel with one vacant room directly above a lesbian bar. I'm not kidding. We check in, and I give Ellen some francs I bought at the Gare du Nord after our uneventful train ride from Marseilles.

I tell her, "You can go to the bar downstairs but do not leave the premises. Go have your fun. Do not bring anyone back to the room. You go to theirs." It's hard to mask the aroma of 5 pounds of Red Lebanese hashish in a little heated Parisian hotel room above a lesbian brasserie. "I'm going out to explore Paris."

Paris possessed everything a new 21-year-old could ask for. Except maybe for one of Henry Miller's sloppy seconds. There were street performers, musicians and mimes just like Marcel Marceau, actual French crepes from a kiosk on the corner, cappuccinos and even student protests (I swear). I'm there alone with my hash pipe and hashish until three in the morning, just walking around Paris on one of the best New Year's Eves I've ever had in my life. As if Jean-Luc Godard was there with a film crew, and I was indeed *Breathless* (in a good way).

I get back to the hotel and try not to wake my sweet little crashed out lesbian drug mule. Eventually, I fall asleep, multiple cappuccinos notwithstanding. It's four in the morning, Ellen's jumping on me screaming, "I can't do it. I know I'm going to get busted. I can't fly to New York with those bricks of hashish on me." She is loud and getting louder, and I'm picturing this giant gendarme army brigade running into the room looking to stop a murder but instead finding all the hash neatly piled up in the closet.

I'm not the type of man to lay hands on a woman except for consensual sexual or healing purposes. In Ellen's case, I made an exception. I choked her. Not a sexually related "Oh-please-choke-me" and certainly not an "I'm gonna kill you" choke. It was the old-fashioned, "Shut the fuck up" choke—just enough to get her to stop screaming.

Now I'm on top of her pleading, "Be quiet, be quiet, shut up! Be quiet, be quiet, shut the fuck up! It's going to be okay. You'll be okay. I promise. You'll be okay. You'll be okay. Don't worry about it. You'll do this. You'll be okay." I had to make this work because I wasn't going to get stuck in Paris with all this hash, and I certainly wasn't going back to the States with it.

I held her and stroked her gently until we both were asleep. The next morning, we talked it through. I reminded her that she was getting a thousand dollars and she had a promise to fulfill. The God of Abraham was not going to let us down. Most of the pot dealers I knew considered themselves to be doing God's work.

I took her to Orly Airport on the Metro. She had calmed down enough to carry on. She flew nonstop back to New York, where my brother and my best friend Jerome anxiously waited for her to get through customs safe and sound. They took her to a nearby motel, had her undress, and marveled not at her perfect bisexual 21-year-old body but rather at how much hashish fell onto the motel's shag carpet. Jerome handed her the grand and said a fond adieu. I never saw or spoke to Ellen again. We were just two brave idiots passing through young adulthood. Risking incarceration while exploring our boundarylessness.

I had to take a flight to London because I couldn't afford to fly home straight from Paris. On the short flight, heavy clouds covered the sky the whole time. It gave me great confidence in radar. I've never worried about flying through inclement weather or thunderstorms ever since. Plus, as a gambler, whenever I think of my plane crashing, I think, *What are the odds?*

There were still some post-holiday winter student flights from London's Gatwick Airport to New York leaving the next day. I was in a pretty good mood. Not only could I afford the student flight home but Ellen had made it back undetected. When I learned that, I took a sigh of relief the size of an asthmatic's first inhale right after getting a shot of adrenaline. She was safe . . . *and so was the hashish.*

While in London, I took in a movie—*Straw Dogs*, a horror film for the college educated, directed by Sam Peckinpah and starring Dustin Hoffman. Films establish a certain mind-set and mood, and Peckinpah was a master craftsman. When I got out of the theater that night, it was a dark and foggy, and the streets felt more suited for Jack the Ripper than a young tourist. That's a polite way of saying I was scared out of my mind.

The film is about a group of British ruffians attempting to brutalize American teacher and mathematician David Sumner (Dustin), just because his flirty, hot-as-hell wife, Amy (Susan George), chose Dustin over them. The film ends in a showdown between the teacher and his jealous adversaries in a ballet of ingenious brutal violence. Filmed in England, it was hitting close to the bone. One reviewer called it, "A violent, provocative meditation on manhood, *Straw Dogs* is viscerally impactful—and decidedly not for the squeamish."

The night's chill cut to my squeamish bone, and I didn't let my guard down until I returned to my hotel room where the only source of warmth was a gas space heater. I turned it on and reached into my pocket for matches. No matches.

Ah, the suitcase, I say, breaking the fourth wall between me, myself, and I.

The gas, hissing away pleasantly, awaits my return as I dig the matches out of my suitcase. Were this a cartoon or a Jerry Lewis movie, you would already anticipate the soot-covered climax. I strike a match, and all the gas that had built up in the fireplace explodes into a fireball that blows me across the room, burning the "l" out of my eyelashes and singeing my eyebrows. I made it back to Philly, regrew my eyelashes, and got a real job.

HIGH

As an artist, I feel that we must try many things - but above all we must dare to fail.
— John Cassavetes

Chapter 6

Picture This FBI Close Call

After I made it back to Philly, I secured honest employment with the Philadelphia School Board in their Audio-Visual Department as a photographer. I photographed people in various occupational settings, such as automobile mechanics, airport workers handling luggage, postal workers sorting mail, and waiters in restaurants. I photographed people in jobs that required training but not a college education. My photos were then used in a multimedia presentation to lure, or encourage, the non- liberal artsy students into vocational/technical high schools to learn a trade.

One of my favorite moments as a photographer was being on an assignment for *The Drummer*, Philadelphia's version of *The Village Voice*. I was having lunch with movie greats John Cassavetes and Gena Rowlands. When I asked Gena to pose for me, she gave me the thumbs up in the air and spitting gesture, just like she did in their film *A Woman Under the Influence*, starring Rowlands, Peter Falk and directed by Cassavetes.

John, seeing this, leans over to me and whispers,

King & Queen Cassavettes
(John & Gena)

"You're the only photographer she's done that for. She must really like you." That compliment from the greatest couple in cinematic America has continued to lift me up during moments or months of despair.

My boss at the school board, a sweet preppy college graduate cat, drove me home one day and wanted to hang out at my place. As we walked in, my roommate took me aside and whispered, "The FBI was just here. An envelope was sent to you from Bogota, Colombia. I think there was cocaine in it. The post office delivered the package, and 10 minutes later, the FBI came through the door. I knew not to open the envelope. Your name was on it! They're coming back to question you or arrest you."

My friend Brad of Israeli ménage à trois fame had sent me 27 grams of coke. We were both under the misunderstanding, false impression, wrong assumption that any envelope under an ounce (28 grams) never got inspected or flagged at the post office. And since my father, Morris, died during a car ride home from his night shift at the main post office, I thought I had a guardian angel looking over my mailing maleficences. In future years, I would call on his blessings many times, as a big part of my business relied on sending pot and coke through the U.S. Postal Service.

I said to my boss, "Ken, something personal has come up. I'm sorry, but I think it would be best if you split. You're not going to want to be here. I'll see you in the morning." (I prayed.)

He gave me a very perplexed and concerned look and left.

Because my roommate said they're going to be back in a half hour, I knew exactly what I needed to do. Take a 5 mg Valium! Because a 10 might have been too much. I know that I'm going to have to calm down for this but not be too drowsy. Sure enough, a half hour later, I'm being interrogated by the goddamn FBI. Yes, they do all wear jackets and ties.

Drawing upon my skills at acting, improv and lying, I concocted a story about a guy I met at Dirty Frank's, a bar I frequented frequently. "We ordered a couple Rolling Rocks and checked out the bar for chicks," I told them. "He said he was a student at

PCA [Philadelphia College of Art] and that he enrolled midterm because he and his girlfriend just moved to Center City from Pittsburgh. We talked about art and shit about Andy Warhol being from Pittsburgh..."

"Okay! Okay!" said the agent, who was trying to shut me up. "How the fuck did he know your address?"

They had already found some weed, so I said, "Oh, we came back here to smoke a joint, and I figured the guy wasn't out to blow me or anything because he said he had a girlfriend. He must have written down the address. It's right next to the front door."

I lived in a 200-year-old trinity house, otherwise called a Father, Son, and Holy Ghost house because they have a spiral staircase connecting three floors and are unique to the very Catholic city of Philadelphia. Each floor is its own room. This particular dwelling was built to house the servants of the Founding Fathers who lived on Pine, Spruce, and Delancey Streets. Those FBI guys searched the place top to bottom.

It took them awhile, but they found some more weed. Not much, but it was the '70s and weed was illegal. Meanwhile, I am in state of shock; on the precipice of passing out or accepting my Oscar. Just then, I realize that one of the agents is Bart Freidman, the son of the fruit and vegetable man who ran the fruit and vegetable store where my mother and I shopped every week. My first thought: I couldn't believe that a Jew had become an FBI agent.

I look at him; he looks at me. At that moment, he realizes he knows me. "Hey, I know this kid and his mother," Bart says. "He's a good kid, leave him alone. Let's get out of here."

They took the package of coke and the weed, and that was the end of it.

In that eternal moment of gratitude, I knew that God was on my side. If it had been a different FBI crew, the story might have ended with the bang of a gavel and the slam of a prison door. After all, they found two controlled substances—including one whose foreign origin broke several federal laws.

Serendipity has played a large role in my life. Dangerous events by chance often reversed to my benefit. Through dumb luck or divine intervention, most of the tense situations in which I found myself ended with magical moments. Was it just fate or some sixth sense I had about navigating such situations?

Looking back, if I had gotten busted that day in the hazy, late-afternoon sunshine, I wonder whether my entire life would have been completely different. If I had a rap sheet or seen the inside of a prison with Bubba as my cellmate, maybe I wouldn't have become a drug dealer. Maybe I would have been better off if fear of going back to prison would have sent me down a more traditional path.

I also think about how life might have turned out had I stayed at the school board, made a decent living, had a job for life (unions in Philly at that time were unbreakable) and retired with a pension. I'm sure I would have still been a drug addict. I just would have had to find other ways to pay for my addictions. In AA they say, "We shall not regret the past, nor wish to shut the door on it." Well, I do regret the past. Smoking pot every day for 26 years was not the sharpest decision I ever made.

When I quit the school board in 1973, I was making $200 a week. (That was the equivalent of $1000 back then.) My boss told me I'd never make that kind of money again.

#

Despite some adverse consequences so early in my profession, I pursued my chosen path with gusto. Being a dealer wasn't just about dealing drugs. It was who I was. My chosen pathway seemed perfectly suited to my God-given talents. Besides, I was now also addicted to expensive nights out on the town—restaurants, concerts, and Broadway shows. And my love of sex and television? (I bought the first Sony Trinitron before anyone else I knew. See photo in Chapter 1.)

Once I was living in a cool Pine Street apartment with cathedral ceilings. I was in the loft bed one afternoon. To be more specific, I was in Patricia, a young and energetic art student who elevated craft services of sex to an artistic multicourse meal worthy of any celebrated chef.

As she and I delved into the delicious main course, the radio DJ announced that Rod Serling had died. Obviously, Patricia and I were too busy enjoying each other to pay any attention to the DJ's obit on the radio. It was 30 minutes later when, relaxing with a postcoital joint, I said, "Hey, did you know Rod Serling died?"

"Yeah," she said. "Died from a heart attack."

We cracked up laughing. Patricia and I had both believed the other was so engrossed in passion, in our conjugal visit, that the untimely death of one of television's premier screenwriters, and host of *The Twilight Zone*, couldn't penetrate our combined crescendos of ecstatic vocalizing.

The Twilight Zone was one of those must-see TV shows that I and perhaps millions of other Americans would look forward to watching once a week. *The Twilight Zone* was the vision of Emmy Award–winner Rod Serling, who was host and writer for more than 80 episodes of the original show's 150-plus episode run. I remember watching an eclectic blend of horror, sci-fi, drama, and humor. It was in black and white, but in my mind, it was bursting with colorful and imaginative content—and for a kid, it could be scary as shit in its darker themes. The extraordinary 1956 TV production of Serling's "Requiem for a Heavyweight," which is one of my all-time favorite tear-jerkers, was made into a full-length film in 1962.

The Twilight Zone brand published novelizations of 19 of Serling's scripts, as well as several volumes of original short stories edited by Serling himself. I read them all. Serling was one of the most radical writers working in television at the time. He dealt with socially relevant, controversial, left-wing issues disguised as *The Twilight Zone*. He was a prophet and died way too young from smoking himself to death. At the end of his short teleplay, "The Monsters Are Due on Maple Street," Serling says:

"The tools of conquest do not necessarily come with bombs and explosions and fallout. There are weapons that are simply thoughts, attitudes, and prejudices—to be found only in the minds of men. For the record, prejudices can kill. And suspicion can destroy. And a thoughtless, frightened search for a scapegoat has a fallout all its own—for the children and the children yet unborn. And the pity of it is ... that these things cannot be confined ... to the Twilight Zone."

#

My drug dealing really took off when my mother opened a family American Express account and gave me a credit card with my name on it. Now I could rent a car to transport the pot I purchased. No one wanted to use their own cars in case they got busted. Now I could move up to the big times.

When I was introduced to The Fox, a dealer in Miami, I became what's known as a middleman. I bought from the people who bought from the smugglers, and I sold to the people who didn't know the people who bought from the smugglers. I preferred to buy weed in south Florida, usually 100 pounds at a time. It cost $300 a pound, and I would drive it or have it driven to Philly and sell them for $400. And make $100 per pound. If I sold them all at once, I'd only make $30 a pound, but that's still $30 x 100, and it was enough to live on for a month.

Drug sales were not always consummated in cash. In 1975, I received a classic 1965 cream-colored, four-door Mercedes Benz sedan as partial payment for a pot sale. About one year later, I was so distracted watching a girl walk down Pine Street that I drove into the rear end of another car. I jumped out, removed my car's license plates, scratched out the VIN number, ran six blocks to Hertz, rented a car, and made it to my appointment to pick up a pound of Thai weed on Front Street. That means I didn't need cash. And I wasn't actually going to Front Street; the dope was being "fronted" to me.

God blessed me with the inborn ability to make friends and influence purchasing opinions. There is nothing like taking a huge buyer, who supplied almost all of Staten Island, into a Ft. Lauderdale pot warehouse with armed Columbian security guards and convincing him he should take an extra hundred pounds on credit because his Winnebago still had some empty space left in the shower compartment.

Any negative stress associated by such scenes was easily dissipated with a vacation to St. Barts, Jamaica, or London, appreciating its museums, theaters, curry houses, brothels, and music venues, from Ronnie Scott's to corner pubs with local troubadours. One time while on St. Lucia, waiting to take a four-day Windjammer Barefoot Cruise, a really cool skinny kid befriended me and showed me around the island before extorting most of the pot I had on me, because he threatened to turn me in the local police, and marijuana possession on St. Lucia was considered an arrestable crime. The little criminal left me with some weed so I could still enjoy the cruise.

Paradise Here I Come

Coming back via Puerto Rico, I was busted in the airport for having one joint on my person. It was my last joint, and I'd planned to smoke it while walking around San Juan. Because I was still in the airport, on federal property, I only got a citation. Had I been caught with it while walking around San Juan, I would have been arrested.

One of my favorite vacation spots became Negril, Jamaica. Reggae music was everywhere, as if it were coming from the jungle at all times. The oceans are clear and great for snorkeling—you can see 20 feet down. The cliffs are to "dive" for. The food is amazing. If the chicken isn't jerked, I don't want it, and the plantains better be hot.

As good as the pot was there, I always took my own. After the plane lands in Montego Bay, it's a good hour and a half drive to Negril. And I had to get high on the way. Plus, the weed I took there was always better than theirs. My Hawaiian always impressed the locals. And, if you're looking for a way to stoke your self-esteem, impressing the local Rastafarian chief with your weed is one of them.

One year on a Full Moon New Year's Eve in Negril, after drinking plenty of vodka and snorting a bunch of Ecstasy, I decided to dive off a 20-foot-high cliff to impress my girlfriend Melissa. I wanted to fly right into the Full Moon. Earlier in the day, I was snorkeling in this very same place. While in mid-air I remembered seeing some thorny black sea urchins while snorkeling. There is no beach here, only a ladder stuck into the side of the cliff that you must climb to get out of the water. That's where the ugly urchins had been congregating—near the ladder.

Simultaneously I saw myself getting stung by said sea urchin, having a deadly allergic reaction, drifting off, corpse-like, into the middle of the beautiful Caribbean Ocean. Then reading the headline in the Jamaica Observer: American Dies in Negril Diving Accident and no one cares. Sort of the way I felt when I thought I was having a heart attack in a bungalow at The Chateau Marmont where John Belushi overdosed and died. Except my obituary would not be on any front pages, it would be one of those little classifieds you have to pay for when someone of no renown dies.

\#

I had adjusted well to my James Bond–type lifestyle of international intrigue and had no regrets for choosing to become a drug dealer, but I still longed to be part of anything cinema. In 1975, I went up to New York City. I was anticipating seeing my buddy Robert Downey

Sr.'s film Greaser's Palace (Bob and I had been friends for over 40 years, until his death on July 7, 2021, left a gaping hole in my heart). The film stars Allan Arbus (Diane Arbus's husband) as Jessie, a man who heals the sick, brings the dead back to life, and tap dances on water, a resurrection story masquerading as a western.

After the screening, I went over to a very famous Brill Building songwriter's apartment and spent the night. I had met her earlier that year at my Genius Cousin Bobb's father's funeral. While the guests were sitting shiva and nibbling on deli snacks in one room of the old apartment in West Philadelphia, the songwriter and I were nibbling on each other in the bedroom. She was about 10 years older than me, a little heavy, and undeniably, a heavyweight seductress. For some reason, the energy at the funeral had elicited a tremendous erotic charge from both of us. It was a crazy afternoon; we were canoodling and moaning while others were mourning over the noodle kugel.

I realized that evening that even if a woman is a little bit older, and has more padding that I'm used to, as long as she's wearing an all-black negligee, she still looks hot. The songwriter was wonderful to me, and I enjoyed every moment we shared. Perhaps she really liked me, or maybe she was simply happy to have a young guy in her antique bed. Either way, I recall her with fondness. That's one of my experiences related to Robert Downey's films. There are more I must mention, completely diverse in content and context.

In October 1975, I went to New York City to see a private screening of a Bob Downey work in progress film. It was first called *Off the Wall*, then *Moment to Moment*, later, *Two Tons of Turquoise to Taos Tonight*, then just *Jive*. Eventually it went back to being called *Moment to Moment*.[1] The event ended at 10:00 p.m. Because the last train to Philly doesn't leave until midnight, I had some time to fill before heading to Penn Station. I dropped down to the downtown IRT line and got off at Fourth Street. The first place I spotted was called Gerdes Folk City. I crossed the street to get a

---

[1]   JUST FOR FUN: *Jive* is "A film without a beginning or an end," in Downey's words.

better look, and I see there's no admission charge. So, what the fuck, I go in. It was open mic night, and a scruffy-looking crowd filled the room. I was deciding whether to stay or go when I saw Tom Waits at the bar. That cinched it. I'm in.

There's a bar in the front room, tables and chairs in back. A girl is singing, but I'm not listening. I'm nursing my Heineken and hoping I have the patience to make it last until 11:45, giving me time to get back to the train station. Still, there is Tom Waits involved in some seriously smoky mind chatter at the bar. I keep walking around, and when I find a seat at a table, I talk to another girl with a guitar around her neck.

Then some little curly-haired guy comes into the bar with a very attractive lady. They looked much like Bob Dylan and Joan Baez. *Holy shit*, it was Bob Dylan and Joan Baez. A small film crew is following them in, and I'm wondering what the occasion is. Allen Ginsberg is also in tow. This was the first time I'd ever seen these icons in person, and what a happy coincidence that I ended up at the same club that night. It was the beginning of Bob Dylan's Rolling Thunder Review tour, and the whole thing was being filmed for *Renaldo and Clara*. It was October 23, 1975.

At first thought, I guessed it was a publicity stunt. Ten minutes later, Ramblin' Jack Elliott and Eric Andersen arrive, and they all launch into "Happy Birthday." It's owner Mike Porco's 60th birthday, and some of the artists he had hired to perform in his club (when no one else would) showed up to celebrate.

Then Ginsberg begins by getting everyone in the club to chant for five minutes, which seemed like an eternity. For the next three hours, not one person left that club. We all just smiled at each other in joyous disbelief that we could all be this lucky. Dylan was doing solos and singing duets with Joan. Roger McGuinn, who was eventually inducted into the Rock & Roll Hall of Fame for his lead work with The Byrds, was also there. And I haven't forgotten Bob Gibson. He was a key part of the folk music revival in the late 1950s and early 1960s.

Joan Baez gets up and jokingly says, "I've known these guys for a long time, and I love them dearly. But everybody is slightly unstable."

Around 3:30 a.m., Patti Smith blows everyone away with the loudest, most modern set of the night and a vision of what the punk rock scene would soon become. Seeing her perform was the most memorable experience of the night. Young and vivacious, she was an incredible punk rocker who was ahead of the movement, and in my estimation, was the best female performer of them all.

Finally, at 4:30 in the morning, Phil Ochs sings his heart out in that unbelievably sad voice. He hanged himself several months later in an alcoholic daze. The last known film footage of Phil Ochs was taken that night. What an honor to have been there, in the presence of a musical artist who wrote hundreds of songs in the 1960s and 1970s and released eight albums.

Ochs is most famous for his antiwar song, "I Ain't Marching Anymore." He did march through life, however, with a diagnosis of bipolar disorder, before committing suicide. And now, like he already said, he's not marching anymore.

The performers weren't singing like in a review. No, it was more like an ensemble. Each was just doing their own thing, which was more than enough for an audience who could not have appreciated it more. These singers are like miracle workers, and they have remained so for many years.

The birthday boy's grandson (blogging in 2011) recalled the night in this way: "A cake was presented to my grandfather and 'Happy Birthday' was sung by all of his friends and admirers. What mattered most to him was that all had a chance to get together again." The night ended in the wee hours with Buzzy Linhart and Bette Midler performing their hit, "Friends." I can't help but say it again—that was an incredibly memorable night.

At about 5:00 a.m. I walk out of the bar into the Manhattan morning mist. Too exhilarated to sit in a taxi, I start walking up Sixth Avenue. Around 22nd Street, for two long blocks, there was nothing but fresh-cut flowers. This is the wholesale florist market for the entire New York area. Trucks from all over are there to load up on the fresh flowers they'll need that day. Flowers in Manhattan by the thousands. What a sight and smell! I'd never been up and out on Sixth Avenue at 6:00 a.m. By 8:00 a.m., all the storefronts roll down their steel doors and wait for the next morning to reveal themselves again. I walked the 30 blocks to Penn Station and dreamt about that night for the 90-minute ride home to Philly.

#

While the night following the screening of Bob Downey's film *Moment to Moment* was pleasurable, my experience appearing in the film was a disappointment. I was disappointed with myself. You see, Bob and I had become good friends. He was shooting in New York, and I was going up there regularly.

He just outright asked me, "Do you want to be in my movie?"

I said, "Of course."

It was more than an honor to be invited to be part of the film. But I had the experience of feeling honored by Bob before. That crossing of our paths started when I saw a notice in *The Distant Drummer*, our local underground newspaper, that underground filmmaker Robert Downey Sr. was showing a work in progress at Temple University. My brother was with me, and I said, "Let's go see the man who made *Putney Swope*." It was one of our favorite films. "He's showing his new movie at Temple tonight."

"You go and bring him back to my place," Brother Bruce said jokingly.

I attended the screening. Afterward, I went up to Mr. Downey and said, "I don't know how you feel about the government of Pakistan. But how do you feel about its hashish?" Bob seemed to like that question. I offered him a ride to the train station so he could get back to New York.

"Sure," he said. But once we were in the car, I told him I had to make a quick stop at my brother's place to borrow a hash pipe. We got to his building and rang the doorbell. He lived on the third floor. Brother Bruce opened the window and looked down.

"What do you want?" Brother Bruce yells.

I yelled back, "I've got him."

"Got who?"

"Here he is. It's Robert Downey."

I saw Brother Bruce's mouth mouth the words, "*Holy shit.*"

He buzzed us in. From the moment the door was opened, an all-night rap session took place. There we were, in the presence of someone we respected and admired. *Putney Swope* was our first exposure to an absurdist work of genius. A comedy that imagined a better world, especially for African Americans. Years later, when Downey first met Richard Pryor, Pryor exclaimed, "You mean you ain't black?"

We spent the next couple hours talking about life and film, the afterlife, religion, sports, gambling, you name it. It was like consulting a human opinionated Wikipedia with questions about every important aspect of life. Eventually, we realized that it was too late to catch the last train for New York. So we brewed a pot of coffee, hot water for tea (for Bob), and kept the conversation going all night. Cocaine wasn't on the scene yet, otherwise I'm sure I would have had some with me. When I did eventually start snorting coke, I had a vial in my pocket for 13 years. *Never* a day without a full vial. You can do that when you're a coke dealer.

A couple months later, I sent Bob a letter asking him if he ever needed any crew members for his next film, I would work for free. I would rather sweep the floor on the set of a Bob Downey film than make a fortune selling stocks for a brokerage company. (Not that that was ever an option.) That's my motto for living. "It's not what you do, it's who you do it for." The letter (real ink, paper, and a first-class stamp) did eventually open the door to a film role for me.

I remember the day we filmed in a downtown loft, because the night before, I was with a girlfriend who was into Arica, a human potential movement started in 1968 by Bolivian-born philosopher Óscar Ichazo. It was based on Sufism, transpersonal psychology and the teachings of Stanislav Grof. She and the other Aricans living in New York all had penthouse apartments because they believed that being as close to the sky as possible was akin to being on a mountaintop. So, they all had the highest apartments they could find in the tallest buildings they could afford. They hired carpenters to build platform beds right at window height. When you looked out at night, you were looking out and down, at all of down-and-out Manhattan. Maybe it's not down-and-out for everyone, just the tens of thousands living on the streets and hundreds of thousands doing hard work for minimum wage. The view was magnificent. She and I stayed up until morning getting higher than her platform bed. She was a little older, and very well versed in keeping a young man up all night, so to speak.

When I showed up on the set the next morning, I had a horrific hangover. I regret not showing up healthier because I didn't do my best acting job. My uncontrolled drug use the night before ruined my scenes, most of which ended up on the cutting room floor. Bob deserved better than what I gave him. I had performed in Philadelphia at local playhouses, and in high school plays, but my performance in Bob's film sorely suffered . . . as did I. I didn't intend to do coke and sex all night, but once we got started, there was no turning back on our backs.

We must accept that this creative pulse within us is God's creative pulse itself.
— Joseph Chilton Pearce

Chapter 7

He Who Strongly Desires to Move Up Will Think of a Way to Build a Ladder

By now, I had devised my own brilliant plan to completely avoid the open-heart surgery business still unresolved from my youth: continual distraction and a slow drip of drug-induced suicidal behavior. If life is about creating our stories on the tabula rasa we are born with then my life as a drug fiend was about to become a chapter full of typos with no Wite-Out in sight.

I never knew what great disappointments or triumphs might greet me when I left the house, so I was always prepared to adjust my mood, alter my perspective or insulate my emotions with a full flask of vodka or tequila, five joints, Valium, Percodan, a vial of cocaine, some 'shrooms and a half-dozen hits of Ecstasy. I never met an intoxicant I didn't like—be it drink or drug—that wasn't temporarily useful, even as it undermined achieving any of my long- term goals.

Goals? They were for footballers and hockey players. Don't get me wrong, I had my share of ambitions, but they were simple and I achieved all three: Make Money. Make Love. Don't Get Caught.

\#

Making love was a priority, but I also spent a lot of time on the road, alone. In 1977, on my way to Big Sur, I was staying at the

Holiday Inn in Carmel, yearning for some company. Before going out to dinner, I looked in the Yellow Pages for a restaurant or nightclub. It was then that I saw the page listing "Escort Services/ Outcall Only." Funny how Marriage Counselors was followed by Massage Parlors. The latter usually precedes the former.

Suddenly, it dawned on me that my future was no longer dark and lonely. I'd go out to the only club with live music on this Sunday night, get some bar food, and have a few drinks. I would do my best to meet someone I could invite back to my room. If I didn't meet a woman, I'd go back to the room and call one of the offerings on the Escort page because I'm in a good mood and I don't want to be alone. Two hours later, back in the room, I make the call.

Forty minutes later, after a joint outside and a half-dozen lines inside, I hear, "Knock, Knock."

"Who's there?"

"Mary."

"Mary? Mother of the Universe?"

Hail Mary.

I paid Mary for two hours upfront. She called her service and told them, "This will be my last call for the night."

I tell her before we get in bed, "We're going to watch the rest of this George C. Scott movie on TV."

It was *They Might Be Giants*. Later, after the hanky-panky session, she says she'll stay all night for no extra money, and asks, "Do you give good sleep?"

I apologized and told her I didn't, but that I appreciated her offer. Under different circumstances, I would have gladly had her spend the night, but I was holding thirty thousand dollars cash stashed in the trunk of my rental car, and the keys were hidden under the mattress of the bed we weren't on. This was in case she had the Pea and Princess syndrome. I couldn't be sure that I wouldn't wake up with no Mary and no money. I did learn that night that you can only experience "free love" after you pay for it.

I also learned that you can usually count on a professional being pleasant to the touch, eyes, and nasal cavity. An excellent call girl, escort, or street worker relies upon her health being in good standing while lying on her back. There is no woman more destined for a night of insufficient revenue than a streetwalker with the aroma of a small Sicilian fishing village before refrigeration.

I carried my tradition of planning ahead into the 1977 football season. Every Monday night I always had a hot plan after going to see the hottest acts in New Wave music, like Elvis Costello and the Talking Heads at the Hot Club on Lombard Street in Philadelphia. I knew the owner, so I always got in free and had access to the Monday Night football game on the TV in the band's dressing room. After the show, in old galoshes traipsing through the snow on my way home, I would regularly stop by a friendly bordello for warm companionship and some laughs with one or two women, depending on my mood and whether the team I had bet on won or lost. It was winter, and on some nights, brutally cold, yet always warm and cozy.

Some people are not always kind to sex workers. I recall back in 1978 my cousin Eric the Rap and I picked up a pair of hitchhiking hookers on Van Ness Street. We took them to our "fancy" motel room where we had sex and played chess all night. Despite the hookers' proficiency at both sex and chess, Eric the Rap, a chess master, would not allow them to win a single game. The bastard.

"I never metaphor I didn't like," someone once said, yet there are two or three escort experiences I found unpleasant, and not from the aroma. One was New Year's Eve, 1985, when my girlfriend Ilene and I had hired an escort for the night. Around three in the morning, things got a little out of hand, and it seemed like everyone was losing their grip.

The escort got naked in the hot tub, refused to leave, and demanded more and more sex. It was a difficult and arduous process getting her out of the tub, dried, and dressed in time for the cab we called to take her away.

We succeeded in getting her ready to depart, but the taxi took longer than anticipated. Each tick of the clock increased the tension because we feared she would refuse to leave and cause more drama. If she did refuse, our next call would be to the police or a hospital. Thankfully, we convinced her to crawl into the cab, which spirited her away into the darkness.

The second upsetting escort experience was distressing only because it forced me to swallow my morals. Alone in a motel in Key Biscayne, 10 miles south of Miami, I had ordered a full-service escort from a full-service outcall agency. With nothing good on TV, all there was to do was get high and do lines. So, I got high and did lines. And waited. And waited. And waited. I called a few times to find out her ETA and the answers were always the same, "She's on her way, she's almost there."

With my heart pounding out my ribcage like timpani drums at the climax of the opera The Ring, I decided the wisest thing to do would be to start taking Valiums. Twenty milligrams later, I finally hear a knock. It's my savior, it's my nurse, it's my relief. Just after we disrobed, she made an anti-Semitic remark. You know, something subtle, such as "Hitler should have finished what he started," or "Hitler wasn't all bad. Look what a good job he did with the Volkswagen."

For the high and mighty, for the high-and-mighty horny, the much-anticipated arrival of an exceptionally attractive professional sex worker overrides the revelation that the woman is one brown blouse away from being the Eva Braun of outcall escorts. I did what any red-blooded American Jewish drug dealer from Logan would do—I paid her, had sex with her, and told her that she should use the money to plant a tree in Israel. As her between-the-sheets performance was stellar, the night was not a total bust. More than my morals got swallowed that night.

#

Breaks were an absolute necessity to maintain good mental and physical health, especially after escapades such as those 24-hour round trips from Boulder to Philly to turn a quick half-kilo of blow and return to the Rockies. After one such escapade, Joe D. picked me up at Stapleton International Airport in Denver and took me right to Boulder's best nightclub. The Paul Winter Consort was playing their unique blend of new age jazz music. For the encore, Paul brought on stage a wolf to howl along with the song, which it did, eerily and happily at the right times, as if on cue. The sheet music must have said, "Howl Here." It was poetic irony since Allen Ginsberg lived nearby.

We were moving and grooving to the music, standing next to a young Buddhist girl. When we offered to buy her a drink, she said, "No thank you. I'm horny enough." She asked if we lived nearby.

"*YES!*" Joe and I yelled out over the music.

Soon enough we were back at our dorm room in Boulder. Actually, an apartment we rented for the summer to attend Naropa University (I guess I did have goals), founded by Chögyam Trungpa Rinpoche, a Tibetan Buddhist meditation master who died at the age of 48 of liver damage caused by severe alcohol (mostly tequila) abuse. As part of Naropa, Allen Ginsberg started the Jack Kerouac School of Disembodied Poetics with poet Anne Waldman. Writers, poets, and seekers came from all over for many magical seminars with some of the best poetry, tai chi and writing teachers in the world.

Speaking of magic, that's what the night turned out to be. Pure magic. Our new Buddhette friend made it clear we were going to a have a threesome. Maybe the Buddha was wrong. Life is *not* suffering. We had good weed, and I had brought back some coke from my overnight trip to Philly. I forget what music we put on, but it was probably more soulful than the smooth jazz the Paul Winter Consort was putting out.

After the poetry of moans and giggles, we reclined by the pool, watching God's free yearly August light show. The three of us were marveling, oohing and aahing, at the Perseids meteor shower, and while lying together there all cosmic and cozy, the girl says warmly, "I think my outbreak is over, so you guys probably don't have to worry about getting my herpes." The true miracle of the evening was that neither Joe nor I contracted the gift that keeps on giving.

#

A lot was happening in Boulder in the seventies. Walking into a party, I said to my friend Joe D., "This is the kind of party that when you see someone who looks like Timothy Leary, *it is* Timothy Leary." Allen Ginsburg called Tim "a hero of American Consciousness." He was also an American psychologist and writer and became an avid club-goer in Los Angeles. Sometimes you just can't get enough of that disco lighting.

Allen Ginsberg and I interacted many times over the years, at Naropa and elsewhere. He scolded me in Boulder, for selling 5" x 7" photographs I had made from Polaroids I owned of Allen and his longtime companion, Peter Orlovsky, naked. Ginsberg was pissed off that I hadn't gotten the photographer's (Elsa Dorfman) permission. I told him I thought since I bought and owned one-of-a-kind Polaroids (20" x 24"), with no negatives in existence, that I could do whatever I wanted with them, including make copies and sell them. He did not agree and was quite adamant. So, instead of selling them, I gave the 5" x 7" prints away. (The Polaroid camera mentioned here is one of the largest format instant cameras ever made—so says Wikipedia—and many well-known photographers have worked with the bulky 235-pound, wheeled-chassis Polaroid to create their art.)

Speaking of great men and great partnerships, you can't do better than Timothy Leary and Dr. Richard Albert, a.k.a. Ram Dass.

Ram Dass was an American spiritual teacher, psychologist, and author. He helped to popularize the spirituality of the Eastern cultures, along with yoga and meditation. He remains popular to this day, even after he let go of his body on December 22, 2019. His super-classic, *Be Here Now* has sold over two million copies and will be considered in a hundred years to have been one of the most significant books of the 20th century. If there is a hundred years from now.

I also took classes with Allen at Naropa University. He gave a class with his teacher Chögyam Trungpa Rinpoche as the guest speaker. In the middle of the class, Gregory Corso bursts into the room with a very unique haircut, and proclaims, "You're not really a completely free man until you can cut your own hair."

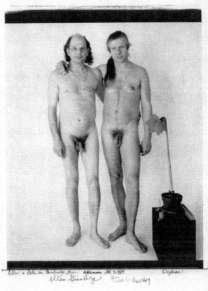

Allen and Peter in Love (20 x 24-inch Polaroids)

Ginsberg says, "Fine, now sit down!"

And he whispers to him, "It looks great Gregory." It did not.

One afternoon, in a stunningly sunny moment, a red Cadillac convertible careens around the corner. Driving is none other than Ken Kesey, author of *One Flew Over the Cuckoo's Nest*, coming to visit his friends on an August afternoon that summer at Naropa. Gary Snyder was giving a reading that night and wouldn't all the local owls be hooting it up and making wise cracks.

\#

I come from a long line of long-winded storytellers, and it is not a contradiction to my rather drug-centered lifestyle that I've always been interested in spiritual concepts.

Since reading Ram Dass's classic *Be Here Now* when I was 18, I've had an interest in New Age thought and ancient teachings. In 2010 I got to experience one of the favorite weeks of my life.

Rev. Michael Beckwith, leader of the Agape International Spiritual Center in Los Angeles, held a five-day retreat on Maui with Ram Dass. My dear friend Renee Lynn, Esthetician to the Stars, gifted me this remarkable gig by Miles Davis and John Coltrane. My nicknames for the Rev. and Ram Dass. They spoke separately and would riff off each other's solos. Everyone in attendance, all 30 of us, could see that these two wise guys, gurus, brothers, teachers, loved each other as much as Tom Sawyer and Huck Finn. Every evening we would sing Kirtan with world-famous musician Jai Uttal. Maui never felt so high. Each day was like watching God pouring God into God.

Back in the early eighties, I especially enjoyed the works of Jiddu Krishnamurti. When the opportunity arose to go to Ojai, California to see him in person, I couldn't say no. My companion on this trip was Karl Abrams, a.k.a. The Professor.

I met Karl Abrams, tenured chemistry professor who knows a lot about a lot, in 1981. His cousin Henry Abrams was Albert Einstein's ophthalmologist. And Karl Abrams tells me Albert's eyes are in a jar at Henry's house in Princeton. See what I mean? The Professor has been my best friend for more than 40 years.

The Professor and I flew from San Francisco to Santa Barbara and rented a car from Avis (always preferring the underdog) and drove to Ojai, where we had the privilege of hearing Krishnamurti speak. He sat in a simple wooden chair, we sat on the ground under a large oak tree. He started giving these talks in 1924 and continued them throughout his life. He died in 1986 at home in Ojai, near the old large oak tree. He was 90. Krishnamurti is credited with having written over 60 books. Most of them I suspect actually transcriptions of his talks. Oh boy, could he talk.

When he ended his rap, and despite having dosed off several times during the enlightened man's talk, I wanted to buy that simple wooden chair. I felt that the chair was now imbued with a solid sense of the spiritual. It wasn't just me who felt the energy during that day. The audience sitting around me felt the vibe they were seeking. They were from all over the world and did not come to

California to ride the Matterhorn at Disneyland. They came for "the truth."

When Krishnamurti finished his talk, he was escorted up to his residence nearby. I immediately rushed up to one of his handlers and asked, "Can I buy that chair?"

"What?"

"Can I buy the chair he just sat in?"

"Well, no, we really don't sell Krishnamurti's chair."

"How about $200?"

"No, Sir, we really don't . . ."

"Listen," I said. "I'll give you $500 for the chair. Nobody has to know." I thought, if a man wants a chair simply because Krishnamurti sat in it, the man must be spiritual, right? I didn't get the chair Krishnamurti gave his talk from.

Years before, my brother and I managed to walk out of the Academy of Music carrying the red velvet chair from the opera box that my brother had sat in during a Van Morrison concert. We formed a V-formation and put the chair between us and managed to make it past the defenders (security) without being tackled. Brother Bruce figured having the chair would preserve the memory of this unforgettable concert. Having to steal it mattered not. He still has it—50 years later. Perhaps, we should have tried to steal Krishnamurti's chair in broad daylight, and if we got caught, we would tell the staff to improve their practice of nonattachment.

Chapter 8

Always Make Way for Fools and Mad Men, Kids and Moms

The one thing we can never get enough of is love.
And the one thing we never give enough of is love.
—Henry Miller

I met Ben's mother, Carlee, in 1977 at about two in the morning at an afterhours club in Philly called the Second Story. There was good energy in the club that night. I guess everyone had their own coke, so nobody was jonesing for any or trying to scam some from all the dealers in the room. Also, famed 76er Julius Erving was sitting alone at the bar having a cocktail. I learned the next morning from *The Philadelphia Inquirer* that on this very night, Dr. J. had the highest- scoring game of his career. Here he was all alone, in a noisy club, quietly celebrating with a drink.

I noticed an exceptionally beautiful woman, also alone, wearing a most stunning, colorful paper-thin silk dress. This was unusual garb for a barhopping woman in the days of disco. I went over to her, and asked, "Where did you get that amazing dress?"

She replied with an international smile that she got it on Portobello Road. I told her that I recently had been to Portobello Road, a flea market in the Jewish district of London, having spent the summer of 1976 in England rather than celebrate America's bicentennial in Philly with the winners of the war to continue slavery, I preferred hanging in the country that let America slip through its fingers 200 hundred years ago. We hit it off. Immediately. She hadn't met that many, if any, men at the disco who knew London or the Portobello Road flea market.

I asked if she would join me for dinner the following night. She accepted. There was something slightly off at the next night's dinner at the only Thai restaurant in Philadelphia. I was trying to communicate with her, but she seemed oddly distracted and disconnected. And she wasn't eating her noodles or the shrimp special.

A year later, she confided in me that she had been so nervous about our first date that she had taken some LSD to take the edge off. To her, the noodles in her Pad Thai seemed to have a life of their own. Despite the psychedelic distractions, we got along well enough that we planned a second date.

She was an equestrian by profession and managed a ranch for a wealthy white songwriter who wrote hits for The Sound of Philadelphia records. Carlee was very adept at everything involving horses (except betting on them). Our second date was at her ranch. She had asked me if I rode, and of course I said yes, no wuss me. When we arrived at the stalls, there were two very large stallions. I waited for her to get some saddles for them, and I waited, and waited.

Eventually she said, "Okay let's get on."

"Where are the saddles?"

"Oh, we mostly ride bareback here."

I had only gone horseback riding a handful of times as a teenager. With all the masculine manhood I could muster, I grabbed the reins, hoisted myself up and on. Away we went. We had another city date the next night, very indoors with no acid. The next time I was at the ranch, still anticipating riding bareback, she suggested we ride in the other direction and do the jumping course.

We dated for a while, but there were some romance-related conflict issues in her life, and we drifted apart. Six months later, Three Mile Island was threatening to melt down near Harrisburg, not too far from Philly. I had my own reactors and decided to be on the next flight to Miami. I was more attracted to the airport's restaurant serving tuna melts than seeing Eastern Pennsylvania melting into the earth. While I was hanging out in Florida, planning a vacation to Jamaica, Joe D., my sidekick, was now also working as my drug mule. He called me one evening from a few blocks away with alluring news.

"Hey, remember that chick Carlee you were seeing for a while? She's here at this jazz club right now."

"Don't let her leave," I said. "I'm on my way."

Long story short, that night I convinced her to go away with me to Jamaica the next morning, where we sunbathed, swam, and had copious quantities of drugs and intimacy. We started a life together, and 10 months later she told me she was pregnant, again. We talked it over, and she decided to terminate the pregnancy.

The day of termination, I said, "You know, you don't have to do this."

"Really?"

"Really."

"Okay, but if I keep the kid, will you promise to take care of us for the rest of my life?"

"Sure. Why not?"

Carlee had already had one or two abortions, and the idea of a third was unbearable and I figured, as long as I was working, I could afford to support them. And if I wasn't working, that would mean I was in prison or shot to death.

I kept my word and took care of her and Ben financially even after Carlee and I broke up, until eventually she married someone else and she became his responsibility.

#

I never had a dad to teach me how to play sports, let alone praise me for my abilities or efforts. When Ben was four years old, I took him to an empty bowling alley.

"The object of the game, Ben," I explained, "is to roll the ball past the pins without knocking any of them over."

With my enthusiastic support, encouragement and guidance, he bowled a perfect game.

Brother Bruce was always fond of Ben, calling him a "wild kid." At age six, my little show-off volunteered to be on stage off Broadway at Penn and Teller's hot new show. They asked him to throw darts at a map of Bible History. When Penn Gillette referred to Ben as a "wild kid," Brother Bruce leaned over to me and said, "See, I told you!"

My son Ben and I have always been close—as close as a father and son can be when Dad loves his son but is also busy selling drugs for the first 14 years of the kid's life so I could support him and his mother . . . and support my voracious appetite for orchestra seats at Sondheim musicals, Zen Macrobiotic workshops with Michio Kushi, sex, drugs, rock 'n' roll concerts once a week and lots of jazz clubs, too.

The night before Ben was born at home in Radner, Pennsylvania, I was in Atlantic City with Bob Watson and Jerome gambling and doing coke. It's not like we were doing coke just because we were in Atlantic City. We could have been sitting shiva or attending a wake or waiting in line at the DMV. We were always doing coke, and we happened to be in AC gambling all night.

When I got home and got in bed at seven in the morning, Carlee rolled over and said, "I think this is it. I'm going into labor."

"No, please, not this morning. Wait until later. I need some sleep."

Two hours later, she wakes me, "The midwife's assistant is out of town. You have to help. Here's a list of things we have to get ready."

The idea of giving birth in a hospital never occurred to us. To start our son's divine existence where people go to die or treat diseases seemed barbarically commercial and all part of Big Pharma's brainwashing endeavors to make mothers think the most natural thing in the world, happening for eons, was only safe in a diseased-filled hospital, where the baby immediately gets his eyes flushed with silver nitrate and taken away from the mother's breast to be circumcised. Imagine the trauma of being taken from Mommy and then whittled like a branch in the hands of an old Okie rocking on the front porch.

I boiled some sheets and got out our prearranged home birth kit with sanitized everything. I just want to make sure the new video camera is set up. I start drinking endless cups of coffee for the rest of the day. I never drank booze in the daytime.

There was a lot of moaning and groaning and consoling. If I tried to say anything funny, Carlee's eyes would shoot daggers at me.

I think we both took a couple of hits from a joint to calm down—to reduce the screaming she was slowly starting to vocalize. The midwife arrived midafternoon, sans assistant. She was all set up with her plastic gloves, peroxide and emergency forceps. Depends, gauze and a plastic sheet—in case I forgot to boil and sun-dry a cotton sheet—and other items as well.

Family lore has it that she forgot her sterilized umbilical cord-cutting scissors, and all we had in the house to cut him loose was the razor off the coke mirror. That probably isn't true.

Oh boy, what a party. Me, Carlee, the midwife, plus Spook and Mia, our two black labs. Carlee hated being filmed, so at six in the evening, right before giving birth to our leading man, she looked at the JVC video camera and it froze for the rest of the night. However, the Nikon was close at hand.

At 7:10 p.m., on the 10th of July, a seven-pound, nine-ounce baby boy was born. I was going to put my thumb on the doula's scale to make it a perfect three 7:10, 7/10, 7 lb./10 oz. But I didn't. Because I don't lie and would never fuck with the scale when weighing cocaine, pot, or family members.

I cut the cord and said, "Please forgive me. I'm sorry I have to do this."

He looked up at me, square in the eye. That night, when I went to pay the midwife in hundreds, I knew what to name the baby: Benjamin. Benjamin Franklin, the greatest of the colonial patriots and one who made his fortune in Philadelphia, creator of America's library system and—check it out—the dude on the hundred-dollar bill; and for Benny Cooper, owner of that corner candy store of my precious and lonely youth. Though Benjamin Franklin loved whores, I did not want Ben to grow up like his father or his namesake.

There was a debate about whether to have the boy circumcised, given that it is a Judaic requirement. Neither of us were traditionalists, but we still scheduled a nip and tuck for Benjamin a couple days later. However, after seeing how incredibly carefree he was, we were afraid that cutting off part of his penis could ruin his day. So, I had to break the news to my mother a few mornings later that the bris had been called off, and we were having a No-Bris celebration. Brisket yes, Bris NO. We had a fabulous party, and all the

Cocaine Baby

Jewish male guests shared a collective sigh of relief to hear I told the mohel to take the day off—not my son's foreskin. I quickly had a little T-shirt made that read, UNCUT. It was the perfect pun for my son's all- natural pecker and his coke-dealing father's ethics.

Avoiding boredom at all costs, within a three-year period, I had two sons, got married and annulled. It took three women for that hat trick. Before there were cell phone cameras, I would tell couples who were about to get married to make sure the wedding photographer was using a Polaroid, so they would be guaranteed they saw photos before they broke up. My marriage broke up during our honeymoon.

Mama Rose, Ben the Son

My firstborn, Joshua, was born to Carol Ann Schwartz. Carol and I also met in 1977, when Robert Downey Sr. invited me to see his new film, a work in progress, at the Los Angeles International Film Exposition, called FilmEx. Always changing careers, I was working at a wholesale female garment gambit at the time. A friendly customer mentioned that one of her designers, a Jewish woman from the Bronx, was now living in Santa Monica and I should look her up.

I looked her up ... and down and from the moment I laid eyes on her, I knew something interesting was bound to happen. I hoped it would be something good, but in any event, I didn't know it would end up being *that* interesting and *that* tragic. Little did I know years later I would wind up as her son's conservator due to his serious developing mental illness. From her apartment we took a romantic walk on the Santa Monica pier in the spring's enticing night air.

Then we drove to The Rainbow Room. As we danced under a mirrored ball with multicolored strobe lights flashing across our faces, our bodies high on cocaine, pot and Donna Summer, we fell in love. Soon to come however would be the winters of my discontent.

We were inseparable for the five days I was in Los Angeles, and a few weeks later she came to Philadelphia to spend a few weeks with me. We went up to Toronto, a lot cooler than Philly, and while at dinner one night, before her first bite, she fell face-first into her snapper soup. For no immediate comprehensible reason, she had passed out cold. The visuals were stunning. It was the first time I had seen someone take a real "header." Embarrassed for her, and me, I wanted to crawl into a shell. I was having mussels.

Once she regained consciousness and took the snapper off her face, we continued on as if nothing was out of the ordinary. We spent the next 10 days in various Canadian hotels and cabin rentals, canoeing on lakes and getting to know each other before we returned to Philly.

A few days later, we were out shopping with a wad of $5 dollar bills. Five dollars bills were almost considered disposable in the drug trade. Way too bulky to fly with or smuggle back to Colombia. No self-respecting dealer would accept them unless they were collecting from street dealers. But I did have one customer who always paid in fives, hundreds of them. He was the main supplier of weed to the organization known as MOVE, a local separatist organization that financed their activities by selling nickel-and-dime bags of pot. The group was a back-to- nature anarchist movement that would like to give America back to the Indians and do away with all governments. Interestingly, all the members shared the same surname: Africa.

When we got home from spending our filthy lucre (the fives were grimy) supported shopping spree, I asked Carol to hand me her newly cut keys so I could open the front door. I guess I was holding all the happily filled shopping bags. She couldn't find them in her purse.

Now, that sort of thing is not that uncommon. Usually, a woman dumps everything out of her purse and then finds them in her coat pocket. This situation was markedly different because she became completely hysterical and unhinged, far out of proportion to the situation of just misplacing some apartment keys.

Her hysteria scared me because it was at a level that only a true hysteric could achieve. I was dumbstruck and dismayed; not because of the lost keys, but because I couldn't stand the thought of being alone with someone so dramatically irrational. It was terrifying. Especially since I was a drug dealer, always adhering to the low-profile way of life. It was as if I was suddenly starring in some low-budget horror movie that, despite the crude lighting and exaggerated makeup, scares you half to death. Sort of like the classic film, *The Three Faces of Eve*. Instead, it was *The Two Many Faces of Carol*.

I began to more closely watch her emotional responses to other situations. For the most part, they were larger than life, over the top, highly charged, inappropriate, and grating on my nerves. This relationship wasn't going to work for more reasons than our irreconcilable mismatched neuroses, and we lived on opposite coasts. I had a thriving drug-dealing enterprise underneath my wholesale garments ruse, and you can fill in the blanks with any other reasonable justifications.

I knew I had to tell her that we could no longer be a couple. I'm not a doctor, despite dispensing massive amounts of unprescribed drugs for self–medication purposes, but I could clearly see that she had significant emotional or psychiatric problems well beyond my coping or caretaking abilities. Such problems are not character defects but medical issues. This did not lessen her beauty, her talent, or her other many splendid qualities. Although she was a very fine commercial artist, and I was an art lover, the outbursts did create a pentimento on my desire to be in a long-term relationship with her.

111

The next day she returned from running and doing some seemingly childish errands and I sat her down and said, "I have something important to tell you."

"I have something important to tell you, too," she replied pleasantly. "You go first."

A glimmer of optimism sparkled briefly as I inferred that we may be on the same page of How to End Your Friendly Failed Relationship. Or, Let's Nip This in the Bud. We were smoking a lot of pot.

"Well," I said with all the warmth I could muster, "it seems obvious to me, and no doubt to you . . ."

She nodded with a sly smile. I waited for her to synchronistically finish my sentence. She did not, so I continued, "that we really should not stay together as a couple."

All the color drained from her face before turning fire engine red. She stood up, looked me right in the eye, and calmly replied, "Well, I just found out I'm pregnant."

With that, she socked me right in the face, knocking me halfway across the room; it was a pretty big room.

Lucky punch.

When we calmed down, she spoke forcefully but without rancor. "I'm thirty-five," she said, "and I'm having this child—with you or without you. Let's make an agreement: You never ask for custody; I'll never ask for child support."

Deal.

My attorney wrote up an agreement that we signed the next day before a notary. Then I bought her a big ol' yellow Chrysler New Yorker (she was after all born in the Bronx) and drove her back to California. I left her with an aging car and a blossoming fetus. Perhaps the biggest mistake of my life was to keep in touch with her. When Joshua was born, I assumed that because she was beautiful and talented, she would soon find a husband, and Joshua would have a daddy and not just a biological drug-dealing father 3,000 miles away.

Carol had called me a few days after Joshua was born, and I wished her well. One year went by, then two. When he was two or three years old, I went to meet the odd couple (I think there was some emotional incest at play) in Key Largo. The next year, I saw them in Big Sur and Joshua was jumping up and down on the bed, yelling "Daddy! Daddy! Daddy!" I never said those words in my *entire* life, so I wasn't sure who he was talking to. Yet here I was hearing them, and it's breaking my heart. I was not his daddy. I was just his

The Schwartz's

father. He was the continuation of my orgasm, not my ward. A man in lust who just never thought much of the future because of his drug addiction, asthma, and aortic stenosis.

Over the next 16 years, I saw Carol and Joshua for a few hours here and there, almost once a year. It was heartbreaking because I think Josh didn't experience abandonment. He experienced rejection.

"Dear Josh, it was never you I rejected, just your mother." It would have been far better if he never knew me, if he believed that his daddy passed away dead when he was three weeks old. Like my dada did do. Living 3,000 miles apart, me in Philly and they in LA, and then 385 miles apart when I lived in Marin County and Carol and Josh were in Santa Monica was not conducive to a steady father-son relationship.

I swear I thought Carol would meet a man, fall in love, and get married so Joshua would have a full-time daddy. She had been married once before so I knew she had it in her, so to speak.

Joshua would see me and know I was his father, but I never took him anywhere because when he was removed from his mother's presence, he reacted like he was being kidnapped (a bit hysterical wouldn't you say?). So I could never have him come stay with me. We never were and would never become a family.

His mother and I remained good friends, mostly because she needed me to send her an ounce of weed every month because she was a marijuana addict worse than me. Sativa and Indica, like Woodward & Bernstein. She was ready for anything, including death.

The most emotionally connected moment in our years of occasional interaction was on a visit to Carol and Joshua's shabby flat in Santa Monica. I was more distant than usual and was suffering from a terrible flu and raging fever. We were sitting together, attempting to communicate through my thick, medicated influenza fog, when Carol's phone rang. The entire atmosphere was rent asunder by the succinct message, "Carol, your mother died." She packed a couple bags for her and the kid, flew to Miami for the funeral for a mother-in-law that never was. I had never met the old lady, the newly deceased woman who raised her daughter to be a bit of an hysteric. At least I was there to drive them to the airport. And you know how much people hate driving friends to LAX.

I once asked Carol about her life in high school, where we all get a chance to figure out who we are and who we wanna be. She told me she couldn't remember anything about being in high school. Not anything. If that's not a sign of some deep-seated psychological trauma, what is? Maybe that's why she smoked pot every day of her life. In fact when I went to her apartment to retrieve Josh's artwork after she died on June 16, 2020, I found two plastic vials of store-bought weed on her nightstand. One sativa, the other indica. Neither could save her life. She died never letting

God shine its light directly into her heart. Clouds block sunlight, pot blocks Love's light.

Back in 1996, Carol, despite her sex appeal and creativity, still hadn't beguiled her Mr. Right right to the Chuppah until Joshua went to college on a full scholarship to CalArts. There, his blazing talent and unleashed creativity rapidly spread his fame and reputation as a future artistic superstar. He was being called the next Basquiat. But by his second semester, the ascending flame of his career was forever extinguished by a complete mental and emotional breakdown. The school called us and said Joshua had given up his dorm room, moved into an art supply closet and often was shouting at professors in class. They thought he was on drugs. That would have been so simple to deal with. Stop the drugs, stop the madness. But it was the madness that ruled everything.

A SWAT team of mental health professionals conducted every known psychological test. He was diagnosed with everything from Bipolar Disorder to Schizophrenia to Schizoid Personality Disorder to Psychosis NOS. It seemed as if he had also had a lot of traits of Borderline Personality Disorder. The list of suspected yet unconfirmed diagnoses was long. No one seemed to be able to put their finger on what evil spirit possessed him. Years later the medical director at Las Encinas Hospital in Pasadena declared, "He's been misdiagnosed for 15 years. He's actually just Autistic!" And artistic!

Years earlier, the head of psychiatry at San Francisco General told me what Joshua needed was a good agent to sell his artwork. "Mr. Buschel, your son is an artistic genius. Don't let what happened to Janis Joplin happen to your son."

I swear that's what he said! Well, she died and her suffering ended. Joshua lives on. He went missing in November 2019 and resurfaced in December 2020, living on the corner of Adams Blvd. and S. San Pedro just adjacent to the official homeless district in downtown LA. He was still sketching and trading drawings for food, not fame.

Joshua, Carol's son, was not invited to his mother's wedding because she was apprehensive about his erratic behavior. Even in his earlier years, he manifested signs and symptoms indicative of disruptive emotional disturbances. His behavior from early adolescence became increasingly unpredictable and concerning. I saw things going off the rails, but I didn't feel I had the right to discipline him or doing anything about it since I only saw him once a year. This included Joshua's refusal to stand for the final prayer at his own Bar Mitzvah, for example.

Strangely enough, I have been Joshua's conservator since the state of California ruled him gravely mentally ill and completely disabled. His mother had moved away to live in the Emerald Triangle amongst the Northern California redwoods, completely abandoning her only son. Joshua became an orphan with two living parents. When he was conceived, such an ignominious destiny was inconceivable.

My dad didn't die on purpose nor did he intentionally cut himself out of my nascent desire for a balanced family. My opportunity to pass out of Joshua's life gave up the ghost the day he bounced on the bed, yelling "Daddy, Daddy, Daddy!"

As a child, Joshua was emotionally married to his mother. Perhaps what some call psychic incest. They rarely had visitors and always were in conflict. While she was smoking pot and watching foreign films, he was in his room playing violent video games and probably harboring patricidal ideations. When Joshua saw me with Ben, my son from the non-Jewish mother, he seethed at our closeness, so clung even harder to his hysterical Jewish mother/ monster/wife/wiccan/Airbnb womb host.

As a deeply damaged adult, he now has only a de facto father, protector and advocate.

His mother abandoned him to me and the California mental healthcare system, which is an oxymoron.

For a few years, whenever Joshua was out of sorts, he would walk over to Cedars Sinai (where I had my open-heart operation and brain surgery) and tell the nurse at the emergency room that he was very unhappy, despondent and planning to kill himself. That act (was it an act?) always got him admitted to the psych ward. On one such 5150, he was speaking to another patient.[2] When Josh asked him what he did for a living, the guy said, "I'm an actor." Josh asked if he'd ever been in anything that Josh (an avid moviegoer) might have seen. "I did play Chaplin in one film."

Joshua responds, "I'm Lee Buschel's son."

"Oh, my God," he says, "that practically makes us brothers." Robert Downey Jr. and Josh palled around like old friends. Robert got out the next day. Before he left, he purchased one of Joshua's drawings that he had brought with him to the hospital. Robert had his manager send a check to the halfway house Joshua was living in at the time. When Joshua got the check cashed he spent all the money on DVDs. He did not own a DVD player or television. Such works the mind of the mad.

That was probably Joshua's only sale to an A-lister. And the sadness just doesn't end. As of the publication of this book, Joshua Theo Schwartz is shelterless. The cop I befriended on the city's Mental Evaluation Unit has been having a team of social workers and one psychiatrist visiting Joshua weekly at his domicile behind the donut shop (not even a Dunkin' Donuts) on S. San Pedro. They have offered him housing and unlimited pharmaceuticals, but he has chosen absolute freedom. Josh loved meeting Robert back then, and whenever I talk to Jr. he always wishes Joshua well.

Josh had taken to living on the street in late 2019. He resurfaced at the end of 2020, spent some time on a psych ward and abandoned living in the California mental health system in June 2021.

As it was, Joshua had previously been confined in a chemical straight jacket for many, many years. He didn't have the Thorazine shuffle so common to those warehoused as "in treatment," but he

---

[2]   5150 refers to the California law code for the temporary, involuntary psychiatric commitment of individuals who present a danger to themselves or others due to signs of mental illness.

had the faraway look of the uncomfortably numb. He's done time in two state mental prison hospitals. Once for attempted kidnapping—a bullshit charge yet he did spend two years at Napa State Hospital awaiting trial, during which time he suffered from selective mutation—he did not speak a single word. It actually worked. He proved himself to be incompetent, so they decided not to try him and let him loose. He also once threatened to kill an on-duty fireman at his halfway house, actually considered an act of terrorism. Josh did two years at Patton State Hospital for that.

Robert Downey Jr. recovered his life and career; perhaps Joshua never had one to recover. By the time he went to college, his future was either all used up or sneaking up on him from behind. These are the lugubrious facts of my life and sorrowful realities of Josh's.

Needless to say, I never had a dad to show me the way, or any way. As shitty as it turned out, I did my best. Is it my fault that Josh has led an incredibly tragic life? Not totally.

Chapter 9

London Calling

One morning in 1980, I was alone in London, extremely entranced with the city. My local BFF Gerry Maguire Thompson told me to go see this new musical called *Sweeney Todd*. Absolutely had to he said! He hoped I could score a single ticket at the Theater Royal Drury Lane.

In my travel journal, I kept track of every "line item" throughout the day, beginning in the morning:

9:15   Instant Miso soup

9:30   One hit of Thai stick

10:30   Another hit

11:00   A shot of espresso and a line of coke

12:00   Two more shots of espresso and half a scone

12:30   Another hit and a spoonful of blow

1:00   Underground to Covent Garden

1:30   Get lucky, buy a single ticket at Theatre Royal Drury Lane and do more blow

2:00   A Carlsberg lager at the pub on the corner

2:15   A mini-bottle of Bombay gin and another toke in front of the theater

2:25   Two more sniffs

2:30   Take my seat, curtain-up—WHAT A RUSH!

For anyone who hasn't been blessed or lucky enough to have seen this explosion of musical theater anytime in the last 40 years, there is an incredibly LOUD high-pitched ship whistle in the first few minutes. I nearly jumped out of my skin and clutched my chest as if I were having a Hollywood heart attack.[3]

I started out in the balcony and then moved down to a gloriously empty seat in the tenth row. No one tried to stop me. I wanted to be as close as possible to everything except myself. Too frightened to internalize, ingest, transform, or transcend, I always sought to be closer to that which was outside of me.

Looking back, I think the encyclopedia of my feelings as a human in this life can all be found referenced in Stephen Sondheim songs. I don't know any artist I have learned more about my feelings from than Sondheim. I've seen all of his shows more than once, except *Assassins*, which I wasn't able to catch live. Of course, I have the CD. Sometimes I wonder who I will mourn the most when they go. Van Morrison, Bruce Springsteen, Stephen Sondheim, or Spike Lee (assuming I outlive them). Spike is the longshot. Black people seem to live forever if they're not pulled over for a traffic stop. Don't get me wrong, I am not obsessed with death, but it's all I think about. I don't really care how I die, hopefully quickly, hopefully painlessly, preferably in my sleep. I just don't want to die during an asthma attack suffocating to death on fresh air, no, not the NPR radio show. Sondheim. When he goes, there won't be much to look forward to on Broadway. Yes, *Hadestown* was great. But it's no *Sweeney Todd*.

#

I was not unhappy or dissatisfied as a drug dealer. I just knew it could end tragically. So I began to pursue every legal opportunity to make a living without jeopardizing my freedom and my life. Once I backed a clothing designer. It didn't work out. I had a video

---

[3]   A cardiac mishap due to a too large ingestion of cocaine hydrochloride, (C17H21NO4), either smoked, snorted, or injected.

studio in Mill Valley, but I really couldn't make a profit with one client, even though it was Peter Coyote. I backed Uncle Vinty's vaudeville career, but that didn't work out. (I wonder why? Wasn't vaudeville making a comeback?) I didn't want all my girlfriends to think all I could ever be was a drug dealer because they knew I would eventually either go to prison or get hurt. I was always looking over my shoulder, afraid my time would be up any day, and the cops would take me away forever. It's not really a sustainable career. And I knew it too. It was just a matter of time. Every new day brought me closer to my demise. Little did I know that all it would take was a bottoming out on Ecstasy (MDMA) and a month at Betty Ford to free me of a futureless future and set me on a new path of love and light.

#

In 1984 my girlfriend was the brilliant set designer Cherry Baker. Years before, when she designed the restaurant and menu at the Yarrow Stalk in Boulder, she was Joe D.'s girlfriend. Cherry was also the chef. She is nothing short of a miracle worker and the author of the cookbook *Delicious Desserts*.

My friend George Wallace (real name) had just released his newest album. He was a composer, performer, producer, vocalist, musician capable of playing any instrument and singing every part for a three-record LP exercise program called FitKids. One night, years later, I took George out to see a performance by Philip Glass at the University of Pennsylvania. George had never heard of him before (George was more of a rock 'n' roller than a Steve Reich kind of guy.) I assured him that this would be the most interesting thing happening in all of Philadelphia that night. True enough, as we entered Irvine Auditorium, Timothy Leary was going in the next door—a rare sighting, especially in Philly. From the first chord, the uniquely round auditorium seemed to spin into space and remain aloft for 90 minutes. Maybe it was Leary spraying the air with an aerosol can of acid.

Anyway, I was interested in buying the rights to license George's FitKids as a video. I contacted the album's executive producer, Rob Rosen. He was a big (tall) New York attorney. We shot a demo in Marin County, starring my four-year-old son, Benjamin, and all his friends. We secured an appointment to pitch FitKids to executives at ABC.

Cherry and I flew to New York and stayed at her brother's Columbus Circle apartment while he was out of town. The night before my meeting at ABC, Cherry and I did some coke— no, a lot of coke. And with a lot of coke comes a lot of alcohol. She passed out at about six in the morning, four hours before my 10 o'clock attempt at noncriminal success.

I tried getting at least a couple hour's shut-eye, but construction crews in the Big Apple didn't adhere to my sleep schedule. There were dozens of jackhammers hammering in front of the building. They rattled the windows and shook down the walls, and my heart, it was a- poundin'.

I thought, as always, that I was going to have a heart attack. This wasn't only drug- induced paranoia. After all, I did have a life-threatening heart condition called aortic stenosis. My reasoning was a bit self-centered; I thought my "defunktive" heart was shaking the building.

I finally discerned that my ventricles were not violently disturbing the concrete and steel of New York, but it was honestly disturbing that I'd forgotten to pick up my business suit at the dry cleaner the day before. With meeting day being on a Jewish holiday, the cleaner was closed, as was most of New York, but ABC was open. So, there I am, waiting to meet my attorney/partner in just a regular shirt and tie with no jacket. It was fall, and it was chilly, but I had no choice.

We went to the ABC skyscraper, otherwise known as ABC News headquarters. I hadn't slept at all. I hadn't eaten at all. I was a mess, to say the least. My partner was a tall imposing figure, handsomely attired and well fed. We made our way to the elevator up to the 48th floor. It seemed as through the elevator itself took delight in speeding us up to our meeting so we could experience our rejection that much faster.

At the same time, I'm imagining the elevator is shooting toward the heavens so fast, it felt like we were on the Saturn V rocket, but instead of taking us to the moon, we would be crashing straight up through the roof into the heavens, and a well-placed parachute would glide us through the air and deposit us in Central Park where we would take a Hansom cab to the Algonquin Hotel and have lunch with Dorothy Parker and share delicious bon bons and bon mots with her friends and thus relieve me of this horrible life of drug addiction and despondency. Instead . . . we were gently frog marched into the executive's office, and we're seated on the other side of his mahogany desk, both pitching the show. Actually, Rob is doing most of the talking while I'm just trying to stay conscious and not throw up. I could feel beads of sweat flying off my forehead, like in a cartoon.

I start feeling really faint, and I'm looking at the executive's desk. I see one of those fancy useless desk pen stands—where two pens with very pointy ends are inserted in a little slab of marble. I'm noticing that the pens are pointed toward me, and I start to think, if I pass out, I'm going to lose an eye by doing a header onto his desk. So I gently, nonchalantly, take the little marble granite pen thing and slide it over, just in case I fall forward.

I manage to keep it together long enough to get escorted out of the office with a "We'll let you know," which rhymes with NO. We did find out a couple weeks later that little gymnast bitch overachieving Olympic Gold medalist slut Mary Lou Retton was in New York pitching her exercise show at the same time. I guess ABC decided they would give it to the Olympian from the Olympics instead of the coke dealer from Philly.

You would like to think I had learned something from that experience. I learned you can always be blindsided by Mary Lou Retton even if you don't lose an eye to a network executive's pen and pencil set. Or, never send a man with a drug hangover to sell physical fitness.

In another appointment-related drama, I made a noon meeting with my attorney, Doug Wurken (still my attorney to this day), to discuss my small video company in Mill Valley, California, I had started. He arrived at my home on time, however I woke up a mere five minutes before the scheduled consultation. Problem was, I was hungover and nauseated and couldn't get out of bed to throw up in the bathroom. But I could lean over and throw up my guts into the waste basket . . . every few minutes. Doug was waiting for me in the garden just outside my bedroom window. Yes, he could hear me vomiting loudly and profusely.

Well, I'm a quick learner. I turned to Cherry, who was living with me at the time, and said, "My God, we need to reassess our relationships with the professional and business worlds. From now on, no appointments before 2:00 p.m. Because, by then, we could at least put on a modicum of looking together and presentable to regular working people."

I didn't take that business meeting. The aftereffect of getting wasted meant Doug's time was wasted on an unreliable and overly intoxicated client (me). The number of meetings cancelled or rescheduled over the years due to hangovers or semi-comatose conditions have never been tallied. Thank God that isn't a problem today. If I make an appointment, you can rely on me showing up in my best condition. Like Johnny Cash used to sing, "If the Good Lord's willing/and the creek don't rise/we'll see you in the morning."

A natural-born entrepreneur, I'd come up with dozens of good business ideas, but my using always got in the way of bringing anything to fruition. Always.

#

A rise in my blood pressure from a jackhammer heartbeat similar to or exceeding my Columbus Circle panic attack happened during a glorious evening of rock 'n' roll at famed Hollywood hot spots the Roxy and the Rainbow Room. It began with a benefit to Save the Whales, but I was the one about to sleep with the fishes.

Thelonious Monster opened for the Red Hot Chili Peppers. I had never heard of Thelonious Monster, and they were amazing. Years later, I had the pleasure of working with the Monster's front man, Bob Forrest, when I screened Bob and the Monster, a documentary film about Bob, at my REEL Recovery Film Festival. Bob was also nice enough to perform at the Experience, Strength and Hope Awards show in 2016, where he did a cutting five-minute spoken word diatribe against rehabs. Just because he had stopped cutting lines didn't mean he'd stopped screaming at the powers that be.

Back at the Roxy, I didn't think any band could be better than Bob Forrest and Thelonious Monster. Boy was I mistaken. Like the shaking of the building under New York construction worker jackhammers, now it was the entire universe shaking. The Chili Peppers had taken the stage and begun their first song. Their performance reached a new zenith, forming a grin on my face that I felt could last forever. Every nerve ending and every brain cell was ecstatic.

They were so exciting. They were so loud, and they were almost completely naked. It took about 10 minutes for Ilene (who is dead now) to yell out, "My God, they're not wearing any clothes! Just socks on their cocks!" (Nice to know that half the band got sober in later years.)

When the show was over, we got our car from valet parking, reluctantly getting in but definitely not wanting the night to be over.

I asked Ilene, "Where to now?"

"The Rainbow Room!"

The Rainbow Room is right next door to the Roxy. The car nudged forward a few inches, we got out, and parked with the same valet. The drive was shorter than my penis.

The Rainbow Room was even more druggie than the Roxy—and so were we: a lot of coke and more than enough tequila. In present tense, it went like this:

We're standing in one of the hallways between the lounges, and my heart is pounding like those jackhammers back in New

York. Once again, I'm scared to death because of my heart condition. I'm just trying to keep my balance and my heart rate under 120.

I turn around and on the wall are various framed LPs, awards and gold records. The one I'm leaning against is by a well-known Los Angeles band called Jack Mack and the Heart Attack. This is it. I just know it.

Yeah, this is going to be my epitaph: He died clutching a mounted album called *Jack Mack and the Heart Attack* on the wall of the world-famous Rainbow Room on Sunset Boulevard where, unlike in *Cheers*, nobody knew his name.

Sweat-drenched and resigned to the inevitable, I wait for my life's most significant moments to flash before my eyes. They do, but not in linear order or arranged by topic or significance. It was as if someone took VHS movies of my life and ran them through a Veg-O- Matic.

In my typical stoned critique mode, I silently ask, *Who the hell edited this reel?* I was so glad for the happy ending that night. I didn't die, and I got laid.

My sexual exploits continued, as did my problems with asthma. In 1985 I was staying in a friend's suburban house in Philly while he was traveling with his band. Ilene was with me and earlier in the day, I had run into my friend Desiree and invited her to visit. I left money with Ilene to pay for Desiree's taxi.

I went out to the liquor store right before Desiree arrived and took my sweet time, knowing that if the two girls met alone, without me there, they would probably be going down on each other before I got back. Right again.

At six in the morning, Ilene had passed out and Desiree had tied me to a chair in the living room and wanted me to do more coke with her. I thought I was having another Hollywood heart attack. I couldn't breathe because my asthmatic bronchia were in full "I ain't marching anymore" mode. I begged her to untie me so I could use my asthma inhaler. I wanted to take some Valiums and go to sleep before the dawn broke. Desiree would have none of that and started to freak out.

I made Ilene wake up and untie me. I grabbed my inhaler, took a few whiffs and we drove Des to Penn Station. We drop-kicked her onto the train platform and dropped a hundred dollars in her purse. In those days, you could pay the conductors with cash. That was before computers controlled our every move, thought, purchase or comprehension of reality.

Ilene and I ran back to the car so we could take off in case Desiree decided to change her mind and wanted to come back to the party house with us. What a long night and morning. Train stations in the morning hold an unreal atmosphere, with well-dressed commuters, whereas we had not even gone to sleep yet. Call me nocturnal, or call me sleep deprived, but call me the happiest man alive because that night was over.

Ilene was a good friend, the kind of woman I could not see for months at a time and then hook up with again as if we hadn't missed a beat. On New Year's Eve 1986, Ilene, two other women and I are at the 4th St. Tavern in San Rafael. Great local band playing. We had already shared a bottle of Tattingers and dabbled in a little sex and had a lot more planned for later. Now we were drinking the hard stuff. Is there anything more elegant than a vodka on the rocks with a squeeze of lime? It's like the moment when Watson and Crick realized they had discovered the design of the DNA molecule. They knew they were right because it was "beautiful." That's how I perceived a vodka on the rocks with a squirt of lime.

About 11:30 p.m., a guy comes up to me bewildered, amazed, and drunk. "How do you rate having three women tonight, and I don't have any?"

"Because I give them what they want: love, laughter, honesty, and sex." Maybe the drugs and champagne had a little something to do with it too. But just a little.

#

Dear Ilene in Heaven,

Do you remember when we went to see 'American In Paris' on Broadway and I stumbled up a flight of stairs coming up from the latrines into the lobby and my head hit the marble wall, then collapsed onto the carpet and the theater manager ran over to offer me first aid, or a ride to the ER?

What a silly memory to think of after all the amazing adventures we had together and you've been dead for three years now.

I remember coming to visit you on your deathbed in Brooklyn. A bitter cold winter's day. You laying in bed so peaceful and guardedly hopeful, yet knowing full well we would never see each other again. When I said I'd be back in New York in the spring and we'd get together, you looked at me like I was such a sweet lying fool. "Sure", you said with beatific smile. "Maybe the new treatments will work." We both knew that was a long shot.

We had visited Earl at Marin General, held his hand and listened to him tell us about his Visigoth ancestors visiting him every night. I didn't know he was already spending time in the next world or the last world.

But you so helpless, with your big gorgeous dog lying on your feet at the foot of the bed, keeping you warm was one of the most beautiful saddest things I'd even seen in my life.

See you soon,
Leonard Heaven-Bound

#

In the taxi from San Francisco International to San Anselmo, after a flight back from a detox de-coking trip to Zihuantanejo, Mexico, I ask Karl, "Once we get home, how long do you think it'll take before we go for the coke stash?"

"How long does it take to open the front door?"

After a half-hour at home, a joint, a few lines, and putting a vial in the vial pocket of my jeans, I got into my car and drove over the forever stunningly beautiful Golden Gate Bridge. It was midnight.

I was driving over the bridge to the Tenderloin. Sometimes I feel like Tom Waits, who famously said on *The Tonight Show*, "I'm so horny, the crack of dawn better watch out."

I picked up a streetwalker. She had a real French name. It was a very long day that started at an airport in Mexico and ended very happily because I was able to get back home without the cops busting me with the hooker, without a DUI and without smashing my car from being blinded by the night. This was my first inkling that my behavior with drugs and sex might one day have disastrous consequences. Now that I know the definition of a sex addict, I think that night I had crossed the line.

I remember once asking my cousin Eric the Rap, who had lived in the Bay Area for 20 years, how long do you have to live in the Bay Area before the thrill of driving over the Golden Gate Bridge fades away. He said, "It never does."

Moments such as these seem fleeting and perhaps inconsequential—or not. And if one is prudish, much of my life is an offense to the senses. Not my senses, of course. I recall making love to some woman after doing a few lines of not very well-chopped coke. I sneezed, broke a blood vessel, and exploded with projectile bleeding all over her pure white canvas-like back. I looked down and thought, I'm Jackson Pollock.

When I became a drug counselor years later, I told this story to a room full of male clients/patients/addicts. For months afterward, when they saw me in the hallway, they addressed me as Mr. Pollock. I didn't realize how colorful the story actually was until I heard them address me that way. Maybe my life looked like a Pollock splatter painting.

#

The 1980s in New York was a charming dichotomy. After checking into the Gramercy Park Hotel at 11:00 p.m., I went out to buy some fresh-cut flowers with no thorns to adorn the room. I was thinking about how cool it was to be able to buy anything you want at any hour in Manhattan. When I got back 15 minutes later, there was a fresh pool of blood in the elevator. Was it cocaine nosebleed blood similar to the one I had on my lover's back or a fresh-cut stabbing?

Stairway to Heaven

It's true, in a 24/7 town, someone could have gotten stabbed in the elevator in the time it takes to go out and buy flowers. At the Gramercy Park Hotel, if you went out to hang in the park, so the housekeeping staff could do its thing, and some lines were on the coffee table in the room, the maid would dust around them. That's New York City. Maids doing maid things, and hotel guests doing everything.

It wasn't until I saw myself in the bathroom mirror of a trendy afterhours club with a joint in one hand and a kamikaze sitting on the sink in front of me, while bending down with a silver straw in my nose inhaling a couple lines of uncut Bolivian cocaine, that I realized my original plan to avoid open-heart surgery was working. I *had* hit on the *ultimate* preventive surgery solution. The solution to my surgery woes was to continue a lifestyle that would kill me first, which wouldn't have been the worst thing that could have happened, except for the lifelong grief I would have inflicted on my mother, brother, and sons.

I was still quite fearful of the possibility of doctors sawing my chest in half, stopping my heart, and replacing defective parts. But if you're dead, the open-heart surgery idea is null and void. It was as if Thanatos himself was whispering a game plan in my ear—the only orifice I didn't put something in to get high.

Chapter 10

Oh Mama, Can This Really Be the END?

Parenting is not as easy as they make it sound in the *Good House-keeping* magazine. As easygoing as she was, my mother had her share of anxiety-provoking moments. Now remember, my mother was not unaware of my vocational aspirations to become a drug dealer. Up to age 79 (her age when I got sober), she always thought something bad would happen to me. There's an old saying that a mother can often share about a son like me: "Every time I hear the phone ring, I don't know if it's the hospital or the police calling, and I often picture you dead in a gutter."

I did have a death-defying incident that even my mother's clair-voyance could not have predicted. The incident was certainly drug related. One night, at age 37, I was nocturnally socializing with my friend and roommate Steve D. and a friend of his in Studio City, snort-ing coke and downing endless bottles of Heineken. When I finally laid down to sleep, as the sun was coming up, and those awful birds were starting to sing, I had a massive asthma attack brought on by dehy-dration and my completely collapsed bronchia.

Luckily, we hadn't taken the usual 6:00 a.m. "let's get to sleep now" 10 mg Valium. When I fell against Steve's bedroom door, he was still awake. He saw that I was suffocating and completely blue. He immediately called 911. I was dying. I could see myself dying. And I didn't want to die. I was dead set against it.

It was the worst, most horrible and frightening experience of my entire life. While dying I was being catapulted through deep space, a million miles of the darkest hell imaginable. I was almost dead. Seconds from the end. No white light, no tunnel shimmering a beckoning plea. I was silently screaming louder than the foghorn on the Titanic. I was hurtling into unimaginable darkness. Blackness, but much blacker than that. Screaming, SCREAMING into the abyss, an abyss so dark and frightening. So horrifying flying through the tunnel of DEATH with NO RETURN. But I did—return that is. I saw my son's DNA floating in the cosmos and knew I had to make it back. I fought the will of death with all my might. I could not let Ben grow up without me. I wasn't going to become my father.

The next thing I was conscious of was my mother's voice. But she lived in Philly, so where was I? Maybe I really had died. Then I heard other voices and realized I couldn't see. I was blind. I thought I was blind. I didn't know it, but my eyelids had been taped shut.

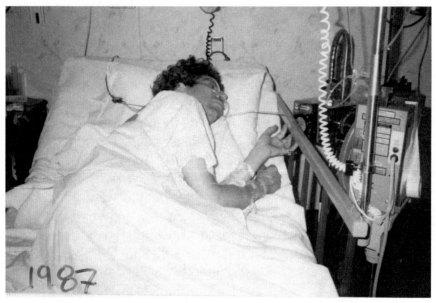

Death Takes a Holiday

I heard the nurse's voice saying, "He's conscious now." She peeled the tape off my eyelids. They had been taped shut because the doctors gave me so much adrenaline and morphine that my eyelids wouldn't close and my eyeballs would've dried up and cracked. My throat was in excruciating pain. The nurse had just taken the ventilator out of my throat after two days of having it breathe for me to keep me alive.

I later found out that the North Hollywood Medical Center had called my mother in Philadelphia and told her that she had better be on the next flight to LA because there was a 50/50 chance she'd be flying home with her son's body. The doctor later told me that if 911 had been called a half-hour later, I would've died in the ambulance, slowed down on Riverside Drive in morning traffic. I was minutes from being pronounced DOA. I had two sons, 8 and 10-years old at the time. Imagine . . . how different their lives would've been had I never woken up from almost dying.

I hope when I die the next time it's not that bad. There are very few records of horrifying near-death experiences. I have to reread *The Tibetan Book of the Dead* and see what it says. I try to rehearse for it. Meditation is a rehearsal for dying, for letting go. Hopefully, I'm inching toward a successful letting go then . . . I don't know when.

When I was released four days later, the thought of not drinking or doing blow never crossed my mind—not even for a split second. My only health-improving lifestyle decision was to switch from vodka to Bombay Sapphire gin, which has herbs in it, so I thought it would be healthy like a tonic.

HIGH

*Let everything happen to you: beauty and terror. Just keep go-
ing. No feeling is final.*
— Rainer Maria Rilke

Chapter 11

Lost Weekend

I am awake. I don't recall being asleep, and I don't know why I am driving a hot red sporty convertible and pulling up to a Miami ATM to withdraw three hundred dollars. I'm not alone. In the passenger seat is an exceptionally attractive woman wearing minimal clothing and exceptionally high heels.

I take the three hundred in twenties out of the ATM and give her the money.

"Thanks," she says, "You're fun. We should do this again sometime."

I'm thinking, *Do what again?* I have no idea who she is or what we did. She shows me where to drop her off.

I go back to my motel room, and I notice that my chest feels sore and irritated. I open my shirt and stare at myself in the mirror, horrified. As the kids today would say, "OMG."

While not quite *The Passion of the Christ*, I look as if nails were pounded through my chest. Sudden memory flash: her shoes/my chest.

Good thing she wasn't a golfer.

These marks are not going away soon—and Ben, age 12, is at his aunt's house. We were planning on going swimming today and I don't want him to ask, "Daddy, what happened to you?" I would have to make up some obvious lie about the love marks on my chest. Instead, I'll make up an obvious lie about why I can't go swimming.

This is humiliating. I'm not ashamed of whatever transpired between the lady(?) and me, but had I not been in a blackout, I would have taken my shirtless future into consideration before having her walk all over me. Her boots were made for walking . . . and that's just what she did.

That night Ben and I flew back to Oakland where my current girlfriend was planning to take us back to her place to take a hot tub. I had to find another excuse to keep my shirt on.

Did the blackout bother me? It never even occurred to me that blackouts were becoming a problem. Honestly, it never crossed my mind.

#

Memories are indelibly etched in my mind like photographs. Some memories are vivid, like a stunning color photo. Some are vague, like a blurry, pixelated image that appears grainy and unclear. And like a photo, once memories happen, they exist forever; unless you accidentally delete the photo or catch Alzheimer's from all the toxic aluminum in your roll-on under arm deodorant.

I always thought the quality of my parenting was contradictory and hypocritical. I provided well and we had a lot of fun, but I knew I could be whisked away by the police at any moment and not see my son again for years. According to my own anecdotal evidence, marijuana can occasionally induce terror and anxiety. Selling pot while smoking pot increases paranoia, such as I experienced years later when living in San Anselmo, one Golden Gate Bridge away from San Francisco, and one Richmond-San Rafael Bridge close to Oakland. Ben, now 14, was living with me. I drove him to Marin Waldorf School every morning and picked him up every afternoon. One morning after dropping him off, I headed to Oakland to do a 20-pound pot deal. I smoked a joint on the way, and I started panic-thinking, *If something happens, and I get busted, there's going to be no one to pick up Ben from school.*

I almost immediately went into a disabling anxiety attack and got nauseated by thinking about what would happen if I got arrested and hauled off to the local police station. The idea of him standing there on the curb waiting, and waiting, and me not showing up was horrifying, but not horrifying enough to change my plans.

"What if . . ." works well for creative writing but living in constant dread of the worst-case scenario drains pleasure from life, triggers debilitating fatalism, and takes all the joy out of a successful drug deal. It's only when it's over and you're back home with your son playing with your dear neighbors and fixing yourself a vodka on the rocks that you can relax. Which really doesn't take much fixing. Ice, vodka, done.

I made it back to school on time, but so unnerving was my constant anxiety that I recall clearly every panic-stricken moment of that uneventful and perfectly normal day.

PTSD = Perceived Terrifying Surmised Disaster

#

Frank Speiser and his girlfriend were asleep in the other room. He was in town performing as Lenny Bruce in his one-man play, *The World of Lenny Bruce*. A month later, Tina Badame and I got a ride from New Jersey to Miami Beach with a drug-dealing gangster named James to see Frank performing in his play. When we got to the Deauville Beach Resort, we met Stacy Keach who did not meet us. He was passed out on a couch in the hotel lobby going in and out of consciousness, waiting for Speiser to get back from scoring for him.

At the time, Keach's career as a film actor was just beginning to take off. It's always an interesting moment when I meet a celebrity, hoping they're decent and genuine and not shitheads. I couldn't tell how Stacy Keach was because he was too drugged up for me to get a sense of what kind of guy he is. Some years later, after being arrested for cocaine possession at Heathrow Airport, he befriended the prison priest, turned to Roman Catholicism, and eventually had an audience with Pope John Paul II.

#

I'm at the Kyoto Inn in Japantown, San Francisco, listening to a ball game on the clock radio. My team, the Phillies, are behind 3–0. Two outs at the bottom of the ninth, and I have $300 that I'm about to kiss good-bye on the game.

"Tonight," I say to my good neighbor Charlene, which rhymes with cream, "I'm going to ignore the myth about losing and sex. We're gonna fuck, no matter who wins this game!"

Gamblers' wives know that when their husband loses a big bet, you can bet there'll be no hanky-panky that night.

"Great," she says, "I'll open the champagne now, okay?"

"Go ahead, we might as well at least get effervescent no matter what happens next."

The Phillies are at home, three runs down, bottom of the ninth against the Giants. While she's getting the bottle out of the ice-cube-filled sink, there is another single, now there's two men on, and while she's peeling off the foil, a walk, she's twisting the cork as the pinch hitter is tapping the nonexistent dirt from his spikes. With the pop of the cork, there's a monstrous crack of the bat and everyone goes running home! Grand slam. It's moments like this you never take for granted and hope you'll remember for the rest of your life. I did. A winning bet, sex, and rock 'n' roll.

I had booked the Kyoto Inn because that night Charlene and I were going to see a concert at the Fillmore West, conveniently located around the corner. After the home run, champagne, and sex, it was the best concert I had ever heard.

#

The Kyoto morphs into the Ramada Inn on Fisherman's Wharf and the ball game now is football. The Miami Dolphins versus the New

England Patriots on ABC's Monday Night Football, December 8, 1980. I'm with several friends when a few take off to see Stevie Wonder perform in Oakland. I stayed with the women in the room to keep drinking and doing blow and to watch the game. Of course, I had a bet on it. The women were two old friends and one new one, Jordie, from Down Under. No comment. Great accent. None of whom I was sleeping with . . . yet.

Patriots kicker John Smith is preparing to kick a field goal.

"Howard," says Frank Gifford, "you have to say what we know in the booth."

"Yes, we have to say it," Cosell replies. "An unspeakable tragedy confirmed to us by ABC News in New York City: John Lennon, outside of the Dakota Apartment building on Central Park West, was shot twice in the back. He was rushed to Roosevelt Hospital, dead on arrival. Hard to go back to the game after that newsflash."

Such somber news coming from the normally ramped up voice of a sports commentator made the overwhelming news feel even more otherworldly. Yet the consummate professional Howard Cosell carried it off extremely respectfully.

All of us in the hotel room burst into tears. We couldn't believe what we had just heard. Who would want to shoot John Lennon? They should have shot Yoko. Kidding.

Our friends heard about it when Stevie Wonder stopped his concert, broke the sad news to the stunned crowd, sang "Imagine" and left the stage. There would be no joy in Oakland that night as the audience exited in silence, disbelief and inconsolable grief. I couldn't stop crying so when Jordie asked if we could lay down and hold each other all night I whimpered, yes. When word of that indiscretion got back to Carlee, she decided to take Ben (six months old), move out of our house in Radner, Pennsylvania, and resettle in Miami, close to her sister. I was devastated. Would I not get to be a dad to my son?

The day after John was murdered, I was alone in my rental car, parked at the top of Nob Hill. The city, magnificent in all directions, and every radio station playing nothing but The Beatles,

John, and John and Yoko songs. My tears rolled down the trolley tracks into the San Francisco Bay.

"Fame" is a killer song, and David Bowie sang it with John Lennon on the record. And now he sings it alone at the Spectrum in Philadelphia. Standing in a pinpoint spotlight singing "Fame" he catches a long-stemmed red rose thrown from the audience. He uses it as a prop and sings to the rose, and when he gets to the line, "Fame, I don't want it/you can have it," he throws the rose back to an adoring woman in the audience.

#

While in Los Angeles, walking down Fairfax Blvd. with Genius Cousin Bobb, a shaggy homeless man asked us to tie his shoe-laces for him. We didn't. As we walked away, Genius Cousin Bobb whispered, "You never know when the Messiah will return or what guise he will take." Since hearing that, I'd like to think I've treated all sentient beings a little bit more kindly.

Chapter 12

Blackmailed, Paris, The Doors, Miles Ahead

My intoxicated fiancée, Laura, had just gotten up on stage to re-create her famous, extremely erotic, almost downright pornographic LA pole dancing moves at New Georges, the local live music dive in San Rafael. At that moment, I am getting a little pissed off over her exhibitionism. My friend Marian Bach invites (really, cajoles) me into the handicapped bathroom to show me her new black garters and seamed stockings.

I don't think I did more than touch something, but the next morning Marian comes over to my house, insisting I made a date with her. I tell her that she must have misheard me because I'm now engaged to Laura, who is asleep in the bedroom. Marian barges into the house and starts yelling about what I did the night before. I ask her to leave to no avail, so I have to pick her up and carry her outside. She starts yelling into my open bedroom window, so I have to choke her to shut her up. Then I carry her to her car by her neck. She takes off, but 10 minutes later, calls me screaming that she wants $1,000 compensation for the bruises on her wrists and neck, and she is coming over in an hour to pick up the damn money, or she'll tell Laura "everything."

She also threatens to call my son's Waldorf School and tell them what his father does for a living. I have a feeling the school knew what I did because whenever there was a class trip to the planetarium or main library, I was always called to be one of the drivers. I guess they knew I worked from home and could usually get away for the day. At that time, a couple of the Dead had their kids in the same school. It was fun seeing Phil Lesh dropping off his little dead head, and Jerry Garcia depositing his daughter at the door on many mornings. They weren't the only celebrity, drug-using parents. The school did a couple musical shows a year, and the house band was made up of the rhythm section of Hot Tuna.

"Laura, Laura, wake up" I said, shaking her shoulder, "There are two important things I need you to do."

"What?" She's groggy but willing.

"In about a half-hour, some girl is coming over. Two things: Give her this thousand dollars."

"Okay."

"And don't believe anything she says."

I would have been happy to have given Marian the $1,000 myself, but Eddie and Steve were picking me up soon because we had a tee time for 11:00 a.m.

Laura agreed without question. Having been a professional stripper in LA, I guess she had heard stranger things than this.

My engagement to Laura was intense but didn't last long. I had to ask her and a daughter to move out because her old Jaguar wasn't really breaking down every other day. She just needed an excuse to go see her mechanic to smoke crack. I had quit freebasing and snorting coke. Taking the high road, I only snorted MDMA. When drug addicts are lying, they're not really lying. They're just surviving.

When I was in Paris with the love of my life du jour, Melissa, and we went to visit Jim Morrison's grave, early in the morning on no sleep, after drinking and clubbing all night with some Parisian bohemians, writers, and scalawags, making memories that have lasted to this day. I was high as could be, the only appropriate way to visit Jim Morrison's grave. I threw up on Chopin, also buried there, and Melissa passed out on Gertrude Stein. (That was fitting. Get it?) As we were leaving Père Lachaise cemetery, there was a full-blown French alcoholic offering us a pull on his unceremoniously, un-chilled half-gallon bottle of rot gut. At least it was French rot gut. We accepted. The man's nose was as bulbous as W. C. Fields, who when asked why he didn't drink water, famously answered, "Because fish fuck in it."

On August 4, 1968, I was 18 years old and saw Jim Morrison and The Doors perform at the Philadelphia Arena. The arena also hosted wrestling shows, most notably Ray Fabiani's *Mat Time*. Some new, enterprising promoter rented the hall and booked The Doors. During their performance it was 100 degrees inside the arena. This new, enterprising promoter decided to save money and *not* spring for the A/C.

Everyone had taken their shirts off, including some of the ladies, but that's not what made the evening so extraordinary. It was . . . his voice. I realized Jim's voice was incredibly beautiful, though the nature of his music was raw and hardcore. His voice was angelic. For me it was witnessing the beginning of time and not The End. If you want to hear a gorgeous song that's not necessarily upbeat, go listen to "The End." When Jim yells, "Father, I want to kill you" and "Mother, I want to . . . (SCREAM) . . . you!" Fill in the Freudian exaltation here. I thought The Doors would last forever. But, as you can see, I had to visit Jim's grave while I was in Paris.

Cool coincidence. On August 4, 1994, EXACTLY 26 years after seeing The Doors in Philly, I went through the doors of Betty Ford and have never gotten high again. Jim died on July 3, 1971. According to Sam Bernett, a Paris nightclub manager, he died of a heroin overdose.

#

It's New Year's Eve 1993. I'm still with, or back with, Melissa and we have a great night planned in front of the fireplace and on our knees. This well-provisioned party was crashed by her son Fang. (A child's name certainly conceived in someone's dark unconsciousness.) At exactly half-past nine, as I'm three-quarters to third base, and only one sheet to the wind, Fang appears in our foyer. We never locked the door because the police station was at the corner, and we knew that would be a good deterrent to the local breaking-and-entering crowd.

"Why aren't you at that party?" we ask in unison, as if an impromptu Greek chorus.

"They kicked me out and said I can't come back unless I bring them some pot."

This poses a moral dilemma. I am a pot dealer, with pounds of weed in a suitcase in the other room. I planned on a cool night of hot romance with the woman I was madly in love with. Except now this kid is the ultimate teenage buzz killer, looking for a bud to go back to the party with. What would you do? Well, I didn't do that. In hindsight, I would have been far happier had I given the kid a lid and taken him back to the party, where redeemed, he would have been joyously included, almost as if they actually valued his presence. But no, I would not give pot to a 15-year-old just so I could have sex with his mother. I must have been temporarily insane or smitten with the morals I always knew I had.

Therefore, with her son home for the duration of the now cancelled inebriation celebration, I did what any disappointed morally trapped drug dealer would do—I took enough Valium to knock me out well before *Auld Lang Syne*. The ball was dropping in Times Square. As were my hopes for a happily ever after with Melissa. I honestly didn't want to greet the California New Year conscious of my emotional vulnerability to overturned expectations. With my sex addiction to Melissa, and her sex addiction to every Tess, Deb, and Harriet, I really thought I could not live without her. With my passion addiction, my codependency, my enabling, my attachment, my obsession, my love, and my need for her, who I could not live without, I felt a despair to my core. In the course of our relationship, suicide was not a regular guest but did do an occasional walk on. An example of my self-serving self-centered view of the universe, I considered that evening one of the "worst nights ever."

Note: It takes 5 mg of Valium to negate, undo, or nullify every four lines of coke snorted. Some of you old coke fiends out there probably think I'm a lightweight. If I wasn't a lightweight, my lights would have been turned off years ago. I valued the moderation techniques I applied to my using career because they allowed me to be high on weed and booze for 26 years and high on coke every day for 13 years.

#

I smoked my breakfast, drank my lunch, and snorted my dinner. Did I have a choice? Of course. Was I consciously choosing to use an endless array of mind and mood- altering substances after weighing all options? Of course not. I didn't get sober for seven more years after I almost died. Even with all my excesses, when I did smoke heroin, about a dozen times, I realized that if I continued, I would be making a choice to ruin my life. Yet I kept using coke and Ecstasy, pushing the envelope, challenging God and these substances to prove me wrong.

Most Americans are not well-versed in moderation. Being very American, the "less is more" concept eluded me. If one line of coke is good, twelve are better. But I never wanted to become a junkie. Everyone knows that HEROIN addiction is bad for you. I hope they teach that in high school! I know most people would say that's too late. There's a fine line between educating about the dangers of drug use and introducing the realities of drug use. YES, it will make you feel a euphoria that only kings, queens and lottery winners experience, and then you quit or die. It's that simple.

A spoonful of sugar helps the medicine go down, but an ounce of sugar may trigger the need for medical intervention. I was into sugar by the spoonful, pot by the pound, and coke by the kilo. And heartaches? I had heartaches with each new relationship—heartaches by the dozen.

There was a painful time in my life when my brother and I weren't talking to each other, until one night he called me to tell me that Miles Davis had just died. He knew I'd rather hear that from a loved one that some Caucasian commentator on the 11 o'clock news. We re-bonded over our undying love for Miles. We were both feeling kind of blue. And we've never been out of touch ever since.

The conversation brought back a vivid memory from Philly years ago. The pink sunlight was peeking in through the frosted apartment window while the phonograph needle on the old cheap record player was stuck in a groove on "Kind of Blue." The same line, over and over and over, while Tina Badame was vomiting, and it became as if her retching was an intentionally overlaid track on Miles Davis's masterpiece. This blending was a most heavenly way to end a perfect night of weed, booze, blow, and sex. The sunlight of dawn, the expansive release (retching) of a gorgeous woman, and the music of Miles Davis, Paul Chambers, John Coltrane, Cannonball Adderley, Wynton Kelly, and Bill Evans. Can there be a better heaven?

After I hung up the phone with Brother Bruce, I grabbed my transistor radio knowing that KJAZ would be playing Miles all night. I grabbed a blanket and my girlfriend's hand and we walked to the park at the end of the block. As we laid down, we saw a star shooting across the sky. I don't know if that was Miles waving good-bye to us or Miles playing his final note in a silent way.

Chapter 13

No Massage for You! Just a Message!!

I never really got to the point where I decided to get help to stop using drugs and become sober. That never happened. That's *not* why I went to Betty Ford. I went because I was having a nervous breakdown due to a shattering breakup of one of the most intense, loving, dysfunctional and sensational relationships I had ever had. *And*, I thought I was about to be arrested by the DEA.

It started the morning after a rough night of downing endless shots of vodka, snorting lines of Ecstasy, and having unsafe sex with a prostitute with bruises on her knees that I didn't put there.

I woke up in a hole, and I could hardly move. I looked at the ceiling and the walls, which seemed to be dripping with limestone, dolomite and gypsum. I thought, *Oh fuck, I'm in a pit, where's the pendulum and I don't know how I got here. I gradually came to and realized I wasn't in a cave.* I was in my bedroom at home. It was like waking up from a nightmare that you're still in.

I looked at the clock and it was already 10:30 a.m. I remembered I had an appointment for a massage with Penny at eleven.

Woke up
Climbed out of bed
Dragged a comb across my head

I got into my car and weaved over to Penny's. Ten minutes into the massage, I had to excuse myself, get up, go outside and throw up. I had a ferocious headache and felt poisoned from the night before. I went back in, layed down and she got back to work. After only five minutes, I had to excuse myself, go outside and vomit again. I went back in, paid Penny for the hour and apologized for my abrupt departure.

I thought to myself, *Self, this is not why I moved to California. What's wrong with this picture?* I was sick as a dog and couldn't even lay through a massage. On my way home, I stopped at the pay phone outside Ralph's Supermarket. I spent a good deal of my life at pay phones, usually arranging drug deals. I saw my friend Karen, arms full of groceries walking over to me with a concerned look. She asked, "How are you?"

I responded, "Pretty good," because I hadn't puked for a half hour. Meanwhile, the sweat on my forehead was flying onto her summer blouse.

She said, "Well, you don't look too good."

"I had a long night."

One Day This Phone Will Be in the Smithsonian

Karen was the only person in the world I knew who had ever been to a rehab. I had been with her the week before she went in. I knew firsthand she was an alcoholic who loved drugs. I asked her if that rehab she'd been to had an 800 number. Cause I wasn't going to spend the money to make a toll call.

"Yes."

"Can you give it to me?"

"I have it at home. I'll call you with it."

I drove home and saw a man taking photographs of my house. I thought for sure it was a detective taking Polaroids of where I lived to show them to a friend of mine who recently got busted with a load of Thai weed sailing up the San Francisco Bay. It was a bad bust. He had been coming to my house regularly for years to buy pounds of Hawaiian pot. I thought for sure they were going to show him the pictures, get him to confirm this was where he scored and then they'd come arrest me.

After this douchebag photographer left, I ran into my house, grabbed everything I would need for a couple weeks away—clothing, toiletries, pot. The usual. And of course some books. I packed up the car and headed south to Big Sur, my go-to getaway.

The next day, safely checked into the River Inn, I went to the pay phone with the 800 number Karen had given me and called the Betty Ford Center. They asked me a lot of questions. When I was done answering, the woman said, "Okay, now how are you going to pay for this?"

"I have some health insurance."

"Okay, we can run the numbers and tell you if we accept it or not."

"Great." I read the number off the Blue Cross card I had, given to me by my mother's boss at the camera store she worked at. As a benefit from an affair she'd had with him years ago, he kept me and my brother on his company's insurance plan.

The intake lady said, "If we don't take your insurance, we will find you a hospital that will."

I said, "Are you fucking kidding me? I'm not sick. I just need a rest. I think I'm having a nervous breakdown because I can't stop shaking."

She said, "And, it also sounds like you have a drug problem."

No shit, Sherlock.

During what I later learned is called "the intake," I never mentioned marijuana because I knew marijuana wasn't my problem. It was the pills, white powders, and the blackouts.

Hello bottom. Good-bye drugs.

Part II

What Happened

Chapter 14

Jung and the Restless

Let go into the Mystery, let yourself go. You've got to open up your heart, that's all I know. Trust what I say and do what you're told, and baby, all your dirt will turn into gold.
—Van Morrison

The only way to make sense out of change is to plunge into it, move with it, and join the dance.
—Alan Watts

Only two people in my life thought I had a problem with drugs or alcohol. I was a potential third, but like a fish in water, it was so much my constant environment and natural habitat that I could not see the forest for the trees. It was right under my nose if you get my snowdrift. Most highly addicted people don't even know they're addicts, the way guppies don't know they're in water.

Although I knew not everyone in the world used drugs, all the everyones I knew did. Years into my recovery, I became a regular at a Marijuana Anonymous (MA) meeting called Heads Above Water. It could have been called Head Out of Ass or Where There's Smoke, There's Brain Damage. Eventually I started an MA meeting in Sherman Oaks, CA, called, Alice B. Tokeless. Shortly thereafter, a group in Marin County adopted the same name. When I met Paul Mazursky, director of said movie, and told him about the two MA meetings named after his film, he did not look pleased, as if we were against pot, *No*. We loved marijuana. Just a little too much.

The two well-meaning commentators and would-be interventionists were my sister-in-law, Bettina, an artist and doctor of psychology, and Misty, a Marin County call girl. They were both experts in their fields. One was born in a penthouse, the other could have worked at *Penthouse*. I had Misty on a retainer for seven years, and no, it wasn't to keep her teeth straight. Misty was worth every penny. At the Nuvos Café at 10 o'clock one night, I was waiting for Misty, my Mistress, to reconfirm an all-night session and call me back on the pay phone on the wall. When the phone rang, I leapt over a guy with crutches and knocked him down. My sexual satisfaction was more important than some athlete's broken leg to me.

Misty could say anything to me. One day she said, "You were doing a lot of cocaine before. Now, I think you're snorting too much Ecstasy."

"That's probably true," I said. The conversation was over and that was the outer limits of my introspection.

"For the past 20 years," Bettina had said, "every time I've seen you, you've been high on marijuana."

"Yeah, what's your point?"

In reality, I only got high once in my life . . . for 26 years. I think people smoke pot to selfishly improve an already enjoyable moment or dull an unpleasant experience. Does it do both? And if so, how does it differentiate between enhance and avoid? Probably the pot doesn't decide. The smoker decides and directs the drug to do whatever the smoker deems appropriate. That probably means the pot contains no properties of enhancement or avoidance on its own.

When a pothead has a good day at work, they smoke a joint when they get home. When a pothead has a bad day at work, they smoke a joint when they get home. So now the good day is not as good and the bad day is not as bad. Weed is the great neutralizer. It takes the edge off. But isn't edginess next to Godliness? If you're not living on the edge, you're taking up too much space.

#

It's July 1994. I'm in the bar at Ventana in Big Sur when I get a call on my cell phone from Betty Ford's admissions office. They have accepted my Blue Cross coverage for the whole $12,000. I burst into tears because I knew the jig was up. Later that month, I'm crossing the lobby of the Benson Hotel in Portland, Oregon, when again, Betty Ford's number comes up on my cell. Now I have an official check-in date: August 3, 1994.

Once I got my check-in date, I had a month to get ready. Part of that included my visiting the Stations of the Cross, as I felt as if I were on the way to the crucifixion of yet another Jew— oh look, it's me.

I knew enough to understand that part of me was probably going to die in treatment. I later learned if a person doesn't "die" in rehab, they're not really getting it. If you're all gung-ho and excited about rehab, you're not getting the message. People in AA have to embrace the St. Francis Prayer to their core. Most people don't want to embrace it. Maybe I'd be leaving rehab clean and sober and with stigmata.

PRAYER OF ST. FRANCIS

Lord, make me a channel of thy peace,

that where there is hatred, I may bring love;

that where there is wrong,

I may bring the spirit of forgiveness;

that where there is discord, I may bring harmony;

that where there is error, I may bring truth;

that where there is doubt, I may bring faith;

that where there is despair, I may bring hope;

that where there are shadows, I may bring light;

that where there is sadness, I may bring joy.

Lord, grant that I may seek rather to

comfort than to be comforted;

to understand, than to be understood;

to love, than to be loved.

For it is by self-forgetting that one finds.

It is by forgiving that one is forgiven.

It is by dying that one awakens to Eternal Life.

My stations included visiting the important people in my life who lived in Northern California, plus my son Ben, who was staying with Carlee in Washington for the summer. I wanted to tell them I needed some rest, so I was going to Betty Ford. It was important to me to let them know in person. I wanted to see the look on their faces. It's an extraordinary feeling when you admit you have a problem and you need help.

Although I was sitting on it the whole time, my bottom came out of the blue, and most people were surprised. It wasn't a dramatic bottom but a long one. When I told my friends that I was going to rehab, most people responded, "What for?" Or, for what? No one ever would have suspected I was going for weed, which I wasn't. I was going for Ecstasy. For years, I was the puppeteer controlling all these substances. Eventually, I became the puppet.

On the phone, Ben was the most supportive: "Dad, you don't have a drug problem, you have a crazy woman problem."

I fly up to Seattle to see Ben and Carlee. When I landed, I saw a sign at the airport bar that said, "Doubles Half-Off." Needless to say I had a couple double Bloody Mary's. I'm not passing up a chance to save money when I see one. When I finally got to Ben's home in rural Washington State, he said, "We got some new scooters. Let's take a ride!" I rarely did sporty things or drove drunk. I couldn't refuse him, but I remember thinking and being overwhelmed with fear that I was so drunk I was going to crash one of these speedy little motherfuckers into a tree and die. I managed to stay in the saddle long enough to impress Ben with my riding skills and not fly off into the woods.

One of my stations was visiting Joe D., who was staying in a cabin on a mountaintop in Big Sur. The cabin had no working phone—and Big Sur had no cell reception at the time. While I was napping, Joe, with the best of intentions I'm sure, had stolen my Volvo and went to Oceanside to score a hooker and some crack, leaving me alone with no car, no phone, and an almost empty inhaler. By late evening, I was scared to death of having a massive asthma attack with no way to call for help. As luck would have it, on this dark and moonless night, I found a big old flashlight sitting out on the middle of the kitchen table. It took me an hour to cautiously maneuver down the steep mountainside road veiled in heavy fog. Any false step near the side of the path would have had me flying over the edge like Evel Knievel.

When I reached the main road and found a pay phone, I called Elyse (Joe's sister), who called a bar and had her girlfriend come and pick me up and take me to a motel. The next day, her friend had no recollection of picking me up. She was in a complete blackout the whole time. I probably could have engaged in sex with her, but I thought she was too hippie-ish.

#

When the day came to check in to the Betty Ford Center, I was at my friend Steve D.'s house in Studio City. He was the one who saved my life by calling 911 back in 1987. Rancho Mirage was about two-and-a-half hours away. I told Steve I had two joints left to my name, one for the drive there, the other for the ride home. He suggested I just take one for the drive there, and he'd hold the other until I got back. I really hope he eventually lit that sucker up and enjoyed it immensely.

When I got close to the facility, I used my fat Motorola flip phone and called for more precise directions. They guided me in ... brought me in out of the cold, so to speak.

When I got to Rancho Mirage, it was a mirage. I got lost and disoriented from smoking a joint of Hawaiian. Dinah Shore Road, Frank Sinatra Way, Bob Hope Drive. I thought I was driving around an endless Republican cul-de-sac. Then I started to hallucinate. Suddenly, I was nine years old, and my mother and I were watching *Your Hit Parade* while devouring a quart of Breyers vanilla fudge ice cream. The last block I drove down should have been named, "End of the Road Rd." (Or Beginning-of-the-Rest-of-Your-Life-You-Just-Don't-Know-That-Yet Street.)

I parked. Found the front desk. I asked, "Is this where I check in?"

The receptionist snorted, "This isn't a hotel. This is where you get admitted."

Soon, I was in the nurse's office, wearing a clear plastic hospital bracelet, and Nurse Jackie was drawing blood. "We want to know exactly what's in your system, in case you're about to go into benzodiazepine withdrawal."

"I haven't had any Valium since last night, and it was only 10 milligrams."

"Do you have any more?"

"Why? You're a nurse—can't you get your own?"

She didn't laugh. Perhaps she thought I was serious. Perhaps I was.

I was almost denied admittance to the Betty Ford Center because they wanted me to surrender my inhaler to be kept in the "med room," where I could get it when I needed it. They didn't understand that when I needed it, I *needed it* right there and then. And suppose I needed it at night, when the med room was locked and the night counselor was on a break? Thank *God* we compromised because I needed rehab as much as that inhaler. I was given a notebook to keep track of every time I took a whiff. The attending physician wanted to make sure I wasn't using it 30 times a day because it had a little ephedrine in it.

Once it was clear I could keep my inhaler, I asked the admitting nurse, suspiciously, "Are they going to brainwash me here?" (Not that my brain couldn't have used a little rinsing.)

She said, "Absolutely not."

Just then, a gentleman came over, greeted me warmly, and said, "Here, this is yours. This is for you." He slapped a hardback book into my hand, which felt like a copy of *Mein Kampf*, or even worse, the Bible.

From the moment I entered the Betty Ford Center, I knew that my chemical kit bag was no longer at my disposal. But that was okay, given that all my thoughts were on the next morning, when I planned on leaving. That first night my primary interest, however, was in falling asleep. Having no sleeping pills called for literary measures—I would read myself to sleep. Luckily, they had given me THAT book that from all indications would be sufficiently boring to induce unconsciousness: *The Big Book of Alcoholics Anonymous*.

I made it to page 25, but I was still awake, just barely. When I got to page 26, I was suddenly wide awake. There, in front of me, was a most familiar name: Dr. Carl Jung. I'd been into Jung and all those who circle within his orbit of influence for years. I regularly attended workshops with Robert Bly and read Joseph Campbell religiously. Carl Jung, I discovered, was credited with having set the course for what today is known as Alcoholics Anonymous.

Asked by a patient if there was any sure way for an alcoholic to truly recover, Jung is quoted as saying, "Yes, there is. Exceptions to hopeless cases such as yours have been occurring since early times. Here and there, once in a while, alcoholics have had what are called vital spiritual experiences. To me these occurrences are phenomena. They appear to be in the nature of huge emotional displacements and rearrangements. Ideas, emotions, and attitudes which were once the guiding forces of the lives of these men are suddenly cast to one side, and a completely new set of conceptions and motives begin to dominate them."

No shit?

I stayed the next day because of Jung, but I was still restless enough to plan a second-day getaway after seeing one discouraging word engraved in a two-by-six-foot marble plaque: **God**. My eyes zoomed in and focused on AA's Step 3: "Made a decision to turn our will and our lives over to the care of **God** . . ." The Eternal One, blessed be **He**, also made an appearance in Step 5: "Admitted to God . . ." Step 6: "were entirely ready to have **God** . . ." and even Step 11: "Sought through prayer and Consternation" (to improve our conscious contact with **God**).

Why am I here? I asked myself. Is this some Christian enclave where an aging Elizabeth Taylor managed to get laid? Not that she ever had any problems in that area, married eight times. *I'm outta here!* Thank God it was Friday. On Saturday, I could use the telephone to call my brother in New York and complain about **God's** omnipresence at the Betty Ford Center.

When I got Brother Bruce on the phone the next day, he reminded me that I had prayed at the Wailing Wall, cried my eyes out at the Anne Frank House, and sought nearness to God in numerous diverse locales such as the temples of Kyoto, a 40-day Sufi retreat on Maui, and Amsterdam's Vondelpark, where I chanted Hare Krishna with hundreds of other seekers.

Despite my obvious track record as a fan of the Almighty, including numerous readings of Be Here Now by transcendental super-Jew Ram Dass, I was inexplicably uncomfortable at the prospect of actually interacting with God while I was straight. Perhaps the explanation for the inexplicable was that never before had I thought of calling upon God to free me from the bondage of drinking and drugging. The All-Knowing and All-Wise had watched me consume intoxicants with wild abandon for 26 years and never once stretched forth His mighty hand to stop me. Then again, I never asked.

The conversation with my brother seemed to center me, reminding me of what I had always really wanted—a connection with the Eternal One. So I decided to drop my defenses, postpone my paranoia, dispense with my disbelief, settle into my seat and stay open to what they were saying.

On my third day, I walked outside into the new morning's light. Suddenly, simultaneously at warp speed and in slow motion, the desire for chemical intoxication completely evaporated. I sensed the change immediately. Like a rotten tooth pulled by a merciful dentist after injecting the perfect amount of high-grade Novocain. I could FEEL all desire for drugs painlessly leave my body.

The psychological sensation, while difficult to describe, was both liberating and slightly disquieting. After all, there is a comforting sense of security in familiar habits and a certain sense of well-being knowing your crutches are always within reach. Although I still thought a drink or two wouldn't kill me. I never got intoxicated alone or by accident. I always had company and planned my benders in advance. And I did not meet the standard criteria for alcoholism set down in the Alcohol Anonymous textbook. Something about a man losing the ability to control his drinking. I never tried to control my drinking. I planned my blackouts in advance (most of the time). Plus alcoholism and drug dealing don't mix. Pot was 24/7 but not booze.

The epiphany that SAVED MY LIFE? "Alcohol is a liquid drug." BOOM. And I am a drug addict to my bone. I am a drug addict through and through. So, if one drink makes me feel a little good, three will make me feel awesome. Yes, I'd like to be suave and sip cognac after dinner and have some ouzo before the moussaka. But I can't, and I *won't*. Like the AA bumper sticker says: "It's easier to stay sober, than it is to get sober."

At that moment I made a vow to never drink again. A vow to who? To the most important non-binary person in my life. Me.

I had always thought one of my old girlfriends, a real barbiturates and booze hound (she called it her Marilyn Monroe pre-suicidal cocktail), would one night succumb at the Money Tree, a jazz bar near Burbank (she worked at Creative Artists Agency - CAA). Factoid: The Money Tree was originally owned by The Three Stooges.

Lori did not die, and in fact, unbeknownst to me, a year before I went to rehab, she had checked herself into the Betty Ford Center. Or, as some of the misinformed called it, Camp Betty. I've heard stories about guys showing up with their golf bags only to be told the only teatime they would see is at mealtimes.

Serendipitously, Lori found out that I was at Betty Ford when she saw me there! She was a guest speaker at the Friday night alumni meeting that all patients were required to attend. There I was in the audience with the rest of the schmucks, being inspired by my Marilyn Monroe—no longer a washed-out bleached blond but a shining example of sobriety with a head of dyed black beauty hair. She was the main speaker.

My first impulse was to slide down under the seat in front of me so she wouldn't see me. But after a few minutes, I liked what she was saying. *Why was I embarrassed being in a rehab with someone who was in the same rehab?*

We talked after the meeting, and I told her I was thinking of going AWOL because I thought the place was too Christian and too Republican. She assured me it was neither, well at least not too Christian. She recited the Lord's Prayer by heart and explained to me Emmet Fox's interpretation of what he considered Jesus's best poem. It all made sense, and just to make sure I stayed the full 28 days, Lori promised she would sleep with me when my month was up.

I was released on the morning of August 31. I still had some prescribed Valium in the toiletry bag they had confiscated when I checked in. The nurse asked me to flush them down the toilet. I was aghast.

"Suppose I need to sleep?"

"You won't need these. You have other methods to help you sleep now."

"Suppose I want to give them to my brother?"

"It's against the law to give prescribed medication to anyone else."

"You're fucking kidding me!"

I followed her suggestion and flushed God's gift to the anxious down the toilet into the Palm Springs groundwater. Curiously, I did have a dozen Mexican Quaaludes in the same kit bag. The nurse didn't know what they were and let me leave with them.

Two amazing things happened after I hit the 10 freeway back to Los Angeles. I drove past a big roadside Liquor Mart, and I watched my hands on the steering wheel to see if they would automatically, on their own accord, steer the Volvo into the parking lot at the store. They did not. It felt like a miracle. And I did not go into the trunk to fish out and swallow a couple of weak Mexican Quaaludes.

So there I was, 44, fresh (one hour) out of rehab and, for the first time since I was 17, *a whole month* without a drug or a drink. And here I was not leaping out of my car into a vodka shop or quickly dropping a few feel-good-fast pills down my gullet. I was watching myself and starting to wonder, *Who was I?*

I knew I was desperate to see a friend and drove right to Bob Downey's apartment. I had written him a letter from the rehab apologizing for thinking it was time for me to quit the team. I also sent the same letter to a couple of drug dealers I knew telling them I needed to retire. The fear and stress had finally gotten to me.

When I got to Bob's he asked, "Now that you've been locked up for a month, what do you want to do? Is there anything you need?"

"Yeah, I could really use a haircut." He said he knew of the perfect place.

Thirty minutes later, we were driving through the gates of Hollywood Park. There was a barbershop at the track called Hollywood Haircuts. At Betty Ford, they drum into you the concept of cross-addiction—replacing one addiction with another— which can eventually lead you back to your drug of choice, your first love so to speak. I thought if I made a single bet, I would immediately have to have a Bloody Mary, which was my designated racetrack drink. I decided to just try and satisfy my soul with food. I ordered a ham on rye. (Please forgive me Jane Velez-Mitchell.) Then I realized I always had my track drink, a Bloody Mary, to wash down the porcine lunch. Of course, I should have been getting a haircut, but the barbershop had no openings that day.

No bet, no booze, no haircut. Just plenty of absurd laughs courtesy of Mr. Downey. *Putney Swope* this was not. More like his film *Moment to Moment*, a.k.a. *Jive*, the film I had a small part in. I made no bets, had no drinks, and didn't lose my shirt or my one month of sobriety.

I spent the night at Bob's and the next day got a room at the Shangri-La Hotel facing the beach in Santa Monica for the aforementioned sober tryst. With a name like Shangri-La Hotel, what could possibly go wrong? Lori met me there around 7:00 p.m., and we did it—and it wasn't part of a coked-up intoxicated threesome, one-night stand or with someone I was madly in love with. Nothing really went wrong. She had to work the next morning and left early. I got to walk and ponder along Ocean Drive and realize that making love to a woman I wasn't in love with felt a little empty. Not completely, just a little. Not unpleasant, just not transcendent. Good drugs and Stoli always made every sexual encounter a peak experience. Love didn't need to be part of the equation. Maybe this hollow feeling goes away after you've been sober for a while. When sex can just be sex. Gore Vidal, author of the early trans novel, *Myra Breckinridge*, once intoned, "Never turn down an opportunity to be on TV or have sex." I should be so burdened with those choices.

On awakening let us think about the twenty-four hours ahead. We consider our plans for the day. Before we begin, we ask God to direct our thinking, especially asking that it be divorced from self-pity, dishonest or self-seeking motives.
— Bill Wilson, co-founder Alcoholics Anonymous

Chapter 15

Temptations: My Girl, Ain't Too Proud to Beg

Betty Ford's 30-day program worked beautifully, and I jumped into the 12 Step program of AA with complete dedication and enthusiasm. My mind and heart were open, and the gifts poured in. After I was set free from behind the oleanders—the hedges Betty Ford kept healthy to keep intruders out and the patients in—I attended the suggested 90 AA or NA meetings in 90 days, made coffee for complete strangers, set up chairs, got an AA sponsor, and worked the 12 Steps as if my life depended on it. Even so, sobriety came with its own set of challenges.

Melissa, the toxic love of my life, was secretary at a Saturday night women's AA meeting, which was perfect because I would stay home and pretend I was at a Broadway musical listening to an Original Cast Recording on my very sophisticated stereo system. Oh, thank God for drug money.

One night, after her meeting, we went to Ralph's Supermarket to buy some groceries. While walking to the dairy section, we were passing the wine aisle. Melissa nonchalantly picked up a bottle of red and put it in our cart. I laughed. I thought she was having fun with me.

As we went about our business of shopping, the bottle of wine in the cart looked out of place and a bit menacing. I knew when we got to the checkout counter, Melissa would move the bottle aside because she was just fucking with me. That's not exactly what happened. She exactly let the girl scan the bottle and put it in our shopping bag. It seemed like the cash register readout suddenly started blinking . . . to me . . . "Dude, you're fucked."

When we got into the parking lot, I said, "I would prefer if you don't drink that bottle of wine with me around."

She said, "Okay. Then I'll have to find another guy to drink it with."

Then how could I possibly say no.

Needless to say, the rest of the evening was very disappointing in every way except the obvious one.

I stopped seeing Melissa because now she wasn't my sobriety buddy but my femme fatale. The following Saturday night, after I knew she gave up her secretary commitment, she knocked on my door with her tears and mascara running down her gorgeous cheeks and her fishnets a little ripped. To me she looked like the red cape to a bull.

She'd been crying. "Can I come in?"

"Come on in!"

We go right into the bedroom, and she politely asks, "Do you mind if I do some coke?"

I reluctantly say, "Okay." Because now there's something in the room that I want as much as she wants her cocaine.

And then to challenge my sobriety even more, she asks me if I can chop up the coke because her hands were too shaky. I was never one to get in between a woman and her addiction, so I said yes.

My first urge was not to snort it. I wanted to stuff it in my face. I missed the taste so much. But I did not. I did start going to Cocaine Anonymous meetings shortly thereafter to be told I was crazy. After all, I had snorted coke every single day of my life for 13 years and never wanted to again.

Years later, I reworded The Lord's Prayer not to say "and lead us not into temptation" but to say "and lead us not into addiction." I realized after my experience with Melissa that temptation was the only way to prove to myself that my sobriety was strong, like bull.

#

What helped me turn the corner to embracing the idea of complete sobriety? Three days after my release from Betty Ford, I was on my way to a friend's Labor Day wine-tasting party in Sonoma County. On the way, I went to an AA meeting (hoping to see there a newly sober, again, Melissa). The speaker—an artist, former drug abuser and retired heavy drinker—said something I'll never forget: "The Dali Lama called Alcoholics Anonymous the most important social and spiritual movement in America."

Similarly, M. Scott Peck, author of *The Road Less Travelled*, said, "Thus I believe the greatest positive event of the twentieth century occurred in Akron, Ohio, on June 10, 1935, when Bill W. and Dr. Bob convened the first AA meeting. It was not only the beginning of the self-help movement and the beginning of the integration of science and spirituality at a grass-roots level, but also the beginning of the community movement."

This is what I had been looking for my whole life. I was, at that moment, experiencing the awareness of an answered prayer.

At a Betty Ford Center anniversary celebration a few years later, the closing event was an outside Al-Anon meeting with Betty Ford in attendance. When the meeting was over, 100 people held hands and recited the Serenity Prayer in unison. I was struck with the memory of seeing an old *Life* magazine in the '60s with an aerial photo of a well-known commune where all the members were in a circle, holding hands, reciting a prayer. This is what I'd been looking for my whole life. Who knew it would be found at a drug and alcohol rehabilitation center in the middle of the God-damned desert!

I got to express my gratitude on national television on July 9, 2011, when a crew from ABC World News Tonight came to my apartment in Studio City to film my reaction to Betty Ford's death the day before. The word *audacious* was being bantered about in the news at that time, referring to Barack Obama. I corrected the news media and told them no. Betty Ford was the most audacious of all. She came out as a pill-popping alcoholic, asked for help, and then started her own rehab.

#

Now, my little ipso facto oedipal secret is: I love being clean and sober as much as I loved my mother. Sobriety is my mother now, always there to comfort and protect me. After I pass, I plan to stick around and have my ectoplasm tickle newcomers at 12 Step meetings.

Even as a proud card-carrying member of Alcoholics Anonymous (psst, don't tell anyone), I have occasionally had to rewrite some of their scripture to make it more applicable to my particular recovery journey. I found the Serenity Prayer too passive-aggressive, so I decided to make it just aggressive.

God, grant me the hostility to reject the things I cannot change,
the cash to change the things I can,
and the woman to know the difference.
Amen.

Chapter 16

A Lot Happens Quickly

One of Henry Miller's famous lines from *Tropic of Cancer* that I've remembered for years and has *never* served me well is, "I have no money, no resources, no hopes. I am the happiest man alive." I think of that line whenever I am broke, with no hope. But I am no Henry Miller. I am just a confused fan of beat poets who wants, really wants to be rich.

Even though sobriety created a new sober me, it did not pay well. And being from humble origins (middle class, single working mother), I needed to make a living. Obviously, it wasn't a good idea anymore to deal drugs, smuggle drugs, use drugs or engage in any shady deals gleaned from my wayward youth. Not that I wanted to. I'd always said that people who use drugs and aren't dealers are addicts, and people who deal drugs and don't use drugs are pushers. I never wanted to be a pusher. So I knew if I wasn't using drugs, I couldn't sell drugs and look at myself in the mirror. Yet giving up my "career" was scarier than quitting drugs. How would I make a living?

I had faith that my family (mother and brother) would help me survive until I found my own pick and vein of gold to extract from society ... legally.

While I loved my job as a dealer, I wouldn't have done it without getting paid. The same way I would never just do a job for money if I hated the job or if it hurt people. I compliment my son constantly about never taking any job that requires ripping people off. Just working for the money is like purgatory. I yearned to do something I loved and get paid for it. Striking that perfect pot of gold has not been easy. I've had a lot more jobs in sobriety than I ever had before.

My favorite entrepreneurial fantasy has always been to have my own cucumber farm. In less than two months you can grow as many cucumbers as you have room for and then in as little as three hours turn them into pickles, sell them at farmer's markets on the weekends, and deliver them to the best local gourmet restaurants during the week. Wouldn't that be a fairytale ending to my otherwise criminalized life?

After two unsuccessful attempts at gainful employment in order to pay my rent—real estate photographer and custom jewelry salesman—it was time to start selling off the art, antiques and my 29 acres in Big Sur.

I bought that mountainside property with a couple of friends in the late 1970s. We purchased the lot so my partners could live on it and grow pot. Poor Ted got busted right before the first harvest. He had to go to drug re-education classes for six months, and we never got a single female plant out of the ground.

Now, being broke, and with my land-owning partners on the verge of a romantic breakup, it was easy convincing them that we should sell. Luckily, there was always some green prospector willing to invest in God's best pot-growing real estate (other than Hawaii) with Pacific Ocean breezes and a ruggedly mild winter that creates an environment to grow some of the best weed in the world. We all felt that the quality of the plants was enhanced because Big Sur growers often played acoustic instruments, flutes, harmonicas and even a harp for their plants on a daily basis.

The art and antiques I had to sell for rent and food included a few 100-year-old Tibetan Thangkas, and two 36 x 42-inch oversized Polaroids of Allen Ginsberg and Peter Orlovsky by the famous Boston photographer Elsa Dorfman. One photo of them wearing suit and tie, incense burning nearby. The second photo is a mirror image of the first except they are completely naked—one cut, the other uncut.

I also had a collection of Mill Valley Film Festival posters, a few antiques, a 100-year- old Japanese tansu, an even older Korean scholar's chest, a dozen pre-Columbian pots and statues, and a 2,000-year-old Roman gold ring with a lion engraved on inlaid jasper.

One of my old fronts was posing as an antique dealer back in old colonial Philadelphia, and here I am now selling antiques again to pay the rent. Even my Victorian port-a-potty, Tiffany lamp, and a bronze Japanese vase with gold and silver inlay I bought in Glasgow had to go.

The possession that broke my heart the most to part with was a pristine 1934 first edition Obelisk Press copy of Henry Miller's *Tropic of Capricorn* in a custom-made box. I had bought this treasure from Joseph the Provider books. They specialized in first editions. It blew my mind that for only $750 you could own an important piece of literary history. Owning it for all those years always made me grateful that my 75-year-old wooden cottage in San Anselmo never burnt down from unextinguished roaches or frayed extension cords. I loved opening the magic box and feeling the cover of my imaginary mentor's writings whenever I was losing my faith in mankind. Henry was one of my adopted literary fathers, so just touching something he created gave me a feeling of well-being. To me he was the tough guy from Brooklyn who never got into a fight. He was a man's man. And even though later in life sex drops a notch on the list of most important and enjoyable reasons to want to live (now it's health, sanity and sobriety), I appreciated that his first publisher in France was called Obelisk Press, a more phallic symbol would be hard to find.

On second thought, what hurt even more was selling off my complete collection of original *New York Post* and *New Yorker* magazines containing J. D. Salinger's *Nine Stories* and *Franny and Zooey*. Imagine me, owning a mint edition copy of *The New Yorker*, published 9 months before I was born, where *For Esmé, With Love and Squalor* first appeared in print. It is regarded by many as a masterpiece of short story writing. No matter what plans you have for your life, whatever goals you may set or dreams you may have, it's difficult to realize them if you're dead and buried. The days come and go, but they never come back.

One day, out of the blue, a single blue-green cell came into my life. I was now on a new path to health, wealth, and well-being—or so I was led to believe.

Penny, my hippie masseuse, always had good sense. She gave me some capsules of Super Blue-Green Algae, known to biologists as Aphanizomenon flos-aquae. It is harvested wild from Klamath Lake in Oregon and has numerous healing properties. I took the sample bottle she gave me and took six capsules three times a day. Before the bottle was half gone, I was feeling more energetic and even-tempered—and God knows people in early recovery can have some periodic bouts of fatigue and pretty dramatic mood swings.

I was also sleeping more soundly since the chlorophyll and amino acids in the algae were helping me to be more nourished. I also stopped eating late at night. Best of all, my sweet tooth was screaming at me less frequently. I bought three bottles of this one-celled algae nutrient and sent a bottle to each of my three best friends: a musician in Los Angeles, a bookmaker in Philadelphia, and my friend The Professor.

Within two weeks, all three were raving about how much better they felt in almost every aspect of their mental and physical conditions. Super Blue-Green Algae was being distributed by a multilevel marketing company, and I thought because it was doing for me so many of the things that weed and other drugs did, I could promote this stuff to everyone I knew who was still using drugs in addition to the uninformed masses I had not yet met.

I became an Official Distributor and started my own "downline" with my three closest friends. Little by little, I got more customers but not enough to make any real money because they weren't actively trying to enlist more sales recruits, a must in the multilevel marketing game. But as faith, providence and a good idea would have it, I came up with something better.

I went to a product convention for the multilevel and perhaps multi-felonious Super Blue- Green Algae company called Cell Tech held at the Cow Palace near Candlestick Park in South San Francisco. There, I discovered there were no actual science books about the product, only pamphlets, fliers and photocopies of photocopies. I also grasped the reality that there were more than five thousand people in attendance.

Like the scene in the thriller/mystery movie *Charade* where everyone simultaneously realizes that the missing $100,000 was actually hidden in a very rare stamp, I instantly grasped the need for a book to help these would-be salespeople and distributors sell their freeze-dried lake scum. I mean that with great affection and humor because it is the most nutritious substance on the planet—*Aphanizomenon flos-aquae*, a.k.a. Super Blue-Green Algae.

Two days later I booked a lecture room at the Chinese Yellow Emperor Natural Healing Center in San Anselmo for Professor Karl Abrams to give a talk on the healing properties of blue-green algae. Then I called Professor Abrams at Saddleback College in Orange County and beckoned him to visit me within the next day or two.

I knew the professor was currently packing up his office to take a well-deserved one-year sabbatical leave. Three days later he arrives in San Anselmo and asks, "So Leonard, do you have anything interesting planned for us to do while I'm here?"

"Not for me, but you're giving a lecture in three days on why Super Blue-Green Algae is the greatest nutritional supplement in the world."

Like the scholar he is, The Professor replied, "Well, I'd better get to a library and start researching."

He spent the next two days at the main San Francisco library and was perfectly and professionally prepared for the event that attracted twenty-five people squeezed into the Emperor Healing Center to be enlightened by America's newest professional professor of nutrition. After the talk/pitch, everyone there bought a bottle of the algae.

The Professor moved into my spare room, and for the next eight months we worked nonstop on what would eventually be known as *Algae to the Rescue! Everything You Need to Know About Nutritional Blue-Green Algae*, copyright 1996 Logan House Publications. Library of Congress Catalogue Card Number: 96-076282. ISBN I-881952-00-5.

When the manuscript was finished, we thought about shopping for a publisher, but first we took it to Big Sur to have William Webb, book publishing genius and very close friend and personal photographer of Henry Miller, read it and give us some instant feedback.

Bill read it in one night and the next morning at breakfast, while overlooking the breathtaking view of the Pacific Ocean, he declared, "This book is too important to wait to find a publisher. They might not understand how critical this information is to get out there. You'll have to self-publish."

That was Sunday morning. Returning to San Anselmo the next day, I went into Michael Whyte's bookstore, bought a copy of Dan Poynter's *The Self-Publishing Manual*, read it and started to follow everything the book told me to do, page-by-page, step-by-step. I named our publishing company Logan House Publications in honor of where I grew up and all my fellow corner loungers who encouraged me to read more.

A month later, we had our Library of Congress ISBN number and a company in Canada printing our first run of 5,000 copies of *Algae to the Rescue! Everything You Need to Know About Nutritional Blue-Green Algae*. We had great graphics, a foreword, and an introduction by two medical doctors who knew and loved the product.

Two months later, Cell Tech, the leading multilevel marketing algae company, was having its annual convention in Klamath Falls, Oregon, right next to the motherlode, Klamath Lake. They were expecting thousands of people looking to enrich themselves by selling this trendy superfood, but without a proper sales manual or any scientific literature to back up their claims. *Bingo!* That's where me and the professor would come in.

Two days before the convention, a large DHL truck delivers 84 cases of books, 60 books in each case. At the ready, we had a large mobile home that slept five, ready to be loaded up for our life or "death of a salesman" journey to Klamath Falls. We put the cases in every nook and cranny of the mobile home.

Loading up the shower stall with six cases of books brought back so many exciting memories of being in Miami, loading up shower stalls in giant mobile homes with bales of Columbian pot to be transported to Staten Island for distribution to the THC-demanding Tri-State area.

Me, Ben and Prof. Abrams - Books to the Rescue

Loading books and not pot, especially with my son Ben there helping us load up, created a feeling in me that was nothing less than a Holy Grail moment. I had escaped my bondage to drugs and drug dealing. Science, books and algae had saved me and given me a new way to enjoy life and contribute something of value to society that I couldn't get arrested for.

Driving our ton of books up Highway 5 into Oregon, arriving in the dead of night, was an unforgettable adventure. I did have a paranoid fantasy that someone else had the same idea and had also been working on a similar book during the last six months. I imagined that they were going to be at the conference selling their books before we arrived. Luckily there was not. I like monopolies, especially if they're mine. The night we pulled into Klamath Lake was also the one- year anniversary of my attendance at Betty Ford's desert getaway. It was my first sober birthday, as they call it in California, and I found a local AA meeting to share my accomplishment. It was all men who feted me like I was a prodigal son. It was very sweet. I was truly touched by these total strangers making me feel part of the global fellowship that calls itself Alcoholics Anonymous.

The next morning, before the algae-heads were awake or making their algae and vanilla smoothies, we unfurled a huge banner on the side of the mobile home that read:

'Algae to the Rescue!' by Professor Karl J. Abrams, $14.95

Over the next three days we sold all 3,500 copies we had brought with us and took orders for the other 1,500 stored in our garage at home. We immediately called the printer in Canada and ordered another 5,000 copies and ultimately sold twenty-seven thousand copies of *Algae to the Rescue!*

The Professor was going out speaking every week, all across the country, doing tons of radio and a few television interviews. I wanted to nickname him Professor One Cell but decided it sounded like prison cell. A year or so later, there was an alarmist report attacking blue-green algae on the Dr. Dean Edell radio program. Syndicated to over 200 markets by Premiere Radio Networks and aired weekday afternoons on America's Talk on XM Radio, the program had around 1.5 million listeners every week. Dean was a notorious opponent of most nutritional supplements.

Dr. Edell's attack on blue-green algae was terribly misleading. He said the algae was contaminated with toxic microorganisms that could cause immediate liver damage. Of course, it's unwise to ingest any unfiltered lake algae, but his complaints about our scientifically regulated product lacked justification. There was absolutely no such concern with professionally harvested food-grade Klamath Lake blue-green algae, but Edell didn't bother to make that distinction.

Although commercially sold blue-green algae is free from any such toxic organisms, this report was enough for the bottom to drop out overnight. Suddenly sales and interest in the health benefits of blue-green algae vanished, along with my dreams of a secure financial future.

This was a great disappointment. I thought I had finally found a gig that I loved. Professor Abrams and I both believed in the Klamath blue-green algae as a panacea for numerous ailments.

I loved selling *Algae to the Rescue!* and thought I could really help people while simultaneously enjoying my role as the professor's manager and booking agent. There was a deep sadness that, once again, I was without a legal livelihood and back to, *What do I do now to earn a living, be of some use to humanity, and enjoy myself in the process?*

We were fortunate to have hit the market before its crash. Of course, time has passed and the momentary health scare based on one radio doctor's inaccurate information is over.

Aphanizomenon flos-aquae, and its cousins, spirulina and chlorella, still play an important nutritional part in many people's diet.

Here I was again with no project, job or gig. Bursting with energy and frustration, actively seeking employment every minute of every day.

#

Not every experience in my memory repository involves a drug or a drink or sex. No, this memory is a sad and poignant one that unfolded on June 20, 1999. That particular day happened to be Father's Day. I'm visiting my 84-year-old mother (I am already 48) while she's in her wheelchair crying silently on the eighth floor of the psych ward at a Hahnemann University Hospital. I'm crying too, through memories of times gone by and feeling heartache this Father's Day, with mom in hospital and Daddy dead.

No Jim Bunning perfect game on that day. If you don't know about it, on Father's Day, in 1964, Phillies pitcher Jim Bunning pitched a perfect game. The Phillies (who at the time had the best record in baseball) were playing a doubleheader at Shea Stadium against the Mets. It was a beautiful hot summer day in New York.

Jim Bunning's perfect game prevented any Mets player from reaching base. The Mets got no hits, the pitcher gave up no walks and the Phillies had no errors. At the end of the game, when Bunning achieved his final strike of the day, perfection had been achieved.

That day at Shea, I can only guess that there were fathers and sons sitting in the stands, focused on the game in quiet apprecia-tion of watching baseball together. I realized that I never had the chance to have an experience like this one while growing up. In fact, I would never have a Jim Bunning–like Father's Day, ever.

In December 1999, when I was busy worrying about Y2K, my 19-year-old son came home one day and says, "Dad, I want to go to treatment." I did a double take. I knew he loved weed (having been busted once in Weed, CA, appealing to our family's appreciation of irony), and he couldn't control his drinking. He knew the expres-sion "go to treatment" because I was working as a drug counselor.

I immediately called my alma mater, and they offered him a very generous partial scholarship. A $13,000 month for only $3,000. *Great deal*, I thought. I told him he had to come up with the extra $3,000 on his own, thereby investing in his own recov-ery. Ben borrowed the cash from Liana Chaouli, a family friend and paid it back within six months of graduating from the rehab program. On January 2, 2000, I had the unscheduled joy and privilege of driving Ben to the Betty Ford Center for his Berlitz-like total immersion course in sobriety.

Only once on the three-hour drive did he turn to me and say, "Dad, I don't think this is such a good idea. Can't we just stop for some sushi and go home?"

I granted one of his two wishes. We stopped for sushi in Azusa. I told him to try quitting for a couple weeks at the rehab and if he didn't like it, I would come pick him up. I knew it was a program of attraction, not coercion. He never made that call. I picked him up a month later and he hasn't had a drink, smoked a joint, or used drugs since.

While he was behind the oleanders, his mother flew in from Olympia, Washington, for family week. I figured I'd let her have the week without me, since Ben had chosen to live with me for middle school, and again, after graduating high school in Vaughn, Washington. She told me while walking around the pond with Ben and seeing the swans spreading their wings in unison imbued them both with a healing energy and sense of freedom.

#

One Sunday morning I was at my weekly house of worship, the Agape International Spiritual Center. My involvement with Agape included attending two services a week and regular classes, volunteering on Sundays and having a profound gratitude (that lives on to this day) that I had found a living spiritual teacher, no less enlightened or as gifted a speaker as Krishnamurti, Alan Watts or Ram Dass, who actually spoke there a few times. For weeks I was in the middle of my shoulder-to-the-wheel of job seeking efforts, Rev. Michael said during a service, "Sometimes you have to take your shoulder off the grindstone to let spirit take over."

So, the next day I flew to Miami to see an old girlfriend. I still don't know if that was spirit guiding me or my cock? A week later when I returned to LA, it was Super Bowl Sunday. I had a moderate bet on the game and a delectable lunch from Whole Foods ready to dive into. Just before the coin toss, my friend Richard Rice calls and tells me a colleague of his who owns a classy French vintage poster gallery in Beverly Hills needs a manager and he recommended me for the position and the owner would like to interview me in an hour at the gallery.

Without a moment's hesitation, I changed out of my jeans and Chucks, into my nerd khakis, penny loafers and powder blue shirt (which really set off my blue eyes) and was presenting myself to Ms. Jane Moufflet at The Antiquarian Antique Mart on Beverly Blvd. When I told her I had read the paperback edition of *Moulin Rouge* about Henri de Toulouse-Lautrec, I got the job. I was home in time to see the last quarter of the game. Just like that. Just like Rev. Michael said it would happen.

I enjoyed working at the gallery for two main reasons. First, there were rarely any customers, so I was alone and could read for hours. I reread *Shibumi*, *Papillon* and other favorites and read some books I had never gotten around to, like *The Great Gatsby* and *The Agony and the Ecstasy*. I was reading or rereading almost a book a week.

Second, when I did have a customer, they were usually in show business and fairly interesting, i.e., Giovanni Ribisi, Courtney Love, Courtney Cox or my favorite customer of all, Michael Caine. I couldn't tell whether he was asking me questions about a poster or reciting lines from *The Man Who Would Be King*. My favorite. I did not try and do my Sean Connery imitation. My stint at the French vintage poster gallery ended when the shop closed down due to poor sales (not my fault).

Living in Studio City with Ben and no income put me in a precarious position. Luckily, we were able to rely on our "eggs, onions and apples" diet to stay sufficiently fed. Eggs for breakfast, a different style every morning, and egg salad on challah for lunch. In the evening, I would sauté a few onions while Ben went to pick up some single pizza slices at the only local pizzeria. They were only $2 each and very large. We'd bury them in sautéed onions and sprinkle on some sun-dried tomatoes for extra sweetness and lots of free oregano. For dessert, we'd bake a couple apples with lots of cinnamon but always with real maple syrup even though it was pricey. Log Cabin Syrup has been banned from my kitchen since my first class in Macrobiotics in 1976.

After a while of not being able to find any appropriate employment for a sober 48-year- old, I decided to move back to San Anselmo and toss Ben out of the nest. He had gotten sober at Betty Ford and took to sobriety and AA like a reincarnation of an Oxford Group member. He got a job as a short-order cook and rented a one-room cottage behind the home of one of our dear elderly women friends we knew from AA in Studio City.

I packed up my car and shipped everything else I owned to a storage facility in Marin County, where I planned to live for the rest of my life. When I returned to San Anselmo without money for first and last, providentially my friend Rose was living at her boyfriend's house most of the time. This meant I could sleep in her bed at her house when she was sleeping in his bed at his house, and on her couch when she was sleeping in her own bed. I lived there for a couple of years with her 16-year-old daughter, Viva, and her 16-year-old stepdaughter, Melanie. I am very proud to report that in all the time I was there, I never went into their hamper even once.

I tried to get a job at the Mill Valley Film Festival. I knew the director because I had helped him to arrange a Robert Downey Sr. screening a few years before. No such luck, their staff was full and no one was going anywhere. So I decided to start my own business. I went to see my ticket dealer and friend (ticket dealer because I used his services so many times over the last 15 years and friend because our sons liked to hang out at his house and play in the hot tub). His name was Wolf and he owned the best travel agency in Marin. (Remember those things, travel agencies?)

Wolf let me use an empty desk at Red Hill Travel to start my brainchild, Sober Holidays Unlimited. The plan was to take tour groups of clean and sober people to culturally interesting places, like a trip to New York to see a few Broadway plays and musicals or a tour of London museums like the Tate Modern and The British Museum. My first planned trip was a *Dìa de dos Muertos* trip to Puerto Vallarta, Mexico. PV is famous for its above-average beaches, great English-speaking AA meetings, a friendly environment, and tours of the location used to film *The Night of the Iguana* with Richard Burton, Ava Gardner and Deborah Kerr, directed by the great John Huston. Who wouldn't want to visit the set of a film about a defrocked alcoholic minister?

We were starting to book reservations to PV just when America needed an excuse to clamp down on its own people, occupy Afghanistan and start a brutal invasion against Saddam Hussein and innocent Iraqi civilians. On the morning of September 11, 2001, Rose called saying a plane had flown into one of the towers of the World Trade Center. I thought, of course, it was a small plane and just an accident. Then I got a call from another friend who was hysterical blabbering about a second plane hitting the World Trade Center. Rose's house, the house I was living in, had no TV. I thought I'd better go someplace where I could watch the news coverage.

I called my friend Marian Bach (of amateur blackmailing fame) and sure enough she had her TV on and was sobbing. I drove over to her house to see the repeated video of the second plane hitting the North Tower. It was a horror. I was thinking about all the people who died, who were dying, getting crushed, leaping to their deaths, dying and how the world had just changed forever. And Marian is rolling another joint. I'm sitting there horrified, as was she, except she's smoking pot—and I'm not.

I thought to myself, *If I were still a pothead, I'd be rolling joints to get high to watch the World Trade Center Towers come down too.* Getting high to watch people die would have felt immoral to me, but I would have done it anyway if I were still addicted to marijuana. Marian was smoking not because she wanted to get high to watch the tragedy. She had to get high for everything, no matter what. Real potheads will get high for a christening, and they'll get high for funerals. They'll get high for weddings and even higher for a divorce.

Marijuana addicts will get high in an ambulance, even if they're the one being rushed to the hospital. I started weeping for joy realizing I was free of that addiction and could experience the travails of life without having to be stoned for every event, good or bad, but never indifferent anymore. This experience is what I later learned in AA is called "living life on life's terms."

Suddenly, the love of my life, marijuana, seemed demonic. I was repulsed by the thought that had I continued smoking pot I might be watching these horrors as if they were a big-budget disaster movies instead of . . . reality. It was like watching the me that I used to be and would never want to be again. I couldn't bear watching my friend getting high to watch people die. So I headed over to the local liquor store—not to drink—but to watch the Towers fall again, and again. The store was owned by Mohammed and managed by his son, Mohammed Jr. I had shopped there for years. It was the closest place to buy my vodka, champagne, rolling papers and Duraflame firelogs. The three of us stood there together in horror and disbelief. I knew their life was going to turn to shit and my new travel business was about to be grounded. The next day at the Chevron station, as I was paying for the petrol with a $20 bill, I saw blood dripping off the bill, knowing that's what 9/11 was really about. And I knew that I would not give up driving and the government would use this event to clamp down on its citizens and create a law enforcement agency with a German-like name. Perhaps, Homeland Uber Alles, or something more authoritarian, like HOMELAND SECURITY.

To make matters worse, three weeks later, my mother died. I had just ordered a grilled chicken sandwich with a side of fries and an iced tea. My cell phone chimed and I saw my sister-in-law's name light up. That was a bit of a surprise. Not that she never called me . . . but she never called me.

"Hi Lee, your mother died."

Rose was 86 and a lifelong Philadelphian. There is a concept in AA that sometimes people just stop drinking because they are "done." I think Mom was just "done" living. She was tired. She had lived alone for 30 years, stopped working when she was 76, endured a fair amount of hospitalizations, and was no longer able to get herself to the salon on Saturday mornings to get her hair done. One son lived in New York, the other (me) in California, 3,000 miles away.

So why go on? I threw a twenty on the table and told the waitress I was leaving and she could give the chicken sandwich to someone else. I remember being in a daze, or a haze, some out-of-body experience as I left Ted's, the local restaurant/watering hole in San Anselmo. I saw Carlo on his bike, and thought, *Carlo is the first person I've seen since I found out my mother died.* I knew that memory would last until the day I died. He wasn't a close friend, just the Volvo mechanic I had used for 20 years. I remembered what a German therapist I knew said about the day her mother died: "When my mother died, I knew it would be a day I would never forget and it would never happen again."

October 3 would forever be the day *my* mother died. 10/3. She was born 3/10. I guess she liked palindromes.

A favorite memory of my mother was the night after I had been suspended from Jay Cooke Jr. High and we (my brother driving) were going past the school. I had my C02 BB gun with me and asked mom if I could shoot at the windows of the principal's office as we drove by. "Sure, go ahead." I asked Brother Bruce to slow down. I shot as many BBs as I could, trying to empty the chamber into the school. We were pretty far away so none of the windows broke, but I was hoping the BBs would at least leave those little holes I had left in other panes of glass I had shot up. My mom cared more about me in that moment than she did for any principle/principal. I knew she loved me that much, and I never did anything to make her lose that love for me.

#

After eight or nine years of sobriety, I was still trying to find my way, winding this way and that way. I realized my previous life and career had prepared me for absolutely nothing in terms of earning a living in the real world. So I decided to do what so many others who couldn't make it in the real world do. I decided to become a drug counselor. I was in my fifties, an age when a lot of working stiffs might be thinking about retirement and Medicare. Here I was back at the starting gate, hoping the starter's gun wasn't aimed at me.

Like Joseph Campbell often said, "Follow your bliss." My bliss had become showing the addict and alcoholic there is a better life to be lived (and certainly a longer one) after a career of wild and obsessive substance abuse.

Having used drugs for decades isn't sufficient qualification to become a drug counselor. There are educational requirements, and I found myself back in school again. Los Angeles City College had a two-year program in Substance Abuse Counseling that would prepare me for the State Examination to receive Substance Abuse Counseling Certification in California.

Our professor, upon graduation, made us redemptified students—mostly ex-cons and ex- addicts—two promises: Upon graduation everyone will be able to get a job. And two, it will never pay enough.

The rewards of helping others in recovery go far beyond the size of a paycheck or the diminution of your ego. I launched into counseling with the same zeal and dedication I have always shown with any project. For a number of years, I worked on the front lines in Los Angeles. I worked in Malibu and I worked in the "hood." I wanted to learn, integrate, explore and master methods and techniques that could serve my clients' needs.

I never judged those I counseled, even those with a sleazier past than I had, but rather saw them as talented and blessed individuals who trusted me, and that was a trust I would not violate. If I could help them resolve issues and face challenges in a manner that made their life more rewarding, I was doing my job. There were times I would witness a client's mind turning the corner after inhabiting a hopeless drug fiend's existence to envisioning a future with no substances to rely on for achieving the basic human need to live in a state of ease and comfort. And they were okay with that.

Part III

What It's Like Now

Breathe when you breathe. Walk where you walk. Talk when you talk. Cry when you cry. Die when you die. Let go when you let go.
— Allen Ginsberg

Chapter 17

Second Breath

It does not matter how slowly you go, as long as you do not stop.
—Confucius

As an adult with an asthmatic's rescue inhaler in his pocket, all the time, I always felt like the little boy in school with an elevator pass. I never let anyone see me use it. I was embarrassed to reveal any physical weaknesses. If I was on a date and suddenly needed to use the inhaler (which I did 20 times a day), I would make up a reason to tell my date to look at someone behind her and sneak a whiff while she was turned away. Today I feel as strong and whole as anyone I meet, work with, or look up to. How did that happen? Some savior creep pulmonologist gave me a sample of a new medication called Dulera.

"Take it two times in the morning and two times at night," he said. By the end of the first afternoon, another Western medicine pharmaceutical miracle happened.

My asthma was gone, and the need for a rescue inhaler vanished completely. I haven't used a rescue inhaler since that day (except when I had a bout of COVID-19, February of 2020). Dulera made me into a man—no longer umbilical cord–like dependent on my pocket inhaler. I use Dulera once in the morning and that's all I need for easy breathing.

Until I was 62, I was that boy with his secret asthma inhaler in his pocket, still embarrassed because I didn't want anyone to see me with a breathing weakness. Now, with Dulera, I can go out for a day or walk from one end of Manhattan to the other or ride around London on the Circle line—with no asthma and no inhaler in my pocket. When I would fly, I always made sure I had an inhaler in my pocket and one in my carry-on in case I lost one. Now, I no longer think that way. I can literally go to a sold-out concert at Hollywood Bowl with no inhaler . . . an extraordinary achievement for me.

No more traumatizing episodes. No more ambulances. Breathing freely is still *so deep and meaningful for me*, and probably wouldn't work so miraculously if I were still smoking pot. Although if I hadn't quit pot, the earthworms and ants would be fighting over which organ or eyeball to devour next. I'm not afraid anymore of suffocating in the fresh air on any day of the week.

Oh, the reason I called the pulmonologist a creep is because when I went back to his office a month later to thank him and tell him how amazing the results of using the Dulera were for me and that I felt, literally, like a new man, he insisted I add another powerful steroid medication to my daily regimen. I told him that I hadn't used the rescue inhaler even once in the last month. From 20 times a day to *zero*. Wasn't that good enough?

"No," he said, as he handed me a sample of Advair and told me to use that too.

"Isn't the point of using medication to use as little as possible and get the best results you can?"

He looked at me as if I were crazy, or an anarchist. "Not at all," he said. "Now take this home and start using it with the Dulera." I guess the kickbacks from the Advair people were very generous.

I didn't verbally tell him to go fuck himself, but the look on my face did. I gave him back his *free* sample and never saw the putz again. As I was leaving I turned to glare at him and he looked like a crustacean. When a pickpocket sees a saint, all he sees are his pockets. When a pulmonologist sees a man, all he sees are his lungs and the medications he can prescribe to get the biggest kickbacks.

Ironically, most of my experiences with doctors and surgeons have been great. When I was 15 years sober, as a sober, much healthier person, I had a new thought that I could actually live through open-heart surgery. This confidence is a gift that sobriety brings. With Ecstasy and vodka, my friends before I became sober, my body would not have been able to withstand the kind of stress that comes with an operation of this magnitude. My body could not withstand the feeling akin to being hit by a Mack truck. But with sobriety in my corner, I knew I was as healthy as I could be and a strong candidate to live a long life with my new bovine valve. Moo moo.

It reminds me of the scene in the short story by J. D. Salinger, "Teddy," when Teddy says: "I was six when I saw that everything was God, and my hair stood up, and all,' Teddy said. 'It was on a Sunday, I remember. My sister was a tiny child then, and she was drinking her milk, and all of a sudden I saw that she was God and the milk was God. I mean, all she was doing was pouring God into God, if you know what I mean.'"

I focus my thoughts on the irony of it all because I have never broken a bone in my body, had an ulcer, appendicitis, or liver or kidney distress. I have only been hospitalized for what has always ailed me. Just had a bad heart valve replaced and, as you will soon learn, a brain tumor removed, that's all. Guess I'm an overachiever. Not to mention the dozen hospital visits to keep my bronchial tubes from closing the show down.

HIGH

The highest purpose of art is to inspire. What else can you do? What else can you do for any one but inspire them?
— Bob Dylan

Chapter 18

Two Eyes to See, One Ear to Hear

Only in art will the lion lie down with the lamb, and the rose grow without thorn.
—Martin Amis

No doubt, joining the merchant class in my late teens allowed me to shape my reality into living passionately for the arts. This fire was ignited during my youth; it burns strongly in me today.

Frankly, it is unquenchable. Of all my romantic interludes, my number-one mistress has always been Lady Cinema.

A life well lived is like a good movie. Like a movie, life has a beginning, a middle, and a conclusion. A great movie has conflict, a turning point and a resolution and so does life. During an exciting film, you sit on the edge of your seat, and you don't leave early. A life well lived is just as engaging and just as riveting and memorable. Such a life is even more satisfying when you've spent time watching great movies. Put a silver screen in front of my eyes, and I have no use for a silver spoon in front of my nose.

Movies provide more than entertainment and diversion. The process of making motion pictures involves craftsmanship. The outcome often elevates the craft to artistry. The arts are powerful, reflective, inspirational and motivational. For those reasons, the arts play a pivotal role both in societal changes and in the process of personal transformation. Seeing your own shortcomings and egregious behavior on the screen is profoundly helpful to understanding your life—and deciding to make some changes.

Nothing compares to the experience of surrendering to a motion picture, as it was meant to be experienced enveloped in the darkness of a theater with close friends or surrounded by strangers who are equally transfixed and sharing a collective dream.

Yes, movies are powerful tools for altering perceptions, challenging assumptions and uniting us with universal issues of identity, longing, transformation, coming of age, sin, redemption and vindication.

It's no surprise that there are a lot of excellent films about great artists who died untimely deaths due to their drug and alcohol use. These films are all worth watching and rewatching. I am thinking of Basquiat, about Jean-Michel Basquiat, with an astounding star-making performance by Jeffrey Wright. Why did Jean-Michel do too much heroin on August 12, 1988?

Then there's Jackson Pollock, with Ed Harris splashing his talent all over this fantastic and heartbreaking biopic. Why did Jackson have to drink and drive his car into a tree and die on August 11, 1956?

And how about the television production of *The Rothko Conspiracy*, on American Masters. Mark Rothko (born Markus Yakovlevich Rothkowitz, oy vey) brought darkness into the light through art. Sit in the middle of the Rothko room at the Tate Modern and see if you don't wonder what it's (life) all about. What made him take a handful of barbiturates and cut the artery in his right arm on February 25, 1970?

In Alcoholics Anonymous, people are often encouraged to write a gratitude list. Books have always been at the top of my list (after family, friends, and pets). Some of the best lessons I learned came not from a classroom but from my favorite authors. They taught me about everything.

With a good book, you can go anywhere. Many years ago, I had an experience waiting in line at the American Express office in Amsterdam. The line was unusually long. As boredom was setting in, I took out my paperback copy of *Stranger in a Strange Land* by Robert A. Heinlein. Suddenly, there I was with Valentine Michael Smith going on adventures with the human-martian. I didn't know that the title was from Exodus 2:22, until I recently saw Cecil B. DeMille's *The Ten Commandments*. Charlton Heston (Moses) says it when he is taken in and comforted by some hip Arabs. The Library of Congress named Heinlein's *Stranger* one of the 88 "Books that Shaped America." And for me, I realized I never had to be bored again as long as I had a book in my hands.

Conversely, two weeks later, I was suffering from a three-day asthma attack, and I found a bed at the free clinic run by student nurses in the Vondelpark. The only book I had with me was H. G. Wells's *A Short History of the World*. It was first published in 1922, right after WWI. I realized the history of the world was about one war after another. I never looked at history like that before, but I guess it's man's inhumanity to man that always gets the most attention and not the kindnesses shared between people.

I'll never forget the experience of reading Alan Watts, *The Book: On the Taboo Against Knowing Who You Are*, sitting under a tree on the lawn at Emily Dickenson's house in Amherst, Massachusetts. I'm sure the pot I smoked enhanced the moment because I thought I heard Emily inviting me in for tea. As the fickle finger of fate would have it, years later I was the guest speaker at an AA meeting in the Alan Watts room at the Esalen Institute in Big Sur. How ironic that there would be an AA meeting room named after Alan Watts since he died of liver disease as the result of too much booze.

I also always had with me *Nine Stories*, the book of short stories by J. D. Salinger. When he died in 2010, my brother and I were on the phone in tears. Salinger was our adopted father. I've adopted quite a few fathers along the way. Not all Jewish. Though I have fallen in love with Philip Roth lately.

Of course, great books also taught me a lot about great people. In December of 1980, I was given a copy of *Naked Came I*, only because the party host forgot to buy me a proper Christmas gift, and she just removed the book from her library and presented it to me as my gift. I pretended I was thrilled with it. Never intended to read it. You can't blame me . . . it's 623 pages long.

On the train home, tired of looking at the passing scenery, I retrieved the book from my luggage on the metal rack above me. It turned out to be a gift from the gods. It's a fictionalized biography (historical novel) about Auguste Rodin. It portrays Rodin as someone who was driven to be an artist because his desire and temperament would allow him to be nothing else. He was a "born artist."

Biographies and autobiographies had never really fascinated me, even though an old friend from Logan, who had done some time, told me that the only books he ever took out of the prison library were of this genre. Now I saw why he loved them so much. I read and loved that giant book! I learned about sculpture, life in France in the late 1800s and Rodin's friends—Edouard Manet, Auguste Renoir and Edgar Degas (not too fond of Jews). I still appreciate how every time Rodin and his wife moved, the first thing she would do on the first day at their new home was plant their vegetable garden (not a single Whole Foods in sight). And when they occasionally had a piece of meat to add to the stew, it was a holiday of gratitude.

In any event, *Naked Came I* started me on my tear of reading historical novels about artists. I soon discovered Irving Stone. He wrote biographical novels about the three artists I mentioned and about Sigmund Freud, Mary Todd Lincoln, Abigail Adams, Charles Darwin and others.

My favorite Irving Stone book is *Depths of Glory*, about Impressionistic pioneer Camille Pissarro. After I read this masterwork, I wanted to see every exhibit of Impressionist paintings I could. Knowing the artists' back stories and their struggles for legitimacy brought the paintings to life. Cézanne said about Pissarro that "he was like a father to me, a man to consult and a little like the good Lord." (Well, he was Jewish after all.)

It felt as if I were with Camille Pissarro as he influenced his fellow artists to exhibit at the traditional venues and exhibit halls. After being rejected by upper-class society, Pissarro encouraged his poor friends (whose paintings would one day sell for millions) to start an alternative exhibition, the *Salon des Refusés*, but only after little art lover Napoleon Bonaparte gave them his approval. Later on, during WWI, Germans were walking all over many of his drawings. Oh, those Nazis bastards!

What I wouldn't have given to have lived in Irving Stone's mind. My other two favs by Mr. Stone are *The Agony and the Ecstasy* (Michelangelo) and *Lust for Life* (Vincent van Gogh).

I never read about George Seurat, but I did see *Sunday in the Park with George* on Broadway (a couple times). I read that Stephen Sondheim devised the whole play in one day during an epiphanic rush while looking at *A Sunday Afternoon on the Island of La Grande Jatte* at the Art Institute of Chicago. I accepted the whole premise as fact. Why not? Or maybe it was James Lapine who wrote the book for *Sunday* who had the epiphany.

Paintings are a passion and a pleasure. Early in my sobriety, I was in Chicago for the 1996 BookExpo America at the McCormick Center, playing hooky and going to the Art Institute to see *Sunday*. Before going in, I had two shots of espresso at a café across the street.

As I entered the hallowed gallery of Impressionism, I was enveloped by *Paris Street; Rainy Day* by Gustave Caillebotte. The painting was done in 1877 and is seven-by-nine feet. I burst into tears. First, because I realized I had not been in a museum sober, not high on weed or coke, in 25 years. And because I really thought the couple in the painting was alive. And the street they walked down had just been rained on, or I had fallen into H. G. Wells's time machine.

What an extraordinary work of art! Was it only now that I could finally see extra lucidly, with no pot in my brain? I used to think I could see more clearly when I was stoned. Clearly, I was mistaken.

And there I was, chilled, goose bumps all over, knowing around the corner was *Sunday Afternoon on the Island of La Grande Jatte.* Dot dot dot dot dot . . . too many to count. What I saw in the painting and in my now sober soul was akin to some lyrics from Sondheim's perfect musical:

Order
Design
Tension
Composition
Balance
Light
Harmony

Standing unadulterated in the windy city, I felt a calm pass through me that defies human understanding. I felt like I was home. I know that sounds trite, but it's true. I'd been high since I was 18. I mean like every-day high. The calm was smooth and sexy to me, like an aphrodisiac. It wasn't the serenity in the famous Serenity Prayer, which always sounded boring to me, and still does. In fact, I replaced the word *serenity* with "surrender." Sounds more proactive.

For reasons mostly apparent to boys in Philly, my first most favorite artist was, and still is, Marcel Duchamp. His major work was the installation piece *Etant donnés* at the Philadelphia Museum of Art, (yes, where Rocky runs up the front steps and raises his hands in victorious jubilation). The English translation of the Duchamp work is *The Waterfall and The Illuminating Gas.*

At first it just looks like a large wooden barn door. When you approach the piece, all you can see "is a tableau, visible only through a pair of peepholes (one for each eye) in a wooden door, of a nude woman lying on her back with her face hidden, legs spread, holding a gas lamp in the air in one hand against a landscape backdrop."[4] Now slow down your reading, for a second. The point

4   Thanks, Wikipedia.

is, in case you missed it, "nude woman lying on her back with her face hidden, legs spread." This was the first vagina I ever saw. I had kept my eyes closed during my birth passage.

Thank goodness Mom was very discreet. (Although she did have me fasten her garter belt to her thigh-high stockings before she went out on date night. I was after all the perfect height at six years old. I didn't have to be on my knees, like in later years.) Once, I engaged with a woman of the night in San Francisco and when I asked her name, she said:

"Rose. Will you help me with my stockings?"

Oedipus Schmedipus.

Imagine a class of twenty 15-year-olds on their school trip to the Art Museum. I'll bet the teachers never had the time to look through the peephole. For you creative types, I must list (again, thank you Wikipedia) the guts of the "assemblage": [(exterior) wooden door, iron nails, bricks, and stucco; (interior) bricks, velvet, wood, parchment over an armature of lead, steel, brass, synthetic putties and adhesives, aluminum sheet, welded steel-wire screen, and wood; Peg-Board, human hair, oil paint, plastic, steel binder clips, plastic clothespins, twigs, leaves, glass, plywood, brass piano hinge, nails, screws, cotton, collotype prints, acrylic varnish, chalk, graphite, paper, cardboard, tape, pen ink, electric light fixtures, gas lamp (Bec Auer type), foam rubber, cork, electric motor, cookie tin, and linoleum.]

I could tell that Duchamp was different. He didn't shop for art supplies at Michael's. No, he shopped at Home Depot. If you ever get to Philly, don't miss it.

I have a little secret for you. I have my own amazing collection of Impressionist art: Manet's *The Ragpicker*, Degas's *Woman Ironing*, Van Gogh's *Portrait of a Peasant*. My favorite is by Matisse, *The Black Shawl*. His Italian model, Lorette, wrapped in a sexy mantilla. Definition? It's a lace or silk scarf worn by women over the hair and shoulders, especially in Spain. She is lying on an oriental carpet composed of the most exotic red I have ever seen. By the way, I also have *The Thinker* by Rodin. I keep that giant paperweight outside. It never snows in Pasadena, so in any season, I can sit and gaze at the statue and think about how blessed I was to get that copy of *Naked Came I* years ago.

I live only 13 miles from Pasadena, which is fortunate because that's where I keep my collection ... at the Norton Simon Museum. I could never afford the insurance. I visit that collection when I have guests in from out of town, after I have been sacked from a job or after a love affair has gone to seed or imploded. The collection offers me solace when I feel defeated and reminds me that reality is still just what you make it.

So, I have saved this next part of my reality until now because I hate to admit that my love of art probably started in the 1960s with psychedelic posters. Peter Max, anyone? When I would go to Jerry's Records, there would be posters lining the walls. They cost a dollar or two, and they jumped right out at you. Some were reprints of famous paintings. Yes, there were some done in Day-Glo. *Yes*, I had a black light. And then came the artists from San Francisco, whose concert posters were artworks dazzling, colorful and phantasmal. This was the first time I ever bought a work of art—unframed, of course. For a dollar.

The first fine art I ever bought was years later at the historic, monumental and sorely missed Sausalito flea market. It was an original photo by Ed Buryn, taken to illustrate his best-selling book, *Vagabonding in Europe*. It was several hundred dollars, but thanks to drug dealing, I could afford to splurge. It still hangs in my living room today. The photo is of a large poster of Count Basie, glued to a wall in Copenhagen, and he's pointing toward the wall next to him, which has written on it, "jaz," next to a woman and her bike. Her face, the bike and "jaz" are hand painted by the photographer. Looking at it reminds me of so many of the things I hold dear in this lifetime.

Rounding out my cultural passion is . . . let's not forget . . . music, and not necessarily of the siren's kind. While the mythological sirens were dangerous creatures who lured sailors with their enchanting music only to cause shipwrecks off the rocky coast, music has never shipwrecked me. The right music can move me to tears or play with my emotions like a fiddle. The right music can free me from the reality of death and remind me of my mortality simultaneously. And music can, in a timeless instant, connect as one, a sea of concertgoers who start out as strangers, creating in them a bond that lasts well after their ears stop ringing. Collective unconscious made into a conscious oneness, through music. What wouldn't you give to have that experience, unless feeling the oneness is just not your thing? It's scary to lose your ego, even temporarily.

It's even scarier to lose your hearing. In 2014 I learned I was growing a tumor on the left side of my brain. Countless MRIs later, the brain surgeon told me if the tumor hit my brain, I would stop breathing because that part of the brain controls the functioning of the lungs. Eventually I had to have brain surgery to remove the acoustic neuroma before it removed me from existence. It was necessary to cut a hole in my head to pluck out the little bastard. I was concerned that my brain was about to get fresh air, (no, not the Terry Gross interview radio show). I wasn't sure it really needed fresh air. I really didn't want to get the surgery, but I knew how much it mattered. Gray mattered. It was never a question of black and white, unless you consider living and dying black and white.

When they took out the neuroma, they removed the hearing mechanism (the hearing canal) from the left side of my head. Completely. I have *no* hearing in my left ear. NONE. You could shoot off a .38 special next to my ear and *nothing*. The lone critter on Earth that has only a unilateral hearing system is . . . the praying mantis. I am in good company. I hope people know it would be bad luck to kill me too.

When John Taylor, cofounder of Duran Duran, heard about my surgery, he was kind enough to give me a complete set of Beatles CDs, all originally mixed in mono (except *Abbey Road*).

Few days goes by without mourning the fact that my *love* for music has been seriously diminished. It's no longer enjoyable to go to a concert, symphony or jazz club. The right ear has over compensated, so I hear things louder than most in my good ear, which makes me recoil at sirens, backfires, noisy people in restaurants, and overly loud trailers in movie theaters.

The left side of my head feels numb at concerts. I still go occasionally when a friend is performing or someone needs a ride or company. I haven't stopped seeing Broadway musicals. Thank God the deafness is not so noticeable in movie theaters or at stage productions.

Some of the absolute best times in my entire life were at rock and jazz concerts. Not just Hendrix, Bob Marley and Miles Davis but amazing bar bands around the world. And blasting music in my car for inspiration and spiritual salvation. It just doesn't do  that for me anymore. When I try, it just makes the left side of my head feel dead. Bummer.

Van, do you have anything to say about this?

Rave on John Donne

Tonight, 'neath the silvery moon, tonight

Tonight, 'neath the silvery moon, tonight

And the leaves, shaking on the trees, in the cool, summer breeze

And the people passing, in the street

And everybody that you meet, tonight

You will understand the oneness

Tonight, you will understand the one

Tonight, 'neath the silvery moon, tonight

Tonight, let it all begin tonight

You will understand

The Oneness,

The Oneness,

The Oneness,

The Oneness,

The Oneness,

The Oneness

The Oneness,

The Oneness

WORDS and MUSIC by VAN MORRISON

Caledonia Music

Let's not cancel Van the Man just because he didn't want to get vaccinated. I've seen Van Morrison dozens of times in small clubs and large outdoor venues. He is like a God to me. My favorite composer, singer, curmudgeon musician of all time. I will mourn his passing like losing a best friend. When Dylan kicks, I will just feel sad.

My first concert after rehab was the Rolling Stones playing outdoors at the Oakland Coliseum, with Seal as the opening act. I had bought the tickets before going away to Betty Ford. The night of the concert, I was in a bad mood because my girlfriend, Melissa, had broken up with me again that afternoon. I was also afraid that even one whiff of weed might make me start craving marijuana and reach for a random joint being passed around near me. Before I got there, I wrapped a thick winter scarf around my face so I wouldn't breathe in the marijuana smoke. I was only 35 days clean. I didn't know how easy it would be for me to return to my 26-year-old habit of daily pot smoking. How much did I love pot? Let Cole Porter answer that:

Night and day, you are the one

Only you beneath the moon and under the sun

Whether near me or far

203

It's no matter, darling, where you are

I think of you night and day, day and night.

Now, I can walk around a reggae club, and the smell of pot doesn't faze me at all. The gift of long-term sobriety. You don't have to avoid anyone or anywhere.

After getting clean and sober, the second concert I attended was Carlos Santana at the Fillmore West. By the time a couple of songs were played, I started crying, streaming tears of joy. I was stoned every other time I had seen Santana. This time, I was sober and amazed that the music still sounded as beautiful. I felt a neighborly connection to Carlos because we both frequented the same breakfast diner, Bubba's, in our little cozy hamlet of San Anselmo. Other regulars included Ram Dass and Ron Kovic of *Born on the Fourth of July* fame. I heard while I was at Betty Ford, Ron was constantly cruising up to my girlfriend Melissa and trying to pick her up. Fat chance.

Music has been my companion on my journey to recovery. Reality is indeed anything you can imagine, anything you can make it. Once in a while, I will click *Anonymous 4—An English Ladymass* on my playlist and set it on autorepeat. Anonymous 4 was an American female a cappella quartet. Their main performance genre was medieval music. Surrounding myself with Gregorian chants for five hours does indeed make my reality my reality.

The trick to overcoming addiction is thus the realignment of desire, so that it switches from the goal of immediate relief to the goal of long-term fulfillment.
— Marc Lewis, The Biology of Desire: Why Addiction Is Not a Disease

Chapter 19

Addiction is Not a Disease, It's an Addiction

*Remember just because you hit bottom doesn't mean you
have to stay there.*
— Robert Downey Jr.

*The most common way people give up their power is by
thinking they don't have any.*
—Alice Walker

*It is no measure of health to be well adjusted to a profoundly
sick society.*
—Jiddu Krishnamurti

I have learned that when you call addiction a disease, most people think of their uncle who died of cancer or of their cousin who died of tuberculosis or their father who died of a heart attack, like my father did. It's a "disease" that people love having until they don't.

How many "diseases" provoke people to commit crimes against others or their property or steal cash out of their mother's purse? In reality, thousands get clean and sober by simply walking into a meeting of AA or NA or checking into a rehab, like what happened to my son and me. The AA expression is "struck sober." In AA meetings sometimes, people will occasionally share that after attending just one meeting, they haven't had a drink ever since.

Is this experience a result of being DONE, being desperate or by receiving God's grace? Maybe it's all of them? It's amazing how sometimes people can stop on a dime. The Japanese have an aphorism, "At its extreme, everything turns to its opposite." Is that what happened to me?

Sobriety is a decision and a "letting go," not a frog march, similar to achieving satori. Recovery starts in your heart or in the frontal lobe. Only after the ice starts to melt around the heart and the mind clears can someone sincerely decide to embrace sobriety. When I worked as a Certified Substance Abuse Counselor, I learned you can't force true recovery. Recovery that starts with judgmental judges in courtrooms or CEOs in boardrooms sending you to rehab, the suspension of your allowance or the threat of being written out of a will or divorced is rarely successful.

In 1994 at Betty Ford, nothing was forced down our throats, neither meds nor the 12 Steps. I listened to my peers' stories, my counselor's advice, the lectures and educational classes and the still small voice within. I realized I had been living an insane existence and had seriously flirted with death on more than one occasion. Most importantly, I learned it was not only possible to go a month without weed, booze or Percodan, it was preferred, advisable, desirable and a winning way to live. No more arrests, emergency rooms, or being numb with staccato heartbeats through frightening frisks at airports and border crossings.

Thank God. Today, I am no longer on the run, fearful, or alone. I marvel at the miracle of a new life in what is truly, for me, a new world.

Alan Watts said, "You can't force enlightenment through the window—but you can make sure the window is open." A treatment center should be a place where you learn to open the window for a healthy lifestyle to come in, and aftercare, with participation in

12 Step programs, is how you make sure the window stays open. Then, it's a lot of vigilance and self-reflection, self-discovery and developing a joie de vivre while using all the sobriety tools you have. Becoming your own sentinel.

Sobriety is a gift. My gift was to be relieved of my cravings; and it's a gift because drugs can ruin your life or kill you. The gift is that I am no longer killing myself or endangering other people.

Sobriety is a miracle. I knew in the bottom of my heart that I did not want or need to do drugs again. Twelve Step programs helped me to see alcohol as a liquid drug, so I stay away from one bourbon, one shot, and one beer. There is something eloquent about living with no substances. Once you have some time being sober under your belt, it's like a reward. Sobriety is like having been given a flower-bearing plant *you have* to water every day. It's like being deputized by God.

Frankly, recovery for me has been a magical thing. Like the time I met a complete stranger who I appeared to have nothing in common with. I was strolling through Central Park and happened upon Strawberry Fields. It's right across the street from where John Lennon lived and where he got killed.

I walk over and see that people have left teddy bears, little guitars and flowers. It's like a continuous shrine there. And I thought, *Well, what do I have that's valuable to me that I could put down?* I had my 15-year sobriety medallion. I set it down on the perpetual impromptu memorial and said a little prayer.

John was a very important human being in my lifetime. Coincidentally I had just gotten my first mini-iPod and had *Sgt. Pepper* on it—the whole album. I sat down on a park bench near the teddy bears and other tchotchkes and started to listen to *Sgt. Pepper* in its entirety with no distractions, right where John Lennon got offed in front of Yoko. Not unlike the other John being assassinated in front of Jacqueline. Halfway through the album, I see another guy looking down at the shrine.

Pondering, he takes something out of his pants pocket and lays it on the ground.

And I thought, *Holy shit.*

I pause the iPod and walk over and say, "Hey, what did you just put down?"

He said, "I put down my 60-day chip."

He said he did that because he saw somebody else had put down a medallion. He said he wondered what's the most valuable thing he has to put down on the ground? It was his 60-day chip.

He was from Boston and I live in LA. And we just had this moment. We didn't fuck it up by saying, "Oh, let's exchange numbers, or are you on Facebook?" It was just like this special moment because I knew he's in Boston and I am in LA. Though we inhabit a fellowship that transcends time and place.

It might have been different if we were both New Yorkers. Maybe we would have hit a meeting together. But it was that moment, that vortex of Universal love energy that sometimes follows those in recovery one day at a time. It was just so damn magical. Sometimes it's not so hard to be a saint in the city.

Afterward, I sat on a nearby bench, recalling a day when I had a ceremony where I literally "married" a quarter pound of hashish . . . talk about love. Unlike a woman, or a father, hashish would never desert or abandon you. But will turn on you eventually. And maybe leave a souvenir tumor in your head. Who knows?

Recovery takes courage. Not really a word I was consciously familiar with as a kid. Courage is woven within Step 4 of the 12 Steps, where we summon the courage to honestly look deep within. For addicts and alcoholics, the prospect of a life without one's main coping mechanism, their "medicine," is unfathomable and unbearable. Not to mention saying adieu to the most important love in their life. It takes courage to decide to break that bond. As novelist James Baldwin wrote, "Nothing is more desirable than to be released from affliction, but nothing is more frightening than to be divested of a crutch."

Recovery takes patience. How long does it take to be sober for a year? 365 days, 8,735 hours, 525,600 minutes. That is where the expression "slowbriety" comes in. I love that. You can only get a year sober by living through 365, 24-hour days. You can't pay off your sponsor or take a class for extra credit. It's not instant coffee or instant gratification, like the first wireless remote-control device Zenith brought to market so you can push a button and change from one show to the next without having to stand up and walk to the set.

Recovery takes commitment. There is a power in passionate commitment. Know what you love, and manifest that love in action. The secret of happiness is no secret. It is living your life in harmony with what you love. I have always loved film, literature, music and multifaceted human interaction, be it erotic or intellectual. Art is manifest when the impetus is self-expression rather than self-indulgence. May God grant me the wisdom to know the difference.

The Greek philosopher Socrates famously said that an unexamined life is not worth living. Canadian Jungian therapist Marion Woodman claims the secret to maintaining long-term sobriety is to constantly strive to get to know ourselves better and realize that our life is more interesting and genuine without drugs. You learn to stay sober from the inside out.

The path of sobriety is never uninteresting.

#

My name is Leonard Buschel and I am an addiction survivor. To this day, all desire for drugs and alcohol have vanished—and it's been that way for 27 years. I learned early on that my odds of keeping sober and avoiding relapse would improve if I was continuously striving to lead a more balanced life. Leading a more balanced life physically, emotionally and mentally is a lifeline toward successful recovery and long-lasting sobriety.

Every morning I sit at my altar and light three sticks of Japanese smokeless incense and flip over a 15-minute hourglass and sit still. Then I do 15 minutes of Dō-In. At least a few mornings a week, I'll attend a 12 Step meeting. I love going to AA meetings.

For me, it strikes a spiritual tuning fork that resonates throughout everything I do during the day. I have a sponsor (who I rarely talk to) and at least two commitments a week. All of this helps keep me grounded in my recovery. I remain an addiction survivor because of AA.

Sometimes at a 12 Step meeting, I look around the room and think: *There are no wimps here. These people are all incredibly courageous. They have been through so much, both in and out of recovery, but they stay on a path that I think can be described as nothing other than holy.* Yes, this is a spiritual movement.

Daily physical exercise like long walks or aerobics will improve your mood. Healthy mental and emotional input garnered from reading good literature, frequenting museums or attending inspirational plays, musicals or performance pieces are also helpful for maintaining sobriety.

Many psychologists believe that a contributing cause of addiction is lack of connection. [See Johann Hari's book, *Chasing the Scream (The Opposite of Addiction is Connection)*] Interestingly, your drug dealer is called your "connection." Addiction creates connection but not to the right things or people.

Has that lack of interpersonal connection been fueled by technology-driven social media, with Twitter's tiny, 280-character messages or Instagram's mindless reinforcement of narcissistic video selfies from teens and pre-teens looking for themselves where there is no one home? Can you imagine having to take the time to find a phone book, look up a phone number, then dial ten numbers on that old rotary phone? Imagine then having to actually talk to someone for more than two minutes.

> *"Now that we have reached a hastier and more superficial rhythm, now that we believe we are in touch with a greater amount of people, more people, more countries. This is the illusion which might cheat us of being in touch deeply with the one breathing next to us. The dangerous time when mechanical voices, radios, telephones, take*

the place of human intimacies, and the concept of being in touch with millions brings a greater and greater poverty in intimacy and human vision."

—The Diary of Anaïse Nin, Vol. 4, *1944–1947*

Lack of connection is not only caused by the advent of technology, which actually has brought us many good things. Like the GE slogan says, "We bring good things to life." (Not to be confused with "COKE Adds Life" or DuPont's brainwashing of the American Soul with "Better Living Through Chemistry," certainly something every addict will perversely agree with.) Still, I cannot help but wonder: Does technology interfere with self-awareness in our lives? For some it's a rhetorical question. For others, they don't know. Still others just don't care.

It's important to release any creative juices you might have had bottled up. Anybody can be creative—a pencil and a piece of paper doesn't cost much. Anybody can look up how to write a Haiku - the Japanese very short form of poetry. Anybody can go to an adult night class to take essay writing or watercolor painting. Walking down the street, observing the leaves on a tree is a meditation; and it's also interactive, if you're sensitive enough to hear their stories. Once you remove drugs and alcohol you have to find other ways to feel alive, without tempting death. Being creative is a high unto itself.

In the early 1980s, an interesting study reported in *Advertising Age* or a similar publication looked at the positive effect of cocaine on creativity. In small amounts, the stimulant was quite effective and beneficial. In larger amounts, with increased frequency, the effect disappeared entirely and actually worked in reverse.

When I worked as a counselor, I used to tell my clients to do something unique. If you used to play guitar, start taking guitar lessons again. Walk around the block and leave your cell phone at home and just be open to your feelings, which can sometimes be very uncomfortable. The wind in the trees—the meditative mind—may offer you unexpected strength.

I was sitting under a tree at Betty Ford one Sunday afternoon when I saw a negative feeling coming at me like a locomotive. The feeling came toward me and seemingly went right through me and out the other side. From that point on I realized that feelings come and go. They won't last forever. I can just observe and even appreciate them. Even be afraid. During years of my addictions, when I felt a "feeling" coming on, I would always be able to heighten it or deflect it, depending on what it looked like and what drugs or booze I had at my disposal.

Recovery—especially if you're going along the steps of Alcoholic Anonymous— suggests prayer and meditation. It's really wonderful. It's not just giving up substances; it's developing yourself as a better person.

I thrive on eating well-balanced meals (and not too many processed food-like substances), sleeping seven to eight hours every night, meditating for a measly (self-judging) 15 minutes every morning, trying to walk two miles a day and making time for reading, writing, films, music and poetry, hobbies and recreation.

Thich Nhat Hanh, a famous Buddhist monk from Vietnam, brought a new form of insight meditation to the West termed Walking Meditation. He said that when you walk you should try to focus on feeling each step and how you are becoming more in touch with Mother Earth, whose energies fill your body with a new sense of awareness. This can happen when you are being open to the energy coming down from the galaxies above and up from the Earth below.

Michio Kushi, with George Oshawa, brought a healthy living practice called Macrobiotics from Japan to America. Macrobiotics means "Big Life." They said if you adopt a macrobiotic lifestyle, eat and practice a certain way, you will become a free man or woman. It was agreed the purpose of life is to play. When I took his class, we were encouraged to look at the dolphins in the sea. Look at the birds—all they want to do is soar and sing (and eat and procreate). On a more physical level, Michio also emphasized stretching and yoga as appropriate means of increasing flexibility in general.

Why? Because exercise can decrease your blood pressure and increase your resolve to stay healthy and lead a longer life.

I have always wanted my clients to learn (or relearn) how to read inspiring books, go to museums and enjoy life. It can help keep you sober if everything in your new life is more interesting, more compelling and inspiring. There is nothing between you and reality. There is a new level of honesty and pride to guide you. So, creativity is a big part of recovery as so many recovering artists have proven personally.

You just have to enjoy it. I don't play an instrument and I can't paint. I don't dance. I don't even recite poetry (an actual sin). But I can cook. And cooking is where my creativity comes out. Luckily no friends have had to be rushed to the hospital to have their stomachs pumped, or severe blood pressure spikes from too much shoyu.

In recovery, you must also learn how to sit with boredom—and lower the bar when it comes to what you feel is exciting. Not much is as exciting as when Melissa and I were searching for drugs in Vieques, Puerto Rico (also known as Isla Nena, or Little Girl Island), a very small Caribbean island populated by hundreds and hundreds of wild miniature ponies. For years the U.S. Navy used Vieques as target practice. The Puerto Ricans could never build any tall hotels there because the navy kept bombing it. But it's a special place, with a phosphorescent bay.

Melissa and I stayed in a small hotel. We didn't bring any coke as I was using this trip as a chance to clean up. While we were there, Melissa insisted we get coke. We went to the bar near the hotel, somehow got into a little four-seater with two strangers and drove into the jungle crammed into the back of the two-door sedan. They promised when we got to their friend's house, he would have cocaine for sale. We naturally thought he would have either cut coke or a machete—something a skillful farmer would know how to chop our heads off with. The only catch turned out to be they wanted $200 for the blow instead of $100. It was too late to renegotiate so we gave them the $200 and rode back to the hotel.

I Don't Even Speak Spanish

That was an exciting night. In sobriety, you're not going to get the we-could-die or we-could-get-high kind of excitement. Newly sober people have to be reminded they're not going to feel that kind of excitement ever again.

You don't get that kind of excitement sitting in an AA meeting. But you've got to learn how to just sit with the stillness. You've got to get comfortable with living without the drama and the challenges and excitement of addiction.

Keep things interesting. Not crazy enough to get arrested. Just crazy enough to have fun.

Do something unique. Follow the suggestions of the 12 Steps.

Marie-Louise von Franz tells us that the "gift of renewal" can suddenly change a "stale and dull life" into a "rich unending inner adventure, full of creative possibilities." The price is too high to not attempt sobriety. Perhaps the most important aspect of healthy living is learning to re-love yourself.

Each day of sobriety gives me a new opportunity to expand and awaken my feelings of gratitude and appreciation for this new and sober life. After all, recovery is all about reawakening and rebirth. The Swiss psychologist and philosopher Alice Miller tells us that "addiction . . . is a sign, a signal, a symptom of distress. It is a language that tells us about a plight that must be understood."

Often newly sober and out-of-work recovering alcoholics can be cursed or blessed with an inkling. When a business idea strikes with a brilliant inchoate thought, it can grow into an idea and after sufficient research and a plan, one could then take action. Focused and sober.

Everything that happens in recovery is magical. As Dr. Gabor Maté has said, "The attempt to escape from pain, is what creates more pain." Recovery begins as you cultivate a new purpose for your life. Don't let the past steal away your present.

For some of us, chronic fear and anxiety (negative thinking) creates pessimism and worry, driving us to continue drinking. Unease and fretfulness often lead to a sense of apprehension or dread. Many people are scared of the "unknown." Even more afraid of the unknown than dying the painful death of an alcoholic.

Sobriety is an awesome adventure and the future does not have to include manipulating fears and insecurities with substances. That future does not include behavior that we've used to cope with life on life's terms. Good or bad. Sobriety is like a reality show, except the stakes are life itself. Everyone's a finalist and everyone can win. It's the ultimate reward when you emerge as a survivor. And it can be done with or without faith in a higher power. It's just a lot easier if you have one, or at least realize that you may be or not be God.

It's beneficial for the addiction survivor (it was for me) to have a structured daily routine. Get up in the morning around the same time (even if you're not working), have dinner early and go to sleep at a set time. You will more easily feel accomplished in the things you do, not feel you're wasting time, experience less boredom and procrastinate less often.

Russell Brand reminds us that our irrational behavior makes us "completely powerless over addiction and unless [the addict has] structured help, they have no hope." Without hope the addict thinks less rationally, behaves less responsibly. Sobriety can seem too far away . . . Like the Zen proverb says, "If we're facing in the right direction, all we have to do is keep on walking."

Be gentle toward yourself and keep in mind that there's no room for perfectionism—a kind of black-and-white form of rigid thinking. In recovery anxiety will diminish, and you'll actually begin to feel good about your imperfect ways.

Joseph Campbell offers a magical reward for your efforts. He says that it is "by going down into the abyss that we recover the treasures of life. Where you stumble, there lies your treasure." It is as if you already are what you are looking for. You too can be an Addiction Survivor.

When you are in recovery you need to understand yourself deeply. A superficial understanding of oneself only leads to more frustration and possible relapse. However, a deeper and more spiritual understanding of oneself can lead to Joy, which is a special kind of Wisdom, that aids sobriety. Great literature, inspiring films and timeless music can also inspire Joy and Wisdom. And getting a therapist wouldn't hurt.

Observation of yourself is always most fruitful in the present moment—at the moment you are hurt or angry, greedy, jealous and worse. And this must happen without criticism, condemnation or judgment. You watch, you observe, it flowers and disappears, it withers away and loses its power over you. You are now free to live a new life and undergo a radical change in yourself that creates a life free from substance abuse.

We are not bad people doing bad things, we are heroes lost like the Lotus-eaters from The Odyssey. Retold here so beautifully in the Marijuana Anonymous guidebook, *Life With Hope*.

The Story of the Lotus Eaters

About 3,000 years ago, the poet Homer told a story about a man called Odysseus and his voyage home to Greece following the Trojan Wars. The story of the Lotus-eaters is found in Odysseus's tale to the Phaeacians in book nine. According to Odysseus, Zeus sent a storm and blew them afar for nine days, before they landed on the island of the Lotus-eaters. There the inhabitants gave them some fruit from the lotus plant. When the men ate this fruit, they lost all desire to make it back home. All they wanted to do was to stay and eat more fruit. They became sleepy and lazy. They would have stayed, lingered, and probably died there, but Odysseus by force of character dragged the men back to the ships to sail homeward. As the men were going, they were weeping. Odysseus even had to tie them up on the ship, lest they escape and stay.

Isn't it time all the drug addicts out there decided to go home? A home that you build on love and compassion. First for yourself, and then the whole world. Be brave. You only live once possibly. Read *The Biology of Desire: Why Addiction is Not a Disease* by Marc Lewis, PhD., and I think you will agree.

HIGH

In the morning
After taking cold shower
–What a mistake–
I look at the mirror.

There, a funny guy, grey hair, white beard, wrinkled skin,
–What a pity–
Poor, dirty, old man!
He is not me, absolutely not.

Land and life
Fishing in the ocean
Sleeping in the desert with stars
Building a shelter in mountains
Farming the ancient way

Singing with coyotes
Singing against nuclear war–
I'll never be tired of life.
Now I'm seventeen years old, Very charming young man.
I sit down quietly in lotus position,
Meditating, meditating for nothing.
Suddenly a voice comes to me:

"To stay young,
To save the world,
Break the mirror."

— Nanao Sakaki, "Break The Mirror" in *Break The Mirror* (North
Point Press 1987)

Chapter 20

Keeping It Reel, Ready for My Close-Up

America is one of the few so-called rich countries without universal health care. That means poor people, more than most, suffer and die before their time. They cannot afford treatment for life- threatening illnesses. Many writers' lives are threatened by the inability to quit alcoholic drinking, substance abuse, and other life-endangering addictions.

I noticed that there were local and national nonprofit organizations to help musicians who needed support for alcohol or drug-related problems, but there wasn't one for those in the worlds of writing and publishing. One trait of successful entrepreneurs is that when they see a vacuum, they strive to fill it. I, on the other hand, see an opportunity to start a nonprofit with absolutely no funding and do it anyway.

I created a mock-up brochure that outlined the mission and vision for Writers In Treatment as if we were already in operation and took it to my dear friend Robert Downey Sr. in New York.

I said, "This is my idea for a new nonprofit. What do you think?"

Bob said, "Leonard, everything you do is nonprofit!" Haha. He thought the idea was sound and agreed to be on the board of directors and be listed as the VP.

Our Advisory Board consisted of the famed criminal attorney and television journalist Darren Kavinoky, Golden Globe

Award–winning actress Joanna Cassidy, Edgar Award–winning true crime writer Burl Barer. Additional members included my brother Bruce Buschel, acclaimed sportswriter, producer, restaurateur and author; Christian Meoli, famed character actor, film producer and theater owner; and Travis Koplow, PhD, international director of communications for an anonymous organization that helps people stay off narcotics. Finally, writer and professional film buff Vernon Scott Jr. was also on the Board.

Writers In Treatment began as a sincere effort to help people in the writing and publishing industries who are experiencing problems due to alcohol and/or drugs. Our goal was also to produce free educational and cultural events that celebrate recovery while reducing the stigma associated with addiction and provide the support individuals need to take their first steps toward health and wholeness. In other words, if someone asked for help, we sent them to rehab. I believe the most and least you can do for someone who wants help is to get them into a 30-day residential program where they can decide if they want to save their lives or not.

The Experience, Strength and Hope Awards show is a part of Writers In Treatment. Every year we present this award to a high-profile individual who has penned a riveting memoir about their addiction and recovery. Celebrities like Oscar-winner Louis Gossett Jr.; John Taylor, cofounder of Duran Duran; Emmy Award–winner Joe Pantoliano; and the second man to walk on the moon, Buzz Aldrin. Also acknowledged: actress and recovery advocate Mackenzie Phillips, television news legend Pat O'Brien, CNN commentator Jane Velez- Mitchell,

I Know a Space Man

and hairdresser to the stars and author of *Upper Cut*, Carrie White. Also, TV star Jodie Sweetin and dearly departed Christopher Kennedy Lawford. These individuals have written very honest memoirs about their careers, their lives, their problems, their addictions, and their recoveries. It is widely acknowledged to be the "sobriety event of the year" in Los Angeles. It starts with a 90-minute buffet and schmooz-athon and ends with everyone in a theater for the awards show. No eating or clinking of tableware as we entertain and honor our honoree. The event is held at the world-renowned Skirball Cultural Center, and clean and sober hipsters look forward to dressing up and having a good time . . . without drinking.

Joanna Cassidy, aka Zhora, always participates doing the thankless job of thanking all our sponsors from the stage and asking these wise men and women to take a bow.

When John Taylor wrote his book, he wanted to include his stay in rehab and his years in AA, because that time was one of the most important in his life. Interesting—sobriety was most important, more than the Grammys and the groupies. Joe Pantoliano, who won an Emmy for *The Sopranos*, wrote a compelling book about mental illness and recovery.

Because I believe it's important for people in recovery, and for those on the cusp, to have entertaining and culturally stimulating events that inspire enthusiasm for living clean and sober, we started the REEL Recovery Film Festival & Symposium to showcase honest, entertaining and genuine portrayals of addiction and recovery to meet that need.

Originally, the film festival served to accomplish two things: create an event we felt was useful and engaging and stimulate funding for Writers In Treatment. Now the primary aims of the film festival are to mitigate the stigma surrounding addiction and mental illness, celebrate recovery through the unique impact of film and expand the dialogue among artists, treatment- industry professionals and the public. After every film we screen, we either have the filmmaker or a clinician engage the audience in conversation or we have an extemporaneous process group.

Our first film festival was for a rapt audience in Los Angeles at the Silent Movie Theater, opened originally in 1942, well after silent films became loud. Opening night was very special and encouraging. We had programmed *Permanent Midnight* based on the true-life saga of TV writer Jerry Stahl, starring Ben Stiller and Maria Bello. After the film, Ben and Jerry sat onstage and interviewed each other for 30 minutes (No ice cream was served). The audience really appreciated the frank conversation and courage of the "behind the scenes" stories. It's a very special experience when the star who portrays the author appears with the author in perfect candor.

We showed *Barfly*, the gem of a film directed by wild man Barbet Schroeder, starring Mickey Rourke (in his prime) and Faye Dunaway (in her element) about writer Charles Bukowski, every perverted/creative alcoholic's hero. After the screening, actress Roberta Bassin talked about making the film and her job of looking after Bukowski when he visited the set, which she said was quite often. I forget the details of what she said about her time with Charles, but I am sure it would not be repeatable here. Having one of the actual barflies addressing the audience after watching *Barfly* was a lovely treat for us fans of Bukowski's poetry and prose.

On the last night we showed a little-known cult favorite, *ivans xtc.* by the director of *Immortal Beloved* about the deaf composer Ludwig van Beethoven. Director Bernard Rose, Mr. haughty Englishman, had made a film about a Hollywood agent (played by Danny Huston) with a drug and personality problem. (Though how could Danny Huston ever have a personality problem?) Danny and director Rose appeared after the film and regaled the lucky audience members with stories of making an independent film about dependency on drugs, alcohol and power. Rose said the film was an update on Leo Tolstoy's *The Death of Ivan Ilyich*. The entire audience, especially clients "druggy buggied" in from various end-of-the-road rehabs, could relate to the film but not necessarily to the Leo Tolstoy reference.

Opening the festival with Ben Stiller and closing with Danny Huston made me realize how powerful and interesting films about substance abuse really are. We were on to something. We had done more than hit a vein. We had the nerve to show honest movies that were interesting, entertaining and perhaps most importantly not bullshit. We know that alcoholics have a very discerning bullshit meter, so all our films are honest depictions of life. Our films don't sugarcoat or exaggerate addiction. They don't judge or justify. They tell it like it is. For many of the films we show, the portrayal of recovery may be about what it was like or what it's like now. Honest and compelling films can powerfully affect us. This is one reason why I have seen many audience members so inspired as to leap passionately and gratefully deeper into their recovery.

I have seen light bulbs go on over people's heads in the audience. I believe some people were rededicating themselves to staying sober either because they saw a person hit rock bottom on the screen or they saw a message of hope. I often see people in the audience become fascinated with filmmakers who share how and why they made the films they did. We don't try to brainwash anybody. We don't do spontaneous interventions on the audience. We show films that teach, not preach. Films that neither condone nor condescend. The films selected are honest depictions of addiction, recovery and sobriety. Anyone who knows me knows that anything I present isn't going to be some heavy-handed, preachy, "beware of demon rum" event. The film festival is not about converting people from one lifestyle to another, nor is it propaganda or a sales pitch for anything. It is exactly what it says it is. An appreciation of film and recovery.

The REEL Recovery Film Festival aspires to meet people exactly where they are— whether that be in recovery or living in the throes of addiction. There's no pressure and there's no agenda. It is not like one of those recovery rallies where people get together and run around in circles for recovery. I don't think someone who gets clean and sober necessarily needs to join the crusade to change the way America thinks about addiction and recovery. They have changed themselves and isn't that the most difficult and reward-ing thing you can do?

The film festival has great appeal to many, in particular to peo-ple in recovery who read books and love films, attend live theater or go to museums when there's a good exhibition. Our intelligence and cultural interests help us to take what we learn in the world into the rooms of AA, and even more importantly, what we learn in the *Rooms* into the world.

We have a lot of clinicians in our audience who treat addicts but have never really witnessed what the day-to-day lifestyle of a heroin or cocaine dependent person looks like from the inside. Films that do not exaggerate can effectively teach and inspire by their realistic portrayals, as long as those movies do not contain far-fetched and maudlin embellishments.

We strongly embrace filmmakers who shine a light into the shadows of alcoholism and addiction. We show numerous films that celebrate freedom from life-threatening behaviors and docu-ment healthier alternatives for the body, mind and soul.

The excitement and feelings I had about the expansion and acceptance of the REEL Recovery Film Festival were far better than a line of coke and certainly more sustainable. As the event garnered more attention, I got a call from a treatment center on the coast of British Columbia. They were interested in bringing the REEL Recovery Film Festival & Symposium to Vancouver, Canada. Wonderful!

After a couple of phone calls, conversations and discussions, we decided on a date and a venue. Four months later, we launched the Canadian premier of the REEL Recovery Film Festival. The mayor of Vancouver was there to cut the ribbon and spoke for about 15 minutes. I was internally overcome with emotions, wish-ing my mother was still alive to see me sharing the stage with a metropolitan mayor who had not signed an arrest warrant for her son.

This was a snazzy event, attended by people from all over Van-couver who came down to the distinctive venue—an art gallery theater on the infamous Eastside of Vancouver. The diversity of attendees was wonderful—we had people from the suburbs, treatment professionals and people in recovery watching interesting films and participating in the Q&A's afterward. All and all, it was an absolute joy and a terrific weekend. And best of all, I got to visit my local friend Dr. Gabor Maté. He took me to his favorite Afghani restaurant where we sat on Oriental rugs, dined on spicy food and solved all the world's ills.

Bringing the film festival to New York, however, contained all the elements of an attempted drug scam but ended like the joyous climax of a Bollywood musical—which is often more enjoyable than what follows a Bollywood meal.

The intrigue began after a business conversation with an ex-wine broker in New Hampshire. He was also part owner of a recovery newspaper in New York City. We started discussions on bringing the REEL Recovery Film Festival to the Big Apple in 2010. Methods and intellectual properties were sent to my new would-be partner. The agreement went back and forth. After amendments were made, my office manager and I were waiting for their deposit check . . . and waiting . . . and waiting.

Seemingly everything was moving forward and we had no apprehension about continuing to share our information, our documents, our contacts and our entire film library, not to mention the expertise we had developed over the years. After a month and a half went by, I'm telling the fellow, "We still have not received that deposit check." His response was unexpected.

"I'm not sending you anything. It was nice knowing you."

The next day, I get a call from a friend at Hazelden, a treatment center in Minnesota, telling me that someone just called him from New York saying that they were putting on a recovery film festival and asked Hazelden to be a sponsor. Hazelden said, "yes." Why? Because they thought it was *my* film festival. When I told them it wasn't, they wanted to know who's scamming who?

I'd hardly set down the phone, when I get another call from New York saying there was a back-page ad in a newspaper called *Together*

New York for a recovery film festival on four dates near the end of September—the dates I anticipated for our New York event.

Dismayed and distressed, I mentioned all this to my brother, who by this point was a *real* New Yorker.

"You're just going to sit back," asks Brother Bruce, "and do nothing about this?"

"Hell no. I'm going to rent the Quad cinema in Greenwich Village for a whole week and put on the best Recovery Film Festival ever."

Why a whole week? Because the owner of the theater told me that the fee for renting the theater for a weekend was the same as renting for a week. I decided to go for it, as we had a sufficient number of submissions to screen films for seven days. We also designated Wednesday night "Pat Dixon's Comedy Intervention" and hired six local sober comics to perform.

To me, the threat of competition was very invigorating. It really made me promise to produce the best REEL Recovery Film Festival & Symposium ever.

A couple days later, I spoke to one of my Board members who said, "Maybe you have some grounds for an injunction to stop these people."

Long story short, even though it could take up to a year to pursue this through the courts, and would be a real pain, I was not about to let this severe lapse of ethics on the part of someone else impact the reputation and future of the REEL Recovery Film Festival. I flew to New York with plans to file legal action against these people, and when I arrived, I met with my friend Dr. Tian Dayton.

"Leonard, I don't think you have to go to court. I got a phone call earlier today saying that there wasn't going to be any other recovery film festival in New York."

"Really?"

"Yes."

"Is that a guarantee?"

"Yes. They folded."

When the treatment industry community found out some New Yorkers were ripping off my idea, the pirates had second thoughts. I was so relieved that I didn't come to New York to have it end up a mudslinging match, and I'm delighted to tell you that our film festival in New York was a wonderful success. Robert Downey Sr. took great joy in introducing his friend Lionel Rogosin's B&W classic docufiction film, *On the Bowery* from 1956. The festival has continued to grow in prestige and participation and remains a weeklong celebration of films that shed light on themes of addiction, alcoholism, behavioral disorders, treatment and recovery.

Nicest Man I Ever Knew, Bob Downey, Sr.

Years go by quickly, and by the time I write this paragraph, the REEL Recovery Film Festival & Symposium has become an international success, featuring filmmakers from around the world. In any given year, we receive 100–200 submissions and pick the best 70–80 to exhibit. With several New York premieres, debuts and films by industry veterans, the film festival represents an eclectic lineup of contemporary films and classic features, documentaries and shorts from the U.S., Canada, Iran, Great Britain, Norway, Ireland and Hong Kong, among others.

The festival is the single longest recovery event of its kind in America: seven days of films, panels, comedy and fellowship. Admission is affordable and no one is ever turned away for lack of funds. That's only possible because of our generous sponsors, whom I love dearly.

Let's party!

A cursory glance at the event program will give you a glimpse into the vast diversity of topics addressed in film and conversation, such as our signature live event, "Chasing the Muse ... Stone Cold Sober." This is a panel featuring some of New York's most creative and successful professional writers and filmmakers addressing the issue articulated in this question: "How do I create now that I'm not getting high, stoned or drunk?"

This question was inspired by the legend that Eric Clapton couldn't pick up a guitar in his first year of sobriety because the guitar itself was a trigger. How does one get back into the creative flow completely "on the natch"? So we had famed *sober* writers and performers address that conundrum.

Through my experience as a counselor and graduate of Betty Ford I've become aware that many treatment centers, sober living houses and clinics make recovery-related films available to their patients and their families.

When I was in treatment at Betty Ford, on the weekends, we were given access to only six VHS tapes. I pulled one out by John Bradshaw on the topic of shame. I sat there and I watched it and wept. I realized I had been walking around with shame my whole life, but I never identified it with a word. Now I had a name for it. That experience facilitated and accelerated my recovery and my healing process. I knew I was in the right place: a safe place to feel feelings for the first time.

Later, when I was a substance abuse counselor in Los Angeles at Beit T'Shuvah, I worked a Saturday night shift and while some of the clients were out at AA meetings and others were out with family members, a lot of clients got left behind. There were often a dozen or two people who were stuck with nothing to do on a Saturday night. I brought in a VHS comedy tape every Saturday night. After 90 minutes of a funny movie that had everyone laughing, it seemed like nobody felt lonely. The levels of despair and stress in everyone diminished. No one seemed to feel like they missed out on something by being stuck inside on a Saturday night. We laughed, had snacks, and it felt like a special evening when most clients thought it would be dull and depressing.

A good movie can create a wide-awake, dream-like experience that can tap into the subconscious mind with truths, insights, and inspirations that might be blocked by denial and fear during normal waking hours—even in the therapist's office.

Watching a film in a darkened room allows one to have very personal reactions to what's on the screen. No one is telling the person what to think. Feelings and thoughts can come and go without constantly being judged and challenged by an all-knowing family member. This was after all, a Jewish facility.

When I started the REEL Recovery Film Festival, I realized that to stay sober, you don't have to check your intellect at the door or leave your love of art and culture behind. I also realized after a few years of sobriety, that films had become my new drug of choice.

Our Addiction/Recovery eBulletin, an electronic news source distributed weekly on Tuesdays, reaches over 23,000 recipients in the US and the UK. The eBulletin newsletter features news and articles from the previous week related to the world of addiction and recovery.

I am both editor and publisher of the newsletter. The publisher may be sober, but the eBulletin is never dry. The diversity of content and sources is wonderful. Every week, it features breaking news, scientific studies, celebrity sobriety, pharmaceutical information, Alcoholics Anonymous, book and film reviews, editorials, medical research, law enforcement stories, obituaries, eating disorder stories, treatment advice, recovery stories, group therapy topics, advocacy initiatives and recovery technology. The articles are relevant, compelling and inspiring. The eBulletin definitely provides "news you can use." Reader response and feedback have been encouraging, which tells me that people like being kept informed while being entertained.

Celebrity gossip isn't gossip in the eBulletin. We do feature public celebrities' personal experiences. Some are dealing with the adverse effects of using, and others are celebrating another day of victory in recovery.

A great thing about the eBulletin is that we are embedding, or linking, to spectacular videos by stellar individuals, such as Dr. Gabor Maté, physician and best-selling author. We also have linked to content by Dr. Carl Hart, Professor of Neuroscience and Psychology at Columbia University and recreational heroin smoker. We adore actor/recovery advocate, comedian, author, and radio host Russell Brand. Until the start of the eBulletin, there wasn't any convenient way for the average or even above average person to keep up with all the addiction and sobriety news.

In 2017, I was blessed with a fantastic associate editor named Ahbra Schiff. A childhood spelling bee whiz and a purveyor of all the news that's sometimes unfit to publish, but we publish it anyway, about addiction, recovery and the decline of Americans' mental health stability. In 2020, 90,000 Americans died from taking too many harmful drugs at one time. That's crazy to me. Or maybe people find copping a buzz worth dying for. I thought life itself was a gift from God, and your two parents. I know I did an awful lot of cocaine in my life, but I never thought one line or even ten lines might kill me. Maybe death is more seductive than I realized.

I knew there was a market for a weekly digest of addiction news, breakthroughs and more, but the immediate positive response after launch exceeded my expectations. In the first six months, the Addiction/Recovery eBulletin attracted 11,000 individual email subscribers, and became the most referred to, linked to, and talked about information and entertainment source within the recovery industry.

The eBulletin has a diverse audience: industry professionals, health and wellness clinicians, treatment centers, doctors, corporate CEO's, MFT's, admission coordinators, members of the press and members of the recovery community. Editions of the eBulletin can be found on http://addictionrecoveryebulletin.org. Each edition is archived, so folks don't have to search back through their email every week to review the stories. Each week, the eBulletin is posted and shared thousands of times on Facebook, Twitter, LinkedIn and Instagram. The eBulletin also draws loyal and supportive advertisers, who help to make the endeavor possible and help to sustain and grow the newsletter.

Once in a while, there is even a crisis with the eBulletin. In October 2015, Sovereign Health, a litigious and corrupt rehab empire, took legal action against me for simply providing a link to a story about them published in the Orange County Register. My error was not checking the publication date of the story. It was from three years earlier. They alleged all sorts of nasty motives on my part and even stated in court documents that I was besmirching their reputation so referrers would send patients to *my rehab*, which of course was ridiculous because I don't have one. I didn't write or publish the original story. The OC Register still has the story available on their website.

It was in court for two years and their plan to sue me for three million dollars for lost referrals barely made it past the initial jurisprudence stage. It cost them a fortune and eventually the CEO Tonmoy Sharma shuttered Sovereign Health and resurrected it under a new name after a wrongful death suit was filed against them.

Chapter 21

Betty Ford Died Sober, I Should Be So Lucky

My life has been a misadventure of minor proportions. I have developed a passion for quality entertainment and the arts in its myriad of manifestations. Some of my life experiences could be considered unfortunate. Who doesn't have some unfortunate experiences? A woman came to Gandhi one day and wailed about losing her son to a terrible accident and wanted the Mahatma to take away her pain. He said he would, but first she had to find someone in her village who had never experienced a similar heartache. She never came back.

I have also experienced many miracles. Being born a white Jewish male to a hip, liberal, working-class mother in the middle of the last great century was only the start. Suffice to say, when I was young, I played with fireworks, cherry bombs and M-80s and still have all my fingers and both eyes. At least I can see in stereo if not hear. I hitchhiked to high school every day for three years without incident. Smuggled hashish from Israel to America, twice! Sniffed cocaine up both nostrils for thirteen years—every day. Dealt drugs for 26 years. Suffered from life-threatening asthma most of my days on the planet (too many 911 calls to remember).

Assisted with the birth of a son who was so sweet and beautiful people said we could start a religion around him. Had a five-hour open-heart surgery to replace a bicuspid valve with some bovine tissue. Moo. Lived with several women (not all at once) who had a history of stabbing their previous partners. Walked into a rehab at 44 and never drank or used drugs again. Had my head drilled open so my neurosurgeon could remove a neuroma that was puckered up against my brain, which could have turned into the Kiss of Death. Survived a mean case of COVID-19 at the very beginning of our global pandemic. Was T-boned by a woman in an SUV at 40 mph who never even hit the brakes. My car flew around and when the vehicle came to rest, passenger air bag detonated, a pedestrian ran over to me and yelled, "I saw the whole thing, she never even slowed down. If you weren't in a Volvo, you would be dead."

Addiction has been a constant theme. Recovery was one of the most transformative powerful turning points in my life.

Along the way, I have been guided by mentors, role models and people who have impacted and influenced me. Authors, poets, filmmakers, playwrights, great philosophers, purveyors of wisdom and close personal friends have all played a role in my evolution. The sweetest friend of all was Bob Downey. May he rest in peace and absurdity.

The Japanese person who did the most to save my life, who has been a continual blessing even after his death, and who I shall never forget or lose my gratitude for is Michio Kushi. One of the most seminal events in my life began in an old colonial style hotel in Boston, Mass. In 1976, I had taken the Amtrak train from the 34th Street station in Philadelphia to attend a three-day symposium on Macrobiotics given by Michio Kushi. The weekend changed my life. It might have saved my life, too. It was, and still is, without a doubt one of the most profound experiences I've ever had. It's not often you can say your life was changed completely over a single weekend . . . and changed in a hotel without a woman. And having that still be true decades later is remarkable.

I learned that Macrobiotics was not about food or diet. The ultimate goal in life was not good health, it was to be free—a free man or a free woman. And to play. Even Albert Einstein said:

"There's no question dolphins are smarter than humans as they play more."

The wisdom of all human existence was imparted to me and the other 60 attendees. Simply put, Macrobiotics means Macro=Big, Biotics=Life, and the goal is freedom and the total acceptance of mistakes, victories and Universal Love.

There is no way I can explain how I was changed that weekend from a 26-year-old Jewish city boy with an appetite for all things processed, meaty, sugary, spicy and myopic into a citizen of the universe. It's not just about yin and yang, brown rice or bancha tea; it's about love and the desire to create One Peaceful World in this or my next lifetime. I see my connection to Alcoholic Anonymous in perfect harmony with this goal. In fact, when I decided to jump into AA with both feet, I did so because I believed that if every country practiced the 12 Traditions of AA, war would disappear and only be read about in history books and seen in old movies.

My first 18 years as a so-called Macrobiotic student were spent in complete hypocrisy. Drug usage was not only not condoned but frowned upon as an affront to one's spiritual development. And certainly *not* very good for your health. I often heard Michio say that marijuana swelled your midbrain. I don't know if there's a connection, but when I needed brain surgery to remove the acoustic neuroma camping out in my head and about to destroy the area of my brain that controls lung function, I could blame no one but myself—or just cross it off to the middle finger of fate.

My one and only marriage was at a Macrobiotic camp in the Pocono Mountains. The special wedding menu consisted of miso soup, brown rice, a bottle of Veuve Clicquot for each guest, and endless lines of coke for my fellow drug dealers.

The officiator was the owner of the best natural foods store in Philadelphia called Essene. Denny Waxman is still very much alive and still teaching the way of Macrobiotics.

Only since I got sober in 1994 have I honestly been a drug-free follower of the Macrobiotic way of life. Which means that

I understand that whenever I get sick, it's because of my sugar addiction, the frequent restaurant food, not chewing enough, excessive amounts of dairy and overeating every day! No yoga, or aikido or tai chi, meditating only as a hobby and only recently as a daily practice and morning ritual.

Not all of us are born with perfect bodies, but it's up to us to nourish and make them as perfect as possible. You can't slow down the aging process with processed foods and soda. Can you believe people still drink sugar-filled chemical-rich carbonated beverages as if they were not pouring pure poison down their gullets? At least we shouldn't harm our bodies too often. I know I messed mine up with drugs and alcohol for quite some time. Living for decades—being high all the time—while suffering from asthma, can only be described as suicidal. I was damaging already damaged lungs.

The travel brochure for AA says you have four destinations to choose from: jail, hospital, morgue, or the road to the path of recovery. Recovery takes you back to your natural state. Takes you to you. And it's as easy as a camel getting through the eye of a needle a mile wide.

I feel at a loss for words to explain how at peace I have felt since that Boston weekend, knowing I am responsible for all my happiness and unhappiness. That weekend was a transcendent experience, yet grounded in fundamental, how-to tools for actual living—how to eat, how to cook, how to meditate and pray. Encoded within these practical arts are ways to approach the powerful dream of Life—how to orient oneself, to cherish the simple pleasures, unite with life's awesome beauty and treasure each moment. Michio gave us permission to walk barefoot like children on the new dew-born grass, to laugh again and trust in the face of ugly and mean appearances, with full confidence in the magnificent Order of the Universe. I know this blip of an interval we call a "lifetime" is an adventure to be lived to the fullest. Michio's whole dissertation ended with the most alluring Q&A of all: Why are we here? We are here to play.

Some of the books Michio has written include:

The Order of the Universe

How to See Your Health: Book of Oriental Diagnosis

The Cancer Prevention Diet

The Book of Macrobiotics

Natural Healing through Macrobiotics

The Book of Dō-In

Nine Star Ki

The Gentle Art of Making Love

Macrobiotics and Oriental Medicine Macrobiotic Palm Healing

AIDs, Macrobiotics & Natural Immunity

Diet for a Strong Heart

And many more . . .

Since that remarkable weekend in 1976, I have attended dozens of camps, lectures, retreats and presentations by someone I am so grateful to call my original sensei. I know I would not be alive today without Michio's teaching, even if I haven't always followed his advice.

That was the weekend Michio Kushi showed me the way. Not his way, but my way. He did suggest that before we retire at the end of the day, we ask ourselves these simple questions:

Did I eat well today?

Did I chew well today?

Did I acknowledge my ancestors with gratitude?

Did I marvel at the wonder of nature?

Would I like to live this day over again?

If you can answer "yes" to all these questions, I believe, as they say, you have hit the cosmic jackpot.

Certainly, Macrobiotics has helped me in life, as has my will and desire to stay in recovery. How have I achieved sustainable recovery for so many years? The cliché answer is One Day at a

Time. That is not just a cliché but also an accurate answer. You have to like being sober more than you like getting high. When someone turns away from a life-threatening path and starts to walk toward life and good health, why turn back?

Even during the unexpected and unrelenting COVID-19 pandemic, I found myself grounded in sobriety. Unfortunately, I have heard of others who returned to drinking or using drugs, partly from the economic pressures and social isolation stressors of the pandemic. Where was the help and support that people with addiction have needed? It does seem like addiction fell off society's radar when the pandemic struck, while so many with addiction continued to struggle, perhaps unnoticed and unheard.

I no longer use drugs or alcohol to enhance, hide, or avoid anything. That's my choice today. Sobriety has opened the door to more adventures than ever. I do what I really love— watching, talking about and scheduling films for REEL Recovery. It's also heavenly slipping into an orchestra seat on Broadway, enjoying a cup of tea while I order up another film on Netflix, Amazon Prime or HBO and of course, having sex. I am a gentleman at all times and under all conditions, unless specifically requested to behave otherwise.

Again, as Joseph Campbell proclaimed—"Follow your bliss." The common interpretation of this maxim is about the selection of a career path and the passion one has for it. I've stumbled through a variety of "careers," from selling pot to promoting blue-green algae to selling French vintage posters (and psychedelic posters when I was young) to being a drug counselor to publishing. It wasn't until the REEL Recovery Film Festival that I realized I'd finally found an intense love for something outside myself and is the reason I love to awaken every morning.

Not every interesting story deserves its own movie. But ask me about personal diaries, and I say they are often a source of page-turning drama that rivals a mystery movie. As they say, "Real life is stranger than fiction."

When my mom passed away, Brother Bruce and I found her diaries, her personal musings on life events, her revelations and her well-kept secrets. Few secrets stay secret after you're dead. Mom never remarried after our father died, but she didn't go without erotic passion. For many years, Mom carried on a torrid affair with a married man, each of them enjoying their many trysts and turns.

Her writings (which so clearly portray the challenges of a Jewish widow with two young headstrong sons) were donated to a Jewish historical society that treasured her heartfelt recounting of life in Logan and sex in motels. The stories of Logan, life, love, arrests, erotica and family drama are a bit of Americana often portrayed, exaggerated and/or skewed by the likes of Philip Roth or Neil Simon.

I digress in my thoughts back to movies. I could go on forever about films I love and movies I didn't like. I could talk about those that stole my heart. In fact, every New Year's Eve, I prepare a year-end list of films I have seen in theaters. It's called "The Loved to Loathed List." These are the movies that moved me, and what movies moved me out of my seat and out of the theater door. I missed publishing my year end list in 2020 because theaters were closed due to the pandemic.

Books and movies, movies and books—how beautiful and blessed are those who cherish movies and books. I can't say everyone agrees with that. Despots and dealers of death attacked the arts, burned books and censored films. Books and movies can be seen as threats or thrilling.

Concluding...

I also enjoy observing human interaction . . . it's fascinating. If you don't believe we can all get along, take a drive on the 101 or 405 freeways in Los Angeles during rush hour. If the assumptions of people not willing to work together was correct, no one would make it home alive. On the highways, there's a blend of Jews, Muslims, Christians, Atheists, Buddhists, Nihilists, Actors, Wiccans, Puerto Rican Separatists and Sikhs always looking for their way home or to work, all merging into oneness from different side roads, changing lanes, modifying their approaches, and signaling their intentions, so that no one is injured or killed. That demonstrates a profound act of cooperation, which overrides presumptions of human differences.

In 1966, Robert F. Kennedy delivered a speech (you can read about it online) that included these words: "There is a Chinese curse which says, 'May you live in interesting times.' Like it or not, we live in interesting times. They are times of danger and uncertainty, but they are also the most creative of any time in the history of mankind."

Orson Welles, playing Harry Lime in *The Third Man* (1949), echoes this sentiment when he tells Holly, the man he's betrayed, "Don't be so gloomy. After all, it's not that awful.

Remember what the fellow said ... in Italy, for thirty years under the Borgias, they had warfare, terror, murder, bloodshed, but they produced Michelangelo, Leonardo Da Vinci, and the Renaissance. In Switzerland, they had brotherly love. They had five hundred years of democracy and peace, and what did that produce? ... The cuckoo clock."

For better or worse, see you on Instagram.

#

Looking back on my life (like rewinding a movie), I would summarize my experiences this way: An ordinary young boy from Philly has serious health problems and stays healthy enough to be a participant in a fun and exciting neighborhood, full of a cast of interesting characters and boyhood friends. He decides that selling drugs is what he really enjoys doing and becomes a drug dealer. Life takes many twists and turns that lead him to many countries, towns and hamlets. To travel or not to travel ... He meets people whom he likes and whom he dislikes, whom he trusts and doesn't trust, and whom he loves and admires. Along the way, life is enhanced by a love for the arts and an appreciation of fine books, marijuana, cocaine, great films, stellar plays and incredible live and recorded music. He also goes through life being addicted, a life that would surely end in his demise. He checks into Betty Ford and comes out a new man. The rest is history, and now his life is an open book.

What's the point of this life review? That sobriety is within the reach of anyone who wants it. I am not some perfect person with astute skills and abilities. I am someone who made the decision to give up substances of abuse in favor of the challenges of unknowingness.

Sobriety is extraordinarily more sustainable than the experience of living with addiction.

I do not pat myself on the back when I say a transformation like mine can be replicated and sustained by others. Take a stand and stand there. Decide you want a better life and then live it. Practice the principles of AA or other spiritual ways of life. Be more in love with others than you are with yourself. You are free to follow any path you want, even to the grave, but wouldn't it be better to die of natural causes as a feeble old man than to be found by your family, slumped over an un-flushed toilet with a needle dangling out of the tattoo on your arm that says Namasté, or slumped over your steering wheel with an iPod on continuous play listening to REM's "Everybody Hurts" with a hose in the window, attached to your own exhaust pipe?

Realize life is a tragicomedy, even absurd perhaps, and find all the laughs you can. Or as Buddha said, "Life is suffering." But then someone like Albert Ellis comes along and says, "Suffering is optional." Infinity. Eternity. Go figure!

I think the book ends here.

I Live My Life In Growing Orbits

by Rainer Maria Rilke

I live my life in growing orbits
which move out over the things of the world.
Perhaps I can never achieve the last,
but that will be my attempt.
I am circling around God, around the ancient tower,
and I have been circling for a thousand years,
and I still don't know if I am a falcon, or a storm,
or a great song.
(Translated by Robert Bly)

More Acknowledgments

Love and affection to all my friends and loved ones who I shared air with:

Buzz Aldrin, Phillip Andrews, Richie Annenberg, Buddy Arnold, Rev. Michael Beckwith, Ed Begley Jr., Lawrence Block, Sabrina Blue, Alonzo Bodden, Nicole Boxer, Marian Brandenburg, Joanna Cassidy, Joseph Chilton-Pierce, William Cope Moyers, Elyse D'Angelo, Joe D'Angelo, Matt Damsker, Bruce Davison, Tony Denison, Robert Downey Jr., Carol Durbin, Renee Echt, Jo Farkas, Tio Hardiman, Bob Ingram, Joelle Jacobson, Greg Laemmle, John Lavitt, Melissa Lawner, Arlene Marinoff, Dr. Gabor Maté, Suzanne Moloney Wright, Roseanne Murphy, Pat O'Brien, Raine Phillips, Karin Purcell Larson, Tim Ryan & Jennifer Gimenez, Dallas Saunders, Carol and Joshua Schwartz, Vernon Scott, John Taylor, Robert Tepper, Jacqueline Twohie, Peter Ty, Mike Tyson, Michelle Vaniver and John West.

And Laura Nyro for making me cry every time I listen to "I Am the Blues."

I Am the Blues

Cigarettes

I'm all alone with my smoke and ashes Cigarettes

I'm all alone with my smoke and ashes Take me night-flying

Maybe Mars has good news Who? . . . who am I?

I am the blues

HIGH

When you get the massage, Hang up the phone.
— Alan Watts

About the Author

Leonard Lee Buschel is a California Certified Substance Abuse Counselor with years of experience working with people struggling with addiction. He attended Naropa University in Boulder, CO. Mr. Buschel is the founder of Writers In Treatment, whose primary purpose is to promote "treatment" as the best first step solution for addiction, alcoholism and other self-destructive behaviors. Leonard is director of the REEL Recovery Film Festival & Symposium, which he founded in 2008, and the editor/publisher of the weekly Addiction/Recovery eBulletin. He also produces the annual *Experience, Strength and Hope Awards* in Los Angeles. He just celebrated 29 years clean and sober.

www.leonardbuschel.com

www.addictionrecoveryebulletin.org

www.reelrecoveryfilmfestival.org

https://en.wikipedia.org/wiki/Leonard_Buschel